GW01167688

The Acquisition of French as a Second Language

Benjamins Current Topics

Special issues of established journals tend to circulate within the orbit of the subscribers of those journals. For the Benjamins Current Topics series a number of special issues of various journals have been selected containing salient topics of research with the aim of finding new audiences for topically interesting material, bringing such material to a wider readership in book format.

For an overview of all books published in this series, please see
http://benjamins.com/catalog/bct

Volume 62

The Acquisition of French as a Second Language. New developmental perspectives
Edited by Christina Lindqvist and Camilla Bardel

These materials were previously published in *Language, Interaction and Acquisition* 3:1 (2012)

The Acquisition of French as a Second Language

New developmental perspectives

Edited by

Christina Lindqvist
Uppsala University

Camilla Bardel
Stockholm University

John Benjamins Publishing Company
Amsterdam / Philadelphia

∞™ The paper used in this publication meets the minimum requirements of
the American National Standard for Information Sciences – Permanence
of Paper for Printed Library Materials, ANSI z39.48-1984.

Library of Congress Cataloging-in-Publication Data

The Acquisition of French as a Second Language : New developmental perspectives /
　　　Edited by Christina Lindqvist and Camilla Bardel.
　　p.　cm. (Benjamins Current Topics, ISSN 1874-0081 ; v. 62)
　　Includes bibliographical references and index.
　　1. French language--Study and teaching--Foreign speakers. 2. French language--
　　　Grammar--Study and teaching. 3. Second language acquisition. I. Lindqvist,
　　　Christina, editor of compilation. II. Bardel, Camilla, editor of compilation.
　　PC2065.A37　　　　　　2014
　　448.0071--dc23   2014008328
　　ISBN 978 90 272 4250 1　(Hb ; alk. paper)
　　ISBN 978 90 272 7007 8　(Eb)

© 2014 – John Benjamins B.V.
No part of this book may be reproduced in any form, by print, photoprint, microfilm, or any
other means, without written permission from the publisher.

John Benjamins Publishing Co. · P.O. Box 36224 · 1020 ME Amsterdam · The Netherlands
John Benjamins North America · P.O. Box 27519 · Philadelphia PA 19118-0519 · USA

Table of contents

Introduction

The acquisition of French as a second language: New developmental perspectives   1
Camilla Bardel and Christina Lindqvist

Synthèse rétrospective et nouvelles perspectives développementales: Les recherches acquisitionnelles en français L2 à l'Université de Stockholm   7
Inge Bartning

Pragmatic use of temporal adverbs in L1 and L2 French: Functions and syntactic positions of textual markers in a spoken corpus   29
Victorine Hancock

La dislocation dans le français oral d'apprenants suédophones: Emploi et développement   53
Hugues Engel

Vocabulary aspects of advanced L2 French: Do lexical formulaic sequences and lexical richness develop at the same rate?   75
Fanny Forsberg Lundell and Christina Lindqvist

Formulaic and proceduralised language in the initial and advanced stages of learning French   95
Richard Towell

The acquisition of additive scope particles by Moroccan Arabic L1 learners of French   117
Georges Daniel Véronique

Development of object clitics in child L2 French: A comparison of developmental sequences in different modes of acquisition   143
Jonas Granfeldt

Subject index   167

INTRODUCTION

The acquisition of French as a second language
New developmental perspectives

Camilla Bardel and Christina Lindqvist
Stockholm University / Uppsala University

Research on French as a second language (L2) has had an important role in second language acquisition (SLA) research for several years and it is constantly developing, especially in the European context. French is one of the most frequently studied foreign languages in European schools and many studies have been carried out on learners with French as target language and a variety of L1s. In France, research on L2 French in recent decades has been a continuation of the seminal work of Klein and Perdue, initiated during the 1980s. Outside France, important work has been carried out for instance in the United Kingdom and in Flanders, where French is a frequently studied school subject. Also in Sweden, French has for a long time been an important foreign language and research on the acquisition of French has a longstanding tradition. In 1988, inspired by the work of Perdue and colleagues in Paris within the ESF project, Inge Bartning started to collect data from Swedish learners of French at Stockholm University. This project (*InterFra*) has grown continuously and now provides data from informants ranging from beginning learners to very advanced L2 users of French, which has made it possible to describe the different developmental stages that the learners go through when acquiring French as a L2. Klein & Perdue (1997) proposed the *basic variety* and, relating her work to their ideas about interlanguage development, Bartning (1997) presented an overview of research on the *advanced L2 learner*. Furthermore, Bartning and Schlyter (2004) identified a scale of developmental stages — from the *initial stage* to the *advanced high stage* — for Swedes' development of morphological and syntactic knowledge in French L2.

All of the contributions in this volume deal with the acquisition of French from different perspectives.[1] The authors are specialized in L2 research, and more

---

1. Several of the studies reported in this volume were presented at a colloquium entitled *French Second Language Acquisition*, which took place in March 2010 at Stockholm University in honour of Inge Bartning at the time of her retirement. Most of these are based on the *InterFra* corpus which will soon be accessible on-line.

particularly in L2 French. Their research interests include morpho-syntax, formulaic language and lexis, and range from formal to functional perspectives on L2 acquisition. The different studies in the volume take into account several different L1s and cover the whole continuum of the acquisition process, from beginners to very advanced, supposedly near-native, L2 users of French. Together they represent a diversity of theoretical perspectives and bring together senior as well as younger researchers, all aiming at a better understanding of the acquisition of French as L2. It is our hope that this volume will be of interest for students and teachers, as well as researchers of French as L2 and SLA researchers in general.

In the first chapter of the volume, **Inge Bartning** presents a survey of the research at Stockholm University during the past 20 years. The first part of her paper is a detailed description of the corpus used in her research and in most papers included in this volume (*InterFra* corpus, see Note 1). The second part concerns the most recent results within the research program *High-level proficiency in second language use*. **Victorine Hancock** examines the pragmaticalisation of certain temporal adverbs, i.e. the development of their different temporal and pragmatic functions in information structure, among highly advanced L2 speakers of French. **Hugues Engel** then investigates the use and development of dislocations in the oral production of Swedish learners of French, ranging from beginners to L2 users who have spent many years in France. Two main kinds of dislocations are analysed: [*moi je* VP] and its syntactical variants, and dislocations referring to third entities such as [NP *il* VP] and [NP *c'est* X]. **Fanny Forsberg Lundell** and **Christina Lindqvist** contribute to the characterization of the advanced learner of French by examining the acquisition of vocabulary and formulaic sequences. This study gives new insights into what is known about the development of Swedish learners of L2 French, which has mainly focused on morpho-syntax in the past. Moving then to another setting for the acquisition of French as L2, **Richard Towell** discusses the acquisition of French by Anglophone learners in Great Britain, focussing on their morpho-syntactic development as well as on the role of formulaic language in L2 French. The chapter illustrates how the model in Towell & Hawkins (1994) can be applied, considering the variety of knowledge sources relied upon in L2 acquisition and the processing demands that consequently distinguish L2 from L1 acquisition. In the next chapter, **Daniel Véronique** aims at identifying the factors that explain the sequence of acquisition and use of additive scope particles (*aussi, même* and *encore*, i.e. 'also', 'even' and 'still') in L2 French by L1 speakers of Moroccan Arabic in France. Investigating the syntactic and semantic differences affecting scope particles in Moroccan Arabic and French, he also brings up other factors such as cognitive saliency and semantic complexity in addition to information structure and finiteness. Finally, **Jonas Granfeldt** analyzes the development of object clitics and the process of cliticisation in French, comparing child L2 learners with different ages of onset to both simultaneous bilingual children and monolingual controls. He discusses the results in relation to the Critical Period Hypothesis.

The aim of this synthesis of L2 French in different settings, from learners of different L1s and of varying age, is to give a picture of research on the topic currently ongoing in Sweden as well as in some other European countries.

INTRODUCTION

L'acquisition du français langue seconde
Nouvelles perspectives développementales

Camilla Bardel et Christina Lindqvist
Université de Stockholm / Université d'Uppsala

Les recherches sur le français langue seconde jouent un rôle important dans l'étude de l'acquisition d'une langue seconde depuis plusieurs années et se développent constamment, surtout dans le contexte européen. Le français est l'une des langues étrangères les plus étudiées dans les écoles européennes et de nombreuses études ont été menées sur les apprenants du français ayant différentes L1. En France, les recherches sur le français L2 au cours des dernières décennies ont prolongé les travaux pionniers de Klein et de Perdue, initiés dans les années 1980. En dehors de la France, d'importants travaux ont été réalisés par exemple au Royaume-Uni et dans les Flandres, où le français est une matière scolaire fréquemment étudiée. En Suède aussi, le français a longtemps été une langue étrangère importante et les recherches sur l'acquisition du français ont une longue tradition. En 1988, inspirée par les travaux de Perdue et de ses collègues parisiens dans le cadre de leur projet ESF, Inge Bartning a commencé à enregistrer des apprenants suédois du français à l'Université de Stockholm. Ce projet (*InterFra*) s'est constamment développé et rassemble aujourd'hui des enregistrements provenant d'informateurs variés, depuis le stade des apprenants débutants jusqu'à celui des usagers très avancés du français L2, ce qui a rendu possible la description de différents stades développementaux que traversent les apprenants qui acquièrent le français L2. Klein et Perdue (1997) ont décrit la variété basique et, à partir de leurs idées concernant le développement de l'interlangue, Bartning (1997) a présenté un survol des recherches sur *l'apprenant avancé d'une L2*. Quelques années plus tard, Bartning et Schlyter (2004) ont identifié des stades développementaux — depuis le *stade initial* jusqu'au *stade avancé supérieur* — pour le développement des connaissances morphologiques et syntaxiques en français L2 des apprenants suédophones.

Toutes les contributions de ce volume traitent de l'acquisition du français, adoptant différentes perspectives.[1] Les auteurs sont spécialistes de l'acquisition de L2, plus précisément du français L2. Leurs intérêts de recherche incluent la morpho-syntaxe, le langage préfabriqué et le lexique, et adoptent les perspectives formelles et fonctionnelles de l'acquisition d'une L2. Les études présentées prennent en compte différentes L1 et couvrent tout le continuum du processus acquisitionnel, des débutants aux usagers de L2 très avancés, potentiellement quasi-natifs. L'ensemble de ces recherches représente une diversité de perspectives théoriques et réunit des chercheurs établis et des chercheurs plus jeunes, ayant tous pour objectif une meilleure compréhension de l'acquisition du français L2. Nous espérons que ce volume intéressera les étudiants et les enseignants, aussi bien que les chercheurs en français L2 ou, plus généralement, en acquisition d'une langue seconde.

Dans le premier article du volume, **Inge Bartning** présente un survol des recherches menées à l'Université de Stockholm au cours des 20 dernières années. La première partie de son article est une description détaillée du corpus sur lequel se fonde ses travaux et la plupart de ceux qui sont inclus dans ce volume (*InterFra corpus*, voir Note 1). La deuxième partie concerne les résultats les plus récents dans le cadre du programme de recherche *High-level proficiency in second language use*. **Victorine Hancock** examine la pragmaticalisation de certains adverbes temporaux, notamment le développement de leurs différentes fonctions temporelles et pragmatiques en relation avec la structure informationnelle chez des apprenants très avancés du français L2. **Hugues Engel** examine l'usage et le développement des dislocations dans la production orale d'apprenants suédois du français, des apprenants débutants jusqu'aux usagers qui ont passé un grand nombre d'années en France (toutes les données sont issues du corpus *InterFra*). Deux types principaux de dislocations sont analysés : [*moi je* VP] et ses variantes syntaxiques, ainsi que les dislocations qui se réfèrent à des entités tierces, telles que [NP *il* VP] et [NP *c'est* X]. **Fanny Forsberg Lundell** et **Christina Lindqvist** visent à affiner la description de l'apprenant avancé du français en examinant l'acquisition du vocabulaire et des séquences préfabriquées. L'étude présente de nouvelles perspectives concernant le développement d'apprenants suédois du français L2, étudié jusqu'à présent principalement du point de vue de la morpho-syntaxe. A partir d'un autre contexte d'acquisition du français L2, **Richard Towell** discute de l'acquisition du français par des apprenants anglophones en Grande-Bretagne, en mettant l'accent sur le développement morpho-syntaxique de leur L2 ainsi que sur le rôle du

---

1. Plusieurs des études figurant dans ce volume ont été présentées à un colloque intitulé *L'Acquisition du français langue seconde* qui s'est déroulé en mars 2010 à l'Université de Stockholm en hommage à Inge Bartning, au moment de son départ à la retraite. La plupart présentent des données issues du corpus *InterFra* qui sera bientôt accessible en ligne.

langage préfabriqué en français L2. L'article montre l'utilité du modèle de Towell et Hawkins (1994) et examine les sources variées de connaissances intervenant dans l'acquisition d'une L2 ainsi que les différentes contraintes de traitement qui en résultent et qui distinguent l'acquisition L2 de l'acquisition L1. **Daniel Véronique** a pour objectif d'identifier les facteurs qui expliquent la séquence d'acquisition et d'usage des particules de portée additives (*aussi, même* et *encore*) en français L2 par des locuteurs d'arabe marocain L1 en France. Examinant les différences syntaxiques et sémantiques des particules de portée en arabe marocain et en français, il montre également le rôle d'autres facteurs, comme la saillance cognitive et la complexité sémantique, hormis la structure informationnelle et la finitude. Enfin, **Jonas Granfeldt** analyse le développement des pronoms objet clitiques et le processus de clitisation en français. Il compare des enfants apprenant une L2, dont le début de l'acquisition se situe à différents âges, avec des enfants bilingues simultanés et un groupe de contrôle composé de locuteurs monolingues. Il discute les résultats par rapport à l'hypothèse de la Période Critique.

L'objectif de ce volume sur le français L2 acquis dans différents contextes et par des apprenants de L1 diverses et d'âges différents est de proposer une synthèse de la recherche actuelle dans le domaine, en Suède et dans d'autres pays européens.

Synthèse rétrospective et nouvelles perspectives développementales
Les recherches acquisitionnelles en français L2 à l'Université de Stockholm

Inge Bartning
Université de Stockholm

Ce chapitre présente une synthèse des recherches en acquisition du français langue seconde/étrangère menées à l'Université de Stockholm. Il fait le lien entre les premiers résultats obtenus au sein du projet *InterFra* (*Interlangue française — développement, interaction et variation*) avec les recherches menées récemment sur les stades très avancés. Le chapitre se divise en trois parties. Les deux premières sont rétrospectives, d'abord une description du corpus *InterFra* — présenté ici dans son intégralité pour la première fois —, puis un bilan des résultats des thèses qui ont utilisé ce corpus, et, finalement, les stades de développement proposés par Bartning et Schlyter (2004). La troisième partie présente un projet sur les stades ultimes d'une L2, *High-level proficiency in second language use,* programme de recherche commun à cinq départements de l'Université de Stockholm et rend compte des résultats d'études récentes concernant trois groupes d'un niveau proche du locuteur natif, des locuteurs non natifs appelés respectivement *avancés, bilingues fonctionnels* et *quasi-natifs*. Le chapitre se clôt sur un bilan de ces études.

1. Introduction

Ce chapitre présente une synthèse des recherches en acquisition du français langue seconde/étrangère menées depuis deux décennies à l'Université de Stockholm. Il propose aussi de nouvelles perspectives développementales basées sur les premiers résultats d'un programme de recherche concernant les stades ultimes en L2.

L'étude se présente sous la forme de trois volets. Les deux premiers sont des parties rétrospectives, d'abord une description du corpus utilisé comme base de données *InterFra* (*Interlangue française — développement, interaction et variation*), puis une présentation des résultats des stades de développement de Bartning et Schlyter (2004) ainsi que des thèses basées sur ce même corpus. Le troisième et dernier volet rend compte d'études récentes sur les stades ultimes dans le projet *High-level proficiency in second language use,* programme de recherche commun à cinq départements à la même université (*cf.* Bartning & Hancock soumis). Il sera donc question de l'acquisition aux stades avancés et très avancés en français L2, stades où il s'agit plutôt de l'usage de la L2 que de l'acquisition proprement dite. On s'intéresse aussi bien aux ressources de l'apprenant très avancé qu'aux obstacles dans son cheminement vers le bilinguisme. On se demande alors quels sont les traits du locuteur natif qui sont toujours en développement chez le locuteur non-natif. On se pose ces questions tant pour la théorisation des stades ultimes que pour une description adéquate des données empiriques de ces stades.

2. Synthèse rétrospective

2.1 Le corpus InterFra 1989–2010

Comme il ressort du Tableau 1, le corpus *InterFra* contient aujourd'hui deux grandes parties, à savoir le Groupe I 'Français langue étrangère' (FLE) avec la production orale de lycéens, de débutants, d'étudiants de 1ère et de 2e année à l'université, de futurs professeurs et de doctorants, et le Groupe II 'Français langue seconde' (FLS) constitué de la production de jeunes suédophones de 20–25 ans, appelés Juniors, qui vivent à Paris depuis au moins 5 ans, ainsi que de suédophones de 40–60 ans, appelés Seniors, qui vivent à Paris depuis 20–25 ans. Tous ces informants ont exécuté les mêmes tâches, à savoir des interviews et des narrations (vidéo et BD) avec les mêmes interlocuteurs. Le corpus inclut aussi un Groupe multi-tâches (II.c), avec des suédophones ayant vécu au moins 5 ans en France et qui ont tous été soumis à des tâches variées (conversations téléphoniques, récits de *Frog story* (Mayer 1969) et de *Modern Times (Chaplin)*, interviews, etc.).

Les apprenants du groupe FLE ont appris le français dans des conditions pour la plupart guidées ou semi-guidées, tandis que ceux des groupes FLS l'ont appris dans des situations non-guidées. Tous ces apprenants ont commencé l'acquisition du français L2 à l'âge de 13–14 ans. Il s'agit donc d'apprenants 'tardifs' ou *late learners* (*cf.* Birdsong 2003).

Ces apprenants/usagers non-natifs (au total 102 informants) sont couplés à des groupes de contrôle de francophones (groupe III, 53 personnes). Le corpus couvre un total de 600 000 mots. Pour transcrire les enregistrements, les principes de la transcription orthographique ont été choisis (selon les travaux de Blanche-Benveniste, par exemple 1997). La plupart des productions du Groupe I

(FLE) ont été étiquetées grammaticalement selon le programme Tagger Beta (voir www.fraita.su.se/interfra).

Du point de vue chronologique, les groupes FLE ont été les premiers à être enregistrés, à partir de 1989. Certains étudiants universitaires ont été suivis pendant quatre semestres, les débutants et les futurs professeurs pendant deux semestres (avec un stage intermédiaire en France), les lycéens deux fois en deux ans. Tous les groupes FLE ont donc été enregistrés de façon longitudinale, hormis les doctorants. L'enregistrement des groupes FLS est plus tardif (2006–2008) ainsi que celui des groupes de LN, sauf les étudiants ERASMUS (1993). Dans le Tableau 1 nous présentons les groupes selon les neuf paramètres suivants : groupes d'apprenants, date d'enregistrement, nombre d'informants, nombre d'années d'étude, durée de séjour dans un pays francophone, âge de l'apprenant, tâches, type d'étude et type d'acquisition. Pour plus de détails sur ces groupes de locuteurs, voir Bartning (1997, 2009).

Le corpus *InterFra* sera, sous peu, converti dans son intégralité en format xml et rendu accessible à la communauté scientifique sur le web.

2.2 La perspective développementale en RAL et les stades de Bartning et Schlyter (2004)

Depuis le commencement des recherches en RAL (Recherche en acquisition des langues), la perspective développementale s'est imposée dans des cadres théoriques différents mais toujours basée sur des données empiriques (R. Ellis 2008, Ch. 4). A titre d'illustration, on peut mentionner les études suivantes : le projet ZISA (Meisel *et al.* 1981), le projet ESF (*European Science Foundation*, Perdue 1993 ; Klein & Perdue 1997), le projet de Pavia (Giacalone Ramat 1992), le projet InterFra (Bartning 1997 ; Bartning & Schlyter 2004), le projet de Lund (Granfeldt 2003 ; Schlyter 2003), la théorie de la « processabilité » (Pienemann 1998), et, notamment pour le français L2, les travaux de Dewaele (2005), Housen et Kuiken (2009), Myles (2005) et Towell *et al.* (1996). Pour des synthèses des résultats sur le développement du français L2, voir Bartning (2009) et Labeau et Myles (2009). Pour des synthèses générales sur la perspective développementale en L2, voir R. Ellis (2008, Ch. 4), Bardovi-Harlig (2006) et Doughty et Long (2003).

2.2.1 *Les stades de Bartning et Schlyter (2004)*
Sur la base d'un échantillon des groupes suivants : les débutants, les lycéens, les étudiants universitaires et les futur professeurs (voir les groupes I. FLE a et b 1–3, Tableau 1), nous avons entamé une collaboration avec Suzanne Schlyter, Université de Lund, qui a abouti à proposer un continuum développemental sur une échelle de six stades pour l'acquisition du français L2 : (1) initial, (2) post-initial, (3)

Tableau 1. Le corpus InterFra — tableau synthétique

Groupes	Date d'enregistrement	Nombre d'apprenants	Années d'étude	Durée de séjour en France	Âge	Tâches	Longitudinal/ Transversal	Type d'acquisition
Locuteurs non-natifs (LNN)								
I. FLE								
a. Lycéens	1996-97	20	3,5	1–2 semaines	17–18	Interview BD, Vid	Longitudinal 2 ans	Guidé
b. Étudiants universitaires								
1. Débutants	1999-2001	18 (10 Long)	0	1–2 semaines	19–30	Interview BD, Vid	Longitudinal 2 semestres Transversal	Guidé
2. Étudiants de 1ère, 2e année	1989	18 (8 Long)	6	3 mois-1 an	19–26	Interview BD, Vid	Longitudinal 4 semestres Transversal	Semi-guidé
3. Futurs professeurs	1992	6	7–8	3 mois-1 an	23–34	Interview BD, Vid	Longitudinal 2 semestres stage	Semi-guidé
4. Doctorants	2003	10	8–9	1–5 ans	23–26	Interview BD, Vid	Transversal	Semi-guidé
II. LNN FLS								
a. 5–15 Juniors	2006	10	(3–6)	5–15 ans	25–30	Interview BD	–	Non guidé
b. 15–30 Seniors	2006	10	(3–6)	15–30 ans	45–60	Interview BD	–	Non guidé

c. Groupe Multi-tâches	2008	10	(3–6)	5–10 ans	25–30	Interview Conv. téléph *Frog Story, Modern Times*	—	Non guidé
Total		102					
III. Locuteurs natifs (LN)							
a. Étudiants d'échange ERASMUS	1993	20	Bac+3	—	23–26	Interview BD, Vid	—
b. LN Juniors	2006	15	Bac+3	—	25–30	Interview BD, Vid	—
c. LN Seniors	2006	8	Bac+3	—	45–60	Int, BD, Vid, JdG	—
d. LN Multi-tâches	2008	10	Bac+3	—	25–30	Int, Conv téléphon *Frog, Modern Times*	—
Total		53					

(*Légende* : Int = interview, BD = Récits de bandes dessinées (Kahlmann 1984), Vid = récits de vidéoclip de Mordillo, JdG = tests de jugement de grammaticalité) intermédiaire, (4) avancé bas, (5) avancé moyen, et (6) avancé supérieur. Ce continuum est fondé sur des itinéraires acquisitionnels de 20–25 critères basés sur deux corpus longitudinaux avec 80 enregistrements de français parlé spontané d'apprenants suédophones. Les critères morpho-syntaxiques et discursifs principaux pour délimiter ces stades étaient (1) la morphologie du syntagme verbal : formes flexionnelles (personne, nombre ; Bartning 1997) ; la morphologie verbale temporelle/aspectuelle (Kihlstedt 1998) ; la morphologie dans le syntagme nominal : le genre (Bartning 2000) ; (2) la syntaxe : le marquage de l'accord sujet-verbe (Bartning 1997) ; celui de l'accord entre noms et adjectifs (Bartning 2000) ; la négation (Sanell 2007) ; la subordination (Hancock 2000 ; Kirchmeyer 2002) ; (3) des phénomènes discursifs : les connecteurs (Hancock 2000).

La perspective de Bartning et Schlyter (2004) était donc développementale et empirique, basée sur deux corpus d'interlangue française différents. Les fondements théoriques étaient les séquences développementales et la perspective fonctionnaliste (Klein & Perdue 1997), la grammaticalisation (relations formes/ fonctions) ainsi que la théorie de la processabilité (Pienemann 1998). Pour souligner l'importance de l'aspect développemental en RAL, il convient de citer Sharwood Smith et Truscott (2005 : 221) : « … it is reasonable to accept that stages must figure in any serious explanation of acquisition ».

Nous avons trouvé des *itinéraires acquisitionnels* qui se développent parallèlement, par exemple pour le système TMA (temps, mode, aspect) : présent > passé composé, imparfait (*être, avoir*) > futur > subjonctif > conditionnel, plus-que-parfait). A partir de tels itinéraires de phénomènes différents et parallèles, très semblables dans les deux corpus, nous avons proposé des faisceaux de traits simultanés en six *stades développementaux*. Ainsi on peut dire que le regroupement en stades est hypothétique ; tandis que les itinéraires sont basés sur des données empiriques des deux corpus (le phénomène A précède B qui, à son tour, précède C, et ainsi de suite). Nous considérons que les stades et les itinéraires reflètent l'acquisition du français de l'apprenant dans des situations à l'oral spontané où il doit avoir recours à ses connaissances implicites et automatisées. (Pour la confirmation 'externe' de ces stades, voir Section 2.2.3.)

2.2.2   Les stades avancés 4–6 de Bartning et Schlyter (2004) — synthèse

Vu le cadre restreint de ce chapitre, nous ne donnons ici qu'un résumé des *stades avancés 4–6*, en renvoyant le lecteur à l'aperçu synthétique de l'intégralité des stades 1–6 récemment publié dans Forsberg et Bartning (2010 : 155–157, Appendice). Le résumé de ces stades de l'apprenant avancé servira ainsi de point de comparaison pour la discussion sur les traits caractéristiques des apprenants très avancés.

Ces stades sont représentés par un éventail plus large de structures d'énoncés et par la grammaticalisation de la morphologie flexionnelle qui devient fonctionnelle mais avec des zones 'fragiles' de développement. La raison pour laquelle nous avons divisé la variété avancée en trois niveaux est qu'au fur et à mesure que l'interlangue se développe, cette évolution crée une richesse d'expressions qui permettent un répertoire plus varié et donc un choix.

Au **stade avancé bas (stade 4)**, plusieurs nouveaux phénomènes émergent : le pronom clitique avant le verbe fini, le conditionnel, le plus-que-parfait, dans des cas isolés. Ces formes apparaissent d'abord dans la syntaxe simple non-subordonnée (Kirchmeyer 2002). On observe aussi l'émergence des formes de la négation *rien*, *jamais* et *personne* (Sanell 2007). **L'application appropriée/inappropriée des règles** : un trait important est que la plupart des formes non-finies (*je *donnE*, *ils *prendre*) ont disparu, ce trait étant très fréquent aux stades précédents. Pourtant les formes courtes IL des verbes irréguliers à la 3e personne au singulier pour le pluriel (*ils *prend*) continuent à co-exister avec les formes correctes. Le genre masculin du déterminant et de l'adjectif est sur-employé et le marquage du genre est plus correct sur le déterminant défini que sur le déterminant indéfini (Bartning 2000 ; Lindström 2008). **L'usage approprié/inapproprié en contexte discursif** : le présent est sur-employé pour les temps au passé et pour le futur (Kihlstedt 1998). Quant aux **traits spécifiques aux apprenants**, on observe un suremploi statistiquement significatif des connecteurs *mais* et *parce que* (Hancock 2000).

Au **stade avancé intermédiaire (stade 5)**, on observe l'**émergence** des énoncés multi-propositionnels et d'un emploi élaboré macro-syntaxique de *parce que* dans les énoncés complexes ; l'émergence de *dont* (Hancock 2000) dont l'emploi se rapproche de celui des LN. Les énoncés elliptiques avec des gérondifs et des constructions infinitivales (Kirchmeyer 2002) émergent également. **L'application appropriée/inappropriée des règles** montre que l'accord du genre (déterminants, adjectifs) est toujours problématique et que l'accord verbal n'est pas toujours marqué sur la 3e personne du pluriel au présent des verbes irréguliers. **L'usage diversifié et approprié en contexte** montre que l'apprenant ici est aussi capable de se déplacer sur l'axe temporel (Kihlstedt 1998). On observe aussi un emploi productif du conditionnel, du futur (simple), du plus-que-parfait et du subjonctif (Bartning à paraître) ainsi qu'un suremploi du passé composé pour le plus-que-parfait. La négation est utilisée en tant que sujet (*Personne ne…*). Enfin, au **stade avancé supérieur (stade 6)**, la morphologie flexionnelle se stabilise, même dans les énoncés multi-propositionnels. Ce stade 6 se distingue du précédent par **l'emploi de formes complexes** (empaquetage, multi-propositions) de façon appropriée et dans des contextes élargis. La fréquence des occurrences d'empaquetage, d'ellipse et d'intégration des propositions traduit une capacité à gérer plusieurs niveaux informationnels au sein du même énoncé (Kirchmeyer 2002). Par ailleurs on observe un emploi natif des connecteurs *enfin* et *donc* (Hancock 2000), ainsi qu'un emploi presque natif des relatives macro-syntaxiques et des subordonnées causales (Hancock & Kirchmeyer 2005). On note aussi des formes '**fossilisées**' et des emplois non standard persistants, notamment la 3e personne du pluriel au présent des verbes irréguliers ainsi que le subjonctif (Bartning à paraître). Des emplois non-standard persistent aussi dans l'accord du genre pour l'adjectif préposé. Le conditionnel et le plus-que-parfait ne sont pas toujours fournis dans les contextes obligatoires.

Comme nous le verrons dans la Section 3 ci-dessous, certains de ces traits typiques des stades 4–6 réapparaissent en tant que difficultés résiduelles chez l'apprenant 'quasi-natif' (voir aussi Bartning & Hancock soumis).

2.2.3 *Confirmation des stades*

Récemment, des études basées sur d'autres corpus européens ont commencé à confirmer les stades. Ces études concernent surtout les stades avancés 4–6, par exemple : Housen *et al.* (2009), pour le français oral, avec le néerlandais comme L1 ; Bolly (2008) pour le français écrit, avec le néerlandais et l'anglais comme L1 ; ainsi que Labeau (2009), français oral et écrit avec l'anglais comme L1. Pour le français écrit et les stades 1–4, voir Ågren (2008) (jeunes étudiants suédophones) ainsi que Granfeldt et Nugues (2007) (adultes suédophones). Pour une application informatique des six stades sous la forme d'un logiciel d'auto-évaluation *Direkt profil*, voir Granfeldt et Nugues (2007). Pour une confirmation générale, voir Véronique (2009). Il y a aussi une mise en rapport récente entre ces stades de développement linguistique et les six niveaux pragmatiques de l'échelle de *CEFR* (*Common European Framework of Reference for Languages*) dans l'étude de Forsberg et Bartning (2010), cette fois sur un nouveau corpus écrit.

Ajoutons que, tout récemment, Lindqvist *et al.* (2011) ont montré des différences significatives en ce qui concerne la richesse lexicale entre les stades 4 et 6 (interviews d'InterFra).

2.3 Bilan des thèses d'InterFra

Après la publication des premiers résultats du corpus *InterFra* dans Bartning (1997), sur l'apprenant avancé, la thèse de Kihlstedt (1998) a porté sur l'acquisition de la référence au passé chez ce type d'apprenant. Dans cette étude longitudinale quatre apprenants ont été suivis pendant quatre semestres, après quoi leurs productions ont été comparées à celles des natifs (total 20 interviews). Il s'est révélé que les formes du temps et de l'aspect sont acquises avant leur emploi fonctionnel stabilisé et étendu, que la multitude des valeurs de l'imparfait en français LC est difficile à acquérir et que l'emploi de l'imparfait est limité à certains verbes et à certaines valeurs aspectuelles par rapport à l'emploi des LN. L'itinéraire acquisitionnel du système TMA, proposé dans la littérature, est confirmé par cette thèse (présent > passé composé > imparfait (*être, avoir*), futur périphrastique > imparfait (verbes lexicaux) > futur simple > conditionnel > subjonctif > plus-que-parfait).

Hancock (2000) a étudié l'emploi de certains connecteurs (*mais, parce que, donc*) et d'expressions épistémiques (*je trouve que, je crois que*) dans les interviews de 22 LNN en les comparant à l'usage des LN (8). L'étude est basée sur des analyses sémantiques, discursives et interactionnelles. Les résultats montrent un suremploi significatif de *mais*, surtout en tant que marqueur de reformulation. Chez les apprenants les plus avancés, l'auteur note un degré plus marqué d'intégration syntaxique/discursive dans les séquences introduites par *parce que*. La thèse montre aussi des emplois très avancés du connecteur *donc* dans le cadre d'une analyse prosodique du paragraphe oral (*cf.* Morel & Danon-Boileau 1998).

Dans une recherche sur la compétence textuelle, Kirchmeyer (2002) a mis en évidence des traits typiques de l'apprenant avancé et pré-avancé (lycéens) dans 36 récits oraux du corpus *InterFra* en les comparant à l'usage des LN et à celui des mêmes apprenants dans leur L1 (suédois). Alors que les apprenants avancés hiérarchisent l'information à travers trois dimensions de la complexité syntaxique : le degré d'empaquetage, d'intégration et d'ellipse (le gérondif), l'apprenant moins avancé a recours à des connecteurs pour hiérarchiser l'information et compenser ainsi le recours à la syntaxe complexe.

La thèse de Lindqvist (2006) porte sur l'acquisition d'une L3, problématique de recherche qui constitue un courant important. On s'interroge sur l'influence des langues antérieurement acquises sur la L3, la nouvelle langue cible. Dans une perspective psycholinguistique, l'auteur examine les influences translinguistiques de la L1 et des autres L2 sur l'emploi du français L3 dans des interviews de trois types d'apprenants : des débutants, des lycéens et des étudiants universitaires (30 apprenants). Lindqvist montre que le niveau en L3 est déterminant pour contrer l'emploi des autres langues acquises : plus l'apprenant est avancé, moins il a recours à d'autres langues dans sa production en L3.

La thèse de Forsberg (2006) s'inscrit dans un autre courant de recherche qui a connu un nouvel essor récemment, à savoir le langage préfabriqué ou les séquences préfabriquées (SP, séquences récurrentes d'au moins deux mots). Sur la base d'un corpus de 66 productions d'apprenants (débutants, lycéens et apprenants avancés) et de quatre variables — le nombre de SP/100 mots, la distribution en catégories de SP, le taux types/occurrences de SP et les types les plus fréquents de SP, l'auteur propose un itinéraire acquisitionnel. Ainsi, elle constate à un extrême, chez les débutants, des SP situationnelles (*je m'appelle*) et des SP idiosyncrasiques (**je ça va bien*) et, à l'autre extrême, des SP lexicales (*rendre un dossier*) qui sont plus fréquentes chez les apprenants avancés et les LN. Les SP discursives (*c'est*) sont de façon générale les plus fréquentes dans la production aussi bien chez les LNN que chez les LN. Forsberg a montré que le développement des SP est lié au niveau acquisitionnel des apprenants.

Sanell (2007), dans une étude longitudinale de la négation et des particules de portée (80 interviews), a montré que la négation de phrase *ne…pas* s'acquiert assez vite en français, à savoir dès le stade 3 (intermédiaire). Au stade initial, la négation *non* est employée de façon idiosyncrasique en tant que négation de constituant et négation pré-verbale, tandis qu'au stade post-intitial la négation *pas* est acquise en position post-verbale. Les particules de portée sont acquises au stade post-initial dans l'ordre *aussi*, *encore* (additif) et *seulement* (restrictif), tandis que les adverbes temporels *encore* et *déjà* sont presque exclusivement employés par des apprenants avancés. Ainsi, Sanell a pu proposer un itinéraire acquisitionnel de la négation et des particules de portée pour le français oral.

Dans son étude longitudinale sur l'acquisition de l'accord du genre des déterminants et des adjectifs dans quatre groupes d'apprenant (débutants, lycéens, étudiants universitaires et futurs professeurs ; 68 interviews), Lindström (2008) a pu vérifier la séquence développementale du genre déjà proposée dans la littérature, avec certaines variantes en ce qui concerne la position de l'adjectif : déterminant défini > déterminant indéfini > déterminant+nom+adjectif > déterminant+adjectif+nom > déterminant+nom *être* adjectif. Elle montre aussi que le taux d'exactitude chez l'apprenant avancé est le plus élevé mais avec une variation interindividuelle très grande. On trouve donc un développement très variable et irrégulier, probablement dû aux phénomènes de séquences non-analysées et de trajectoires individuelles.

La thèse de Engel (2010), sur l'acquisition de la dislocation en français parlé (*Pierre, il est venu hier*), s'appuie sur la quasi-totalité des groupes d'apprenants du corpus InterFra, depuis les débutants jusqu'aux apprenants très avancés/'quasi-natifs', ces derniers avec une période très longue en France, en passant par les étudiants universitaires et les futurs professeurs. Cette étude longitudinale, elle aussi, compare les LN et les LNN. Les résultats mettent en avant l'influence des deux tâches, interviews (80) et récits (78), sur l'emploi des structures, avec des différences significatives. Les structures étudiées sont, d'une part, *moi je SV* (avec variantes syntaxiques) et, d'autre part, *SN il SV* et *SN c'est SN*. Les résultats montrent un parcours développemental, mais l'apprenant maîtrise déjà, dès le début, la dislocation lexicale se référant aux entités ainsi que les règles d'emploi pragmatiques. La fréquence de *moi je SV* est fortement corrélée aux niveaux acquisitionnels et son émergence constitue un trait relativement tardif.

2.4 Hypothèses explicatives

Pour ce qui est des résultats du développement mis en évidence par les stades, on peut proposer que l'émergence des moyens linguistiques pourraient s'interpréter par des besoins discursifs dans une perspective fonctionnaliste (Klein & Perdue

1997): l'émergence graduelle du système temporo-aspectuel attesté surtout aux stades 4–5 en est un exemple (voir 2.2.1). Par contre, les phénomènes tels que l'application appropriée des systèmes formels, comme le genre et l'accord sujet-verbe lié à la complexification de la phrase, s'interprètent bien par la théorie de la processabilité de Pienemann (voir l'application de cette théorie à l'acquisition de l'accord adjectival dans Bartning 2000). D'autres phénomènes encore s'expliquent par le poids cognitif (mémorisation), comme le met en évidence l'accord sujet — verbe dans les phrases complexes (*cf.* Bartning, Forsberg Lundell & Hancock 2012). Dans la section suivante on abordera la question de tels phénomènes de complexité.

3. Recherches actuelles : le projet *High-level proficiency in second language use* ou 'Acquisition très avancée en langues secondes' — nouvelles perspectives développementales

On a vu depuis quelques années un intérêt grandissant pour les stades ultimes en RAL après une longue période de recherches sur les stades précoces et intermédiaires. La description de ces stades ainsi que les explications avancées sur la possibilité d'atteindre des niveaux 'natifs' (*native-like*) en L2 ont été abordées sous différentes perspectives. L'influence déterminante du facteur de l'âge comme base d'explication a fait l'objet de vives controverses entre deux positions. La première n'exclut pas la possibilité qu'un locuteur non natif puisse atteindre une maîtrise quasi-native après l'âge de la puberté (par exemple, Birdsong 1999, 2003 ; Bongaerts 1999 ; Muñoz & Singleton 2007 ; Montrul & Slabakova 2003). L'autre position, à l'inverse, soutient que l'acquisition d'une L2, pour des raisons de maturation, est plus ou moins impossible après la puberté et qu'il faut commencer l'acquisition à des âges précoces (entre autres, Abrahamsson & Hyltenstam 2009). Ces auteurs ont proposé qu'après avoir identifié les locuteurs qui passent pour des natifs dans les tests d'écoute, le chercheur doit faire une analyse linguistique approfondie pour voir en quoi ces 'quasi-natifs' diffèrent des natifs.

Les études portant sur les 'quasi-natifs' en français L2 commencent à être nombreuses, notamment celles menées par Birdsong (1999, 2003, 2005, 2006), Bongaerts (1999, 2003), Singleton (2003) et, plus récemment, Donaldson (2011), sans omettre l'article original plus ancien de Coppieters (1987). Pour d'autres L2, mentionnons les études sur le *near-nativeness* de Sorace (2003) et de Montrul et Slabakova (2003). S'inscrivant dans d'autres perspectives, citons les études de Lambert (1997, 2006), Dimroth et Lambert (2008) et von Stutterheim (2003) sur les traces de l'influence de la L1 et la conceptualisation/choix de perspective des apprenants très avancés en français, anglais et allemand (voir aussi Hyltenstam & Abrahamsson 2003 et Paradis 2009).

3.1 Vers le locuteur natif — projets actuels

L'objectif du programme *High-Level Proficiency in Second Language Use/Acquisition très avancée en langues secondes* à l'Université de Stockholm est de mieux comprendre les conditions qui permettent aux apprenants d'une L2 d'atteindre les très hauts niveaux d'acquisition en abordant cette problématique sous diverses perspectives théoriques, à savoir psycholinguistiques, linguistico-structurales et sociolinguistiques. La tâche de l'un des projets, concernant le français, est d'identifier les traits morpho-syntaxiques, discursifs et lexicaux spécifiques au locuteur non-natif très avancé par rapport aux LN. Pour ce faire, comme on l'a vu, nous avons constitué de nouveaux corpus de locuteurs quasi-natifs de français pour les comparer aux locuteurs natifs (voir ci-dessus, Tableau 1, les groupes FLS). Par locuteur *quasi-natif* nous entendons, dans notre programme de recherche, une personne qui est perçue comme locuteur natif, dans le cadre d'une interaction orale normale, mais qui peut être distinguée d'un locuteur natif par certains traits lors d'une analyse linguistique détaillée de sa production langagière (Bartning *et al.* 2009).

Le premier objectif des travaux récents menés dans ce projet est de contribuer au débat sur la possibilité pour un apprenant d'atteindre le niveau quasi-natif en L2, en cernant tant les ressources que les zones fragiles dans l'acquisition très avancée. Nos études se distinguent aussi d'autres travaux, notamment ceux de Abrahamsson et Hyltenstam (2009), du fait que les informants du corpus *InterFra*, même les FLS, ont été exposés au français à l'âge de la puberté ou après. Comme on l'a vu, ce sont donc des 'apprenants tardifs'. Le deuxième objectif est de trouver et de caractériser des traits pertinents spécifiques aux apprenants avancés par rapport aux LN et de les combiner pour discerner des stades éventuellement plus 'tardifs' se situant au-delà des six stades de Bartning et Schlyter (2004). (Pour un aperçu de traits 'tardifs' de l'acquisition du français L2 dans la littérature internationale, voir Bartning 2009, 2012).

3.1.2 *Trois domaines 'tardifs' — morpho-syntaxe, séquences préfabriquées et structure informationnelle*

Afin de contribuer au débat concernant la possibilité d'atteindre un niveau *quasi-natif*, Bartning *et al.* (2009) ont proposé une analyse combinant trois phénomènes différents, à savoir l'emploi des séquences préfabriquées, qui relèvent du lexique, le recours à l'organisation informationnelle de l'énoncé en préambules et en rhèmes, et les phénomènes morpho-syntaxiques, à savoir les déviances (ou erreurs) dans la morphologie nominale et verbale, ici appelées déviances morpho-syntaxiques (DMS).

L'étude part de plusieurs hypothèses. Premièrement, nous supposons que les séquences préfabriquées sont des composantes importantes dans le langage des

LN et des LNN, dont on a pu retracer le développement en L2 (Forsberg 2006). Ces séquences sont utiles dans la production orale spontanée dans la mesure où elles sont 'traitées' plus vite que des constructions à règles créatives (Conklin & Schmitt 2008). Deuxièmement, en ce qui concerne l'organisation discursive et informationnelle en français parlé, on part de l'idée qu'il existe des parties thématiques longues (la juxtaposition d'informations nombreuses) avant la partie rhématique. Ces parties thématiques, ou *préambules* (PA), sont construites par des segments/constituants exprimant la modalité, le point de vue, le cadre temporel (Morel & Danon-Boileau 1998) (voir exemple 1, partie préambule (PA), pour un exemple natif). Il a été constaté (Conway 2005) que le LNN ne dispose pas des mêmes moyens pour construire des PA que les LN, mais que les constituants des PA augmentent durant le développement de ses connaissances. On sait aussi que les PA sont suivis par la partie rhématique où le locuteur présente ce qu'il veut dire relativement au thème. C'est dans le rhème qu'on trouve souvent le verbe fini 'principal' de l'énoncé pour la production duquel l'apprenant doit appliquer des règles morpho-syntaxiques telles que l'accord verbal et nominal (nombre et genre) (voir exemple 1, partie rhématique (RH)). La différence est dans l'association de ces deux parties (thématiques et rhématiques) à l'oral (*cf.* voir plus bas et Bartning *et al.* 2012). Troisièmement, on s'attend, selon nos études antérieures, à des zones fragiles, c.-à-d. des déviances morpho-syntaxiques, dans certains contextes des productions orales spontanées des usagers non-natifs (Bartning 2009).

(1) (PA) Euh moi / de mon point de vue euh je pense que oui en Espagne / en Italie/ et cetera (RH) ce sont des gens qui sont plus euh peut-être / dynamiques entre guillemets ou avec un peu plus de #/ virulents euh et peut-être / un peu plus individualistes (LN)

Notre base de données est constituée du sous-corpus suivant du corpus *InterFra* (voir Tableau 1): Groupe 1: 10 locuteurs non-natifs aux stades 5–6 de Bartning et Schlyter, 5 apprenants de chaque stade (Gr I, FLE), nombre d'années d'études 6–9; Groupe 2: 10 locuteurs non-natifs ayant vécu en France 5–15 ans, les Juniors (Gr II, FLS); 3–6 années d'étude; Groupe 3: 10 locuteurs non-natifs ayant vécu en France 15–30 ans, les Seniors (Gr II, FLS); 3–6 années d'étude; Groupe 4: 10 locuteurs natifs, dont 5 Juniors et 5 Seniors (Gr III, LN).

Résultats
L'étude de Bartning *et al.* (2009) a montré, d'une part, un développement des séquences préfabriquées (SP) d'un groupe à l'autre, et d'autre part, une utilisation significativement plus fréquente d'une sous-catégorie des SP, à savoir les SP lexicales, par les groupes 2–3 et les LN que par le groupe 1. Précisons que Forsberg (2008) a pu identifier plusieurs catégories de SP, parmi lesquelles les SP lexicales

et les SP discursives. Les SP lexicales sont des SP référentielles (*rendre un dossier*) relevant de la compétence lexicale encyclopédique en L2 tandis que les SP discursives (*c'est vrai que, au niveau de, disons que…*) relèvent de la compétence discursive. Les premières, on l'a vu, sont soumises aux 'règles créatives' ou positions ouvertes (Forsberg 2008) et les secondes sont constituées de séquences holistiques sans variations formelles des constituants. (Pour la distinction SP lexicales/discursives, voir Bartning *et al.* 2012). En ce qui concerne la structuration informationnelle, le nombre de mots/préambules est plus élevé dans les productions des LN que chez les LNN. Par ailleurs, chez les apprenants, les LNN du groupe 1 utilisent au plus cinq constituants tandis que les LNN des groupes 2 et 3 en utilisent jusqu'à six-sept. A titre d'illustration chez les natifs de six constituants en préambule, voir l'exemple 1 (ci-dessus) ainsi que la suite de sept constituants dans l'exemple (2) :

> (2) (PA) : *mais / un quartier / qui soit aussi mixé euh chinois / maghrébin / comme ici / à Paris / Belleville /* (RH) : *il y en a pas à ma connaissance à Marseille* (Luc, LN)

Quant à la morpho-syntaxe, nous avons constaté, à notre surprise, qu'il n'y avait pas de différences entre les trois groupes LNN en ce qui concerne les déviances morpho-syntaxiques, bien que la durée de séjour en France varie sensiblement d'un groupe à l'autre. Nous partions de l'idée que ce facteur distinguerait les trois groupes, en nous basant sur des recherches en français L2 très avancé qui stipulent qu'à ces stades les locuteurs ne produisent plus d''erreurs grammaticales' mais connaissent des problèmes exclusivement au niveau du discours et de la conceptualisation (von Stutterheim 2003 ; pour d'autres études de productions très avancées avec erreurs morpho-syntaxiques, voir par ex. Hyltenstam 1992 ; Lardière 2007 ; Hopp 2010). Ce qui nous semble intéressant, c'est que les DMS sont du même type que celles trouvées aux stades 4–6 du continuum dans Bartning et Schlyter, en morphologie nominale (**un image*) ainsi qu'en morphologie verbale (*ils *prend*) (voir la Section 2 ci-dessus). Il y a chez les LN quelques rares exemples d'erreurs de ce type mais qui ne sont pas systématiques. Le non respect des règles d'accord du genre et celui du sujet-verbe à la troisième personne du pluriel au présent des verbes irréguliers ne semble pas remis en cause par des interactions en milieu naturel.

L'hypothèse concernant l'impact de la durée de séjour en France n'a donc été confirmée que partiellement par des différences significatives entre le groupe 1 et les deux autres groupes dans le recours à des séquences préfabriquées lexicales (augmentation dans les groupes 2–3) et aussi par la capacité à construire des préambules plus complexes. Les DMS, par contre, sont toujours des difficultés résiduelles, malgré l'exposition importante à la langue cible dans les groupes 2 et 3. Les DMS constituent par conséquent un domaine qui ne semble pas être sensible à un séjour, même très long, dans le pays de la langue cible.

3.1.3 Interaction entre les trois domaines

L'étude de Bartning *et al.* (2009) a pu identifier trois domaines (DMS, SP ainsi que PA et Rhèmes) spécifiques de l'acquisition très avancée, que nous avons aussi envisagés dans la deuxième étude (Bartning *et al.* 2012), dans le contexte linguistique de leur occurrence et dans leur *interaction*. La principale question de recherche est de savoir si la distribution et les propriétés de deux phénomènes linguistiques, à savoir l'organisation de la structure informationnelle ainsi que le langage préfabriqué, peuvent offrir des explications contextuelles à la présence d'erreurs morphosyntaxiques.

Les résultats de cette étude, basés sur les mêmes groupes de locuteurs que ceux étudiés précédemment, montrent d'abord que les DMS sont rares à l'intérieur des SP et, comme on l'a vu ci-dessus, qu'elles apparaissent dans des SP lexicales qui sont des constructions à positions ouvertes par opposition aux SP discursives (non-analysées).

De plus, les résultats montrent que la complexité de la structuration informationnelle influence l'apparition des DMS quand il y a obligation d'appliquer des règles grammaticales (choix du sujet ou choix des formes flexionnelles du verbe fini). La partie rhématique attire donc plus de DMS que les PA dans les trois groupes d'apprenants, comme dans l'exemple 3 :

(3) PA : c'était assez rocambolesque parce que RH : bon c'était nous **qui** *devai(en)t (LC: **devions**) les accueillir en premier (I:mhm). et donc on savait rien (LNN)

Ce résultat est dû au fait que la partie rhématique est généralement plus complexe syntaxiquement que le PA, ce qui implique une charge cognitive plus élevée. Cette complexité a été mise en évidence par l'analyse comparative approfondie de la subordination et du degré d'intégration des propositions subordonnées dans les rhèmes ainsi que dans les PA. Une autre explication qui relève de la complexité tient à la longueur moyenne de la partie rhématique par rapport au PA : les rhèmes contiennent le double de mots. Enfin la présence des DMS dans les rhèmes trouverait une explication aussi — explication qui de nouveau concerne l'interface entre les trois domaines — dans la mise en rapport de la distribution des SP et de la structuration informationnelle. Il s'est révélé que la partie rhématique contient une proportion moins élevée de SP que les PA. Le rhème contient ainsi plus de SP lexicales, constructions qui ont plus de positions ouvertes pour le choix des mots (*poser **une** question ou **la** question*) que les SP discursives (*disons que*). Ainsi, les occurrences des DMS, même à des niveaux très élevés d'acquisition, peuvent être prédites par leur contexte linguistique et par la distribution des éléments pertinents.

Cette étude prend aussi en compte les notions de *complexity, accuracy* et *fluency (CAF)* proposées, par exemple, par Housen et Kuiken (2009), facteurs qui se sont avérés importants en RAL. Les trois phénomènes observés sont en relation directe avec les notions de complexité, de taux d'exactitude (*accuracy*) et de fluidité (*fluency*) (SP).

3.1.4 Bilan

L'étude de Bartning *et al.* (2009) a ainsi montré que le langage préfabriqué, le nombre de segments dans le PA et les propriétés du rhème constituaient des mesures pertinentes pour évaluer l'état des ressources disponibles à des niveaux très avancés du français L2. Ainsi, la fréquence des SP lexicales a montré une différence significative entre les trois groupes. De plus, le nombre maximum de constituants dans les PA a mis en évidence une différence (toutefois non significative) entre le groupe 1 et les autres.

Par contre, contrairement à nos hypothèses, la présence des DMS ne s'est pas avérée discriminante entre les trois groupes de LNN. Le facteur de la durée de séjour n'a joué que pour les deux premiers domaines.

En ce qui concerne la question de recherche posée dans la deuxième étude (Bartning *et al.* 2012), à savoir si la distribution et les propriétés de deux phénomènes linguistiques — l'organisation de la structure informationnelle et les séquences préfabriquées — peuvent offrir des explications contextuelles à l'apparition des déviances morpho-syntaxiques, on a pu répondre par l'affirmative. Les deux études ont montré qu'il est nécessaire de tenir compte *et* des propriétés des trois domaines *et* de l'interaction des phénomènes lexicaux, discursifs et morpho-syntaxiques pour expliquer l'acquisition des locuteurs très avancés ou quasi-natifs (*cf.* Sorace 2003).

Enfin, quelle est la relation entre nos résultats et les trois mesures *CAF*, complexité, taux d'exactitude et fluidité ? La deuxième étude a montré que la fluidité (les SP) est liée au taux d'exactitude, à savoir l'emploi des SP discursives (produites sans choix ouvert) contribue à éviter les DMS. Par contre, les SP lexicales qui exigent l'application des règles — et qui sont ainsi plus 'lourdes' à traiter — entraînent les DMS et donc l'inexactitude. De façon générale, la complexité, à son tour, a un effet négatif sur l'exactitude, puisque la plupart des DMS sont produites dans des contextes linguistiques complexes. De plus, les phénomènes de fluidité, comme les SP, ont une certaine distribution dans la structure informationnelle (surtout dans les PA), ce qui suggère un lien entre complexité et fluidité. Il est probablement plus facile de traiter un PA, même s'il est long puisqu'il est composé d'entités figées rendant ainsi le traitement plus flexible, avant d'attaquer le rhème, qui, à son tour, contient plus de syntaxe complexe et moins d'entités préfabriquées.

4. En guise de conclusion — l'avenir

Pour les recherches futures sur l'apprenant très avancé, nous avons vu qu'il serait nécessaire de postuler encore des stades pour capter les ressources et les zones fragiles de ces stades ultimes d'acquisition du français. A partir des résultats de nos deux études, et depuis déjà Bartning *et al.* (2009:206), nous avions suggéré encore un stade au-dessus du stade 6 (stade avancé supérieur), à savoir le stade 7, correspondant à des locuteurs que nous avons appelés *bilingues fonctionnels*, qui ne sont pas encore des quasi-natifs selon notre définition ci-dessus (voir 3.1). Le *bilingue fonctionnel* serait dans ce cas, et comme nos études l'ont montré, quelqu'un qui a une L2 plus élaborée et plus riche que l'apprenant avancé au stade 6, avec une quantité 'native' de SP et avec une quantité 'native' de constituants dans le PA, deux traits acquis pendant de longues durées de séjour dans le pays de la LC. Pourtant ces *locuteurs bilingues fonctionnels* du stade 7 ne passent pas encore pour des natifs dans des tests d'écoute par des évaluateurs natifs selon notre définition du locuteur quasi-natif.

Pour être en mesure d'évaluer ce passage au *native-likeness* de nos locuteurs des groupes 1–3, nous sommes en train d'analyser le résultat des tests d'écoute qui ont été évalués par 10 natifs selon les mêmes principes que ceux proposés par Abrahamsson et Hyltenstam (2009:264: un extrait de 30 secondes d'un entretien jugé par 6 des 10 natifs comme 'natif'). Ainsi nous disposerons de critères qui s'ajouteront aux mesures DMS, SP, PA/Rhème et au test d'écoute, à savoir la richesse lexicale et la fluidité, pour étayer notre proposition de stades à des niveaux avancés, à savoir les stades 7 (*bilingues fonctionnels*) et 8 (*quasi-natifs*), avant les natifs (*cf.* Forsberg Lundell *et al.* soumis).

Notre groupe, qui est toujours à la recherche des traits de l'apprenant avancé et quasi-natif, continue ce travail, dont les résultats plus récents sont présentés dans ce volume, par exemple, dans les chapitres de Hancock sur la pragmaticalisation des adverbes temporels, de Forsberg Lundell et Lindqvist sur le développement des séquences préfabriquées lexicales et de la richesse lexicale et de Engel sur l'acquisition de la dislocation.

Remerciements

Recherches effectuées au sein du projet *High-level proficiency in second language use* (La banque nationale suédoise, 2006–2012, M2005-0459 :1, M2005-459 :1-PJ). Ce chapitre est basé sur les études de Bartning (2009), Bartning *et al.* (2009), Bartning *et al.* (2012), Bartning et Hancock (soumis). Je tiens à remercier les trois évaluateurs de leurs remarques précieuses.

References

Abrahamsson, N. & Hyltenstam, K. (2009). Age of acquisition and nativelikeness in a second language — listener perception vs linguistic scrutiny. *Language Learning* 58, 249–306.

Ågren, M. (2008). *À la recherche de la morphologie silencieuse. Sur le développement du pluriel en français L2 écrit*. Thèse de doctorat. Université de Lund: *Études romanes de Lund* 84.

Bardovi-Harlig, K. (2006). Interlanguage development. Main routes and individual paths. *AILA Review* 19, 69–82.

Bartning, I. (1997). L'apprenant dit avancé et son acquisition d'une langue étrangère. *Acquisition et Interaction en Langue Étrangère* 9, 9–50.

Bartning, I. (2000). Gender agreement in L2 French — pre-advanced vs. advanced learners. *Studia Linguistica* 54, 225–237.

Bartning, I. (2009). The advanced learner variety: ten years later. In E. Labeau & F. Myles (Eds.), *The advanced learner varieties: the case of French L2*, 11–40. Berne: Peter Lang.

Bartning, I. (2012). High-level proficiency in second language use. Morphosyntax and discourse. In M. Watorek, S. Benazzo & M. Hickman (Eds.), *Comparative perspectives to language acquisition: a tribute to Clive Perdue*, 170–187. Clevedon: Multilingual Matters.

Bartning, I. (à paraître). Late morpho-syntactic and discourse features in advanced and very advanced L2 French — a view towards the end state. In S. Haberzettl (Ed.), *The end state of L2 acquisition*. Berlin: Mouton.

Bartning, I., Forsberg, F. & Hancock, V. (2009). Resources and obstacles in very advanced French L2: formulaic language, information structure and morphosyntax. In L. Roberts, G.D. Véronique, A. Nilsson & M. Tellier (Eds.), *Eurosla Yearbook*, 9, 185–211. Amsterdam: Benjamins.

Bartning, I., Forsberg Lundell, F. & Hancock, V. (2012). On the role of linguistic contextual factors for morphosyntactic stabilization in high-level L2 French. *Studies in Second Language Acquisition* 34, 243–267.

Bartning, I. & Hancock, V. (soumis). Morphosyntax and discourse at high-levels of second language acquisition. In K. Hyltenstam (Ed.), *High-level proficiency in second language use*. Berlin / New York: Mouton de Gruyter.

Bartning, I. & Schlyter, S. (2004). Itinéraires acquisitionnels et stades de développement en français L2. *Journal of French Language Studies* 14, 281–299.

Birdsong, D. (1999). *Second language acquisition and the critical period hypothesis*. Mahwah: Erlbaum.

Birdsong, D. (2003). Authenticité de prononciation en français L2 chez les apprenants tardifs anglophones: analyses segmentales et globales. *Acquisition et Interaction en Langue Étrangère* 18, 17–36.

Birdsong, D. (2005). Nativelikeness and non-nativelikeness in L2A research. *International Review of Applied Linguistics in Language Teaching* 43, 319–328.

Birdsong, D. (2006). Age and second language acquisition and processing: a selective overview. In M. Gullberg & P. Indefrey (Eds.), *The cognitive neuroscience of second language acquisition*, 9–49. Oxford: Blackwell.

Blanche-Benveniste, C. (1997). *Approches de la langue parlée*. Paris: Ophrys.

Bolly, C. (2008). *Les unites phraséologiques: un phénomène linguistique complexe? Séquences (semi-)figées construites avec les verbes prendre et donner en français écrit L1 et L2. Approche descriptive et acquisitionnelle*. Thèse de doctorat. Université Catholique de Louvain.

Bongaerts, T. (1999). Ultimate attainment in L2 pronunciation: the case of very advanced late L2 learners. In D. Birdsong, (Ed.), *Second language acquisition and the critical period hypothesis*, 133–159. Mahwah, N.J. Lawrence Erlbaum.

Bongaerts, T. (2003). Effets de l'âge sur l'acquisition de la prononciation d'une seconde langue. *Acquisition et Interaction en Langue Étrangère* 18, 79–98.

Conklin, K. & Schmitt, N. (2008). Formulaic sequences: are they processed faster than non-formulaic language by native and non-native speakers? *Applied Linguistics* 29, 72–89.

Conway, Å. (2005). *Le paragraphe oral en français L1, en suédois L1 et en français L2. Étude syntaxique, prosodique et discursive*. Thèse de doctorat. Université de Lund: *Études romanes de Lund* 73.

Coppieters, R. (1987). Competence differences between native and near-native speakers. *Language* 63, 544–573.

Dewaele, J.-M. (2005). *Focus on French as a foreign language*. Clevedon: Multilingual Matters.

Dimroth, C. & Lambert, M. (2008). La structure informationnelle chez les apprenants L2. *Acquisition et Interaction en Langue Étrangère* 26. Special issue.

Donaldson, B. (2011). Left dislocation in near-native French. *Studies in second language acquisition* 33, 399–432.

Doughty, C. & Long, M. (Eds.) (2003). *The handbook of second language acquisition*. Oxford: Blackwell.

Ellis, R. (2008). *The study of second language acquisition*. Oxford: Oxford University Press.

Engel, H. (2010). *Dislocation et référence aux entités en français L2. Développement, interaction, variation*. Thèse de doctorat. Université de Stockholm: *Cahiers de la recherche* 43.

Engel, H. (ce volume). La dislocation dans le français oral d'apprenants suédophones: emploi et développement.

Forsberg, F. (2006). *Le langage préfabriqué en français parlé L2. Étude acquisitionnelle et comparative*. Thèse de doctorat. Université de Stockholm: *Cahiers de la recherche* 34.

Forsberg, F. (2008). *Le langage préfabriqué. Formes, fonctions et fréquences en français parlé L2 et L1*. Berne: Peter Lang.

Forsberg, F. & Bartning, I. (2010). Can linguistic features discriminate between the communicative CEFR-levels? A pilot study of written L2 French. In I. Bartning, M. Martin & I. Vedder (Eds.), *Communicative proficiency and linguistic development: intersections between SLA and language testing research. Eurosla Monograph Series* 1, 133–158. European Second Language Association.

Forsberg Lundell, F. & Lindqvist, C. (ce volume). Vocabulary aspects in advanced L2 French — do lexical formulaic sequences and lexical richness develop at the same rate?

Forsberg Lundell, F., Bartning, I., Engel, H., Hancock, V., Lindqvist, C. & Gudmundson, A. (sous presse). Beyond advanced stages in high-level spoken L2 French. *Journal of French Language Studies* 24 (2).

Giacalone Ramat, A. (1992). Grammaticalisation processes in the area of temporal and modal relations. *Studies in Second Language Acquisition* 23, 387–417.

Granfeldt, J. (2003). *L'acquisition des catégories fonctionnelles. Étude comparative du développement du DP français chez des enfants et des apprenants adultes*. Thèse de doctorat. Lund: *Études romanes de Lund* 67.

Granfeldt, J. & Nugues, P. (2007). Évaluation des stades de développement en français langue étrangère. In N. Hatout & P. Muller (Eds.), *Actes de la 14e conférence sur le traitement automatique des langues naturelles*, vol 1, 357–366.

Hancock, V. (2000). *Quelques connecteurs et modalisateurs dans le français parlé d'apprenants universitaires*. Thèse de doctorat. Université de Stockholm: *Cahiers de la recherche* 16.

Hancock, V. (2007). Quelques éléments modaux dissociés dans le *paragraphe oral* dans des interviews en français L2 et L1. *Journal of French Language Studies* 17, 21–47.

Hancock, V. (ce volume). Pragmatic use of temporal adverbs in L1 and L2 French: functions and syntactic positions of textual markers in a spoken corpus.

Hancock, V. & Kirchmeyer, N. (2005). Discourse structuring in advanced French interlanguage. In J.-M. Dewaele (Ed.), *Focus on French as a foreign language*, 17–36. Clevedon: Multilingual Matters.

Hopp, H. (2010). Ultimate attainment in inflection: performance similarities between non-native and native speakers. *Lingua* 120, 901–931.

Housen, A., Kemps, N. & Pierrard, M. (2009). The use of verb morphology of advanced L2 learners and native speakers of French. In F. Myles & E. Labeau (Eds.), *The advanced learner varieties: the case of French*, 41–61. Berne: Peter Lang.

Housen, A. & Kuiken, F. (2009). Complexity, accuracy and fluency in second language acquisition, *Applied Linguistics* 30, 461–471.

Hyltenstam, K. (1992). Non-native features of near-native speakers: on the ultimate attainment of childhood L2 learners. In R.J. Harris (Ed.), *Cognitive processing in bilinguals*, 351–368. Amsterdam: North Holland.

Hyltenstam, K. & Abrahamsson, N. (2003). Maturational constraints in SLA. In C. Doughty & M. Long (Eds.), *Handbook of second language acquisition*, 539–588. Oxford: Blackwell.

Kahlmann, A. (1984). *Rédactions françaises*. Stockholm: AWE International.

Kihlstedt, M. (1998). *La référence au passé dans le dialogue. Étude de l'acquisition de la temporalité chez des apprenants dits avancés de français*. Thèse de doctorat. Université de Stockholm: *Cahiers de la recherche* 6.

Kirchmeyer, N. (2002). *Étude de la compétence textuelle des lectes d'apprenants avancés. Aspects, fonctionnels et informationnels*. Thèse de doctorat. Université de Stockholm: *Cahiers de la recherche* 17.

Klein, W. & Perdue, C. (1997). The basic variety or: couldn't natural languages be much simpler? *Second Language Research* 13, 301–347.

Labeau, E. (2009). An imperfect mastery: the acquisition of the functions of *imparfait* by Anglophone learners. In E. Labeau & F. Myles (Eds.), *The advanced learner varieties: the case of French L2*, 63–92. Berne: Peter Lang.

Labeau, E. & Myles, F. (Eds.) (2009). *The advanced learner varieties: the case of French*. Berne: Peter Lang.

Lambert, M. (1997). En route vers le bilinguisme. *Acquisition et Interaction en Langue Étrangère* 9, 147–172.

Lambert, M. (2006). Pourquoi les apprenants adultes avancés ne parviennent-ils pas à atteindre la compétence des locuteurs natifs? In G. Engwall (Ed.), *Construction, acquisition et communication. Études linguistiques de discours contemporains*, 151–171. Acta Universitatis Stockholmiensis. Romanica Stockholmiensia 23. Stockholm: AWE International.

Lardière, D. (2007). *Ultimate attainment in SLA. A case study*. Mawhaw: Erlbaum.

Lindqvist, C. (2006). *L'influence translinguistique dans l'interlangue française. Étude de la production orale d'apprenants plurilingues*. Thèse de doctorat. Université de Stockholm: *Cahiers de la recherche* 33.

Lindqvist, C., Bardel, C. & Gudmundson, A. (2011). Lexical richness in the advanced learner's oral production of French and Italian L2. *International Review of Applied Linguistics in Language Teaching* 49, 221–240.

Lindström, E. (2008). *L'acquisition du genre en français L2 — l'accord des déterminants et des adjectifs.* Thèse de fil. lic. Université de Stockholm.

Mayer, M. (1969). *Frog, where are you?* New York: Dial Press.

Meisel, J., Clahsen, H. & Pienemann, M. (1981). On determining developmental stages in natural second languge acquisition. *Studies in Second Language Acquisition* 3, 109–139.

Montrul, S. & Slabakova, R. (2003). Competence similarities between native and near-native speakers: an investigation of the Preterite/Imperfect contrast in Spanish. *Studies in Second Language Acquisition* 25, 351–398.

Morel, M.-A. & Danon-Boileau, L. (1998). *La grammaire de l'intonation. L'exemple du français.* Paris: Ophrys.

Muñoz, C. & Singleton, D. (2007). Foreign accent in advanced learners. Two successful profiles. In L. Roberts, A. Gürel, S. Tatar, & L. Marti, (Eds.), *EUROSLA Yearbook* 7, 172–190. Amsterdam: Benjamins.

Myles, F. (2005). The emergence of morphosyntactic structure in French L2. In J.-M. Dewaele (Ed.), *Focus on French as a foreign language*, 88–114. Clevedon: Multilingual Matters.

Paradis, M. (2009). *Declarative and procedural determinants of second languages.* Amsterdam: Benjamins.

Perdue, C. (Ed.) (1993). *Adult language acquisition: cross-linguistic perspectives.* New York: Cambridge University Press.

Pienemann, M. (1998). *Language processing and second language development: processability theory.* Amsterdam: Benjamins.

Sanell, A. (2007). *Le parcours acquisitionnel de la négation et de quelques particules de portée en français L2.* Thèse de doctorat. Université de Stockholm: *Cahiers de la recherche* 35.

Schlyter, S. (2003). Development of verb morphology and finiteness in children and adults acquiring French. In C. Dimroth & M. Starren (Eds.), *Information structure, linguistic structure and the dynamics of learner language*, 15–44. Amsterdam: Benjamins.

Sharwood Smith, M. & Truscott, J. (2005). Stages or continua in SLA: a Mogul solution. *Applied Linguistics* 26, 219–240.

Singleton, D. (2003). Le facteur de l'âge dans l'acquisition d'une L2: remarques préliminaires. *Acquisition et Interaction en Langue Étrangère* 18, 3–15.

Sorace, A. (2003). Near-nativeness. In C. Doughty & M. Long (Eds.). *The handbook of second language acquisition*, 130–151. Malden/Oxford: Blackwell.

von Stutterheim, C. (2003). Linguistic structure and information organisation. In S. Foster & S. Pekarek Doehler (Eds.), *EUROSLA Yearbook* 3, 183–206. Amsterdam: Benjamin.

Towell, R., Hawkins, R. & Bazergui, N. (1996). The development of fluency in advanced learners of French. *Applied Linguistics* 17, 84–119.

Véronique, D. (Ed.) (2009). *L'acquisition de la grammaire du français, langue étrangère.* Paris: Didier.

Abstract

This chapter presents a synthesis of research on the acquisition of French as a second and foreign language undertaken at Stockholm University. It relates the earlier results of the project called *InterFra (French interlanguage — development, interaction and variation)* with more recent research on ultimate attainment in SLA. The study is presented in three parts. The first two are retrospective: first a description of the corpus *InterFra* (www.fraita.su.se/interfra) — the integral corpus is here introduced for the first time — then follow the results of the doctoral theses and the continuum of the developmental stages as proposed by Bartning and Schlyter (2004), which all build upon the *InterFra* corpus. The third part accounts for a recent research programme about the last stages in SLA, namely *High-level proficiency in second language use*, a common programme between four departments at Stockholm University. The chapter gives the latest results from studies in this programme using three learner groups near the native borderline, called 'advanced', 'functional bilinguals' and 'near-natives'.

Pragmatic use of temporal adverbs in L1 and L2 French
Functions and syntactic positions of textual markers in a spoken corpus

Victorine Hancock
Stockholm University

This paper deals with the functions of a number of frequent temporal adverbs and their placement in the information structure produced by highly advanced L2 speakers of French. The study concerns both structural and pragmatic aspects of learner language that seem relevant for characterizing the highly proficient French L2 user. The *pragmaticalization* of these adverbs, i.e. the development of different pragmatic functions in L2, is investigated. The adverbs can occupy different positions in the utterance and we expect that the pragmaticalization of the adverbs entails their syntactic isolation in the information structure. The analysis of positions showed that, for two adverbs, argumentative functions in outer positions were absent even in the most advanced speaker group.

1. Introduction

This exploratory paper looks at the use of temporal markers in a corpus of advanced L2 French (*InterFra* corpus). It investigates the development of the pragmatic use of six temporal adverbs in four advanced learner groups. The most advanced group represents speakers with near-native proficiency in French. The aim of the paper is first to characterize the pragmatic use and development (*pragmaticalization*) of *déjà*, *encore*, *toujours*, *alors*, *après* and *maintenant* ('already', 'still', 'always', 'so', 'then' and 'now'), and we ask whether the learners develop textual and pragmatic uses of these adverbs during the course of L2 acquisition (see Hancock & Sanell 2010). We also investigate the syntactic positions of the textual markers in order to better describe subcategories of functions and differences in the use among learners and native speakers. Thirdly, we investigate whether the pragmatic use of the temporal adverbs is a feature that could characterize the 'highly proficient user' above stage 6 (see Bartning & Schlyter 2004 and Bartning this volume).

The starting point for this chapter, as regards the pragmatic development in L2 of the above listed adverbs, is the recent studies of polysemy and diachronic/historical pragmaticalization of discourse markers (Hansen 1998; Dostie 2004; Hansen & Rossari 2005; Dostie & Pusch 2007). There might be parallels between the two processes, in so far as both processes reflect language change over time. The historical process could hopefully shed some light on the development of discourse markers in L2 (*cf.* Giacalone Ramat 2000). However, the diachronic process is considered as only one potential explanatory factor among others, a question to which we will return.

Studies of diachronic pragmaticalization have shown that syntactic isolation (or detachment from the inner clause/rheme) is one of the criteria of the development of discourse markers, and a relevant property for the roles that markers play in the management of conversation (e.g. turn-taking, topic structuring, interpersonal management). We expect that the progressing L2 pragmaticalization entails a syntactic isolation of the items, i.e. the marker would be detached from the inner clause (or rheme) of the utterance, and placed in outer positions, the pre-front field or post-end field. This prediction is compatible with the notion that spoken French is highly *decondensated*, i.e. that connectives, modalizing and other interpersonal expressions are detached from the rheme (Morel & Danon-Boileau 1998) and sometimes form long sequences in front of the rheme. Example (1) from the corpus illustrates the syntactic detachment of the temporal adverb *d'abord* ('first') in its textual, argumentative use. The speaker, who is a painter and a 3D-animator, explains how easy animals are to represent three-dimensionally in a realistic way, in comparison to food. In (1) *d'abord* is detached, placed in the pre-front field (in bold) and introduces a first argument.[1]

(1) **parce que / bon /** *d'abord* **/ tout ce qui e:st animal et cetera / je veux dire / à part les spécialistes de la grenouille** on on nous fera jamais le reproche que que le petit doigt-là ben est un peu plus long ou que la tâche sur euh ce type d'espèce ne devrait pas être exactement comme ça / enfin bref. (Nic, NS)
('**because / well /** *first* **/ all that has to do with animals and so on / I would say/ except the experts in frogs** they will never blame us by saying that little finger is a little longer or that the spot on that species shouldn't be exactly like that / well that's it.')

---

1. See Appendix for transcription conventions.

2. Discourse markers: Polysemy and pragmaticalization

The polysemy of discourse markers and the diachronic development of this polysemy in a linguistic unit, *pragmaticalization*, have been thoroughly studied recently by a number of authors, in L1 French and other languages (Dostie 2004; Hansen & Rossari 2005; Fischer 2006; Dostie & Pusch 2007; Beeching 2009; Defour *et al.* 2010). In general, three features that characterize this diachronic process of semantic change are *semantic bleaching, phonological reduction* and *syntactic isolation* (Erman & Kotsinas 1993; Traugott 1995; Hansen & Rossari 2005; Fischer 2006). Although semantic bleaching is described as a loss of semantic content, the linguistic unit becomes pragmatically more complexified, with a gain of communicative and metacommunicative properties. A first step in such a process could thus be described as a development from (in our case) a temporal marker, with a propositional and anaphoric content, to a textual marker with an argumentative and discourse organizing role. The second step would be development from the textual to a discourse marker, which has a subjective or expressive meaning, and could have communicative functions (e.g. for expressing the speaker's attitude or for conversational management purposes). Phonological reduction could be exemplified by the reduction of *you know→y'know* and because→*'cause*. Syntactic isolation have been illustrated by example (1) above. The detachment of the item is linked to another property of the pragmaticalized marker: It has often a larger scope than the original item. In example (1) the scope of *d'abord* is the whole utterance that follows the item.

The order of appearance of the adverbs as *encore, toujours, alors, après* and *maintenant* in the oral production of L1 and L2 French, was studied by Schlyter (2005). Schlyter's study showed that adult L2 learners used all these adverbs from the lowest levels of proficiency, although the author does not discuss pragmatic aspects in the use of the adverbs in detail.

Romero Trillo (2002) investigated the pragmatic use of a number of discourse markers (among others *well, I mean, you know, you see*) in four corpora of L1 and L2 English. He observed that proficient L2 speakers lacked a competent use of the pragmatic functions of involvement markers needed in daily conversation, and this seems to lead to "pragmatic fossilization" of markers both in quantity and diversity. Romero Trillo argues that the lack of explicit focus on the markers in foreign language teaching is the source of the pragmatic fossilization.

3. Data

We analyze here the adverbs in (semi-formal) interviews from four different acquisitional levels (see Tables 1 and 2). The data stems from the *InterFra* learner corpus of Stockholm University. The three lower levels (low, medium and superior advanced) were assessed by applying the Bartning and Schlyter (2004) scale. The fourth presumed highest level represents the ultimate stages in the acquisition of L2 French, and consists of the production of Swedish speakers who have lived in the Paris region for 15 to 30 years (NNS P = non native speakers from Paris). The

Table 1. Interviews from the *InterFra* corpus

Group	N of informants	N of years at a French university	Years in a French speaking country	Age	N of words of informants
1. Stage 4 (low advanced)	8	1 semester	0–2	20–25	8712
2. Stage 5 (medium advanced)	8	1–3	1–2	25–35	16561
3. Stage 6 (superior advanced)	8	2–5	2–3	25–30	14371
4. NNS P	8	0–1	15–30	45–60	27757
5. NS E (exchange students)	8	n.a.	n.a.	20–25	21027
6. NS P (from Paris region)	8	n.a.	n.a.	30–35 45–60	21191
Total	48				109619

Table 2. Total N of tokens of markers in the study

Group	*alors*	*après*	*maintenant*	*déjà*	*encore*	*toujours*	Total
1. Stage 4	12	14	38	5	15	7	91
2. Stage 5	56	21	29	6	6	18	136
3. Stage 6	18	17	40	10	14	29	128
4. NNS P	20	66	42	41	21	65	255
5. NS E	49	8	12	30	26	25	150
6. NS P	42	40	26	16	28	34	186
Total N	197	166	187	108	110	178	**946**

NNS productions were compared to two NS groups that had a similar age distribution (NS E = native speakers, exchange students, and NS P = native speakers from Paris).

4. Results

In this section the textual and interactive functions derived from the temporal adverbs will be presented. As mentioned above, we focus here on the development of the pragmatic aspects of the markers and their degree of pragmatic use. As regards the (original) semantic content of the temporal adverbs, we refer to Hancock and Sanell (2010) and to Sanell (2007), where also temporal-aspectual uses of the adverbs are considered in more detail.

We will then look at the degree of pragmatic use of the investigated adverbs across the development of the different groups from the lowest to the most advanced groups of speakers. The measurement of the degree of pragmatic use will be explained in Section 4.2. Thereafter the positions of the items in the information structure are considered and we will ask in which respects the NNSs use the syntactic positions for the same functions as the NSs. Finally, the relevance of the investigated adverbs as an indicator of a highly advanced level of L2 use is evaluated.

4.1 Textual use of the adverbs in the corpus

Our analysis of the textual uses of these highly polysemous adverbs is based on the categories proposed by Hybertie (1996), Hansen (1998, 2004, 2008), Hansen and Strudsholm (2008), and Buchi (2007a, 2007b). The categories found in the *InterFra* corpus are also presented in Hancock and Sanell (2010). *Déjà, encore* and *toujours* are aspectual adverbs and all three have scalar functions. These three adverbs will be analyzed first, and then *alors, après* and *maintenant* will be examined.

4.1.1 *Déjà*

The three non-temporal functions of *déjà* are the *scalar*, the *argumentative* and the *interactive* (*cf.* Buchi 2007b; Hansen 2008). The scalar use does not function on an objective time-scale, but is metaphorically applied on an evaluative scale with a value which reflects the speakers' expectations, as exemplified in (2). Its semantic content could be rendered by 'always', 'already'.

> (2) C'est *déjà* bien! En fait, c'est même super! (Hansen & Strudsholm 2008).
>   ('That's *already* good! In fact, it's even great!')

Argumentative *déjà* introduces the first one in a set of arguments and is a *discourse connective* in a pre-verbal position (Hansen & Strudsholm 2008: 186).

> (3) J'aime bien ce film : *déjà*, c'est original, **et puis** il a de très belles photos (Hansen & Strudsholm 2008).
> ('I like this movie: *first of all*, it's original, and it **also** has beautiful images'.)

Interactive *déjà* contains at the same time an interrogative speech act and a request. The speaker signals that s/he has forgotten the information known before and asks the hearer to remind him/her about it, as exemplified in (4). *Déjà* corresponds here to 'again' in English.

> (4) Comment c'est le nom de ce pays, *déjà*? Bezoncourt? Bezancourt? (Buchi 2007b: 213).
> ('What's the name of that country *again*? Bezoncourt? Bezancourt?')

Argumentative *déjà* is the far most used function in the corpus and is found only in the most advanced group together with the interactive use (NNS P). Examples of the scalar, argumentative and interactive use are shown in (5–7).

> (5) je vais / je vais quand même travailler eh / un an en Suède / (I:mm) avant d'aller en France parce que je pense que c'est *déjà* bien d'avoir une éducation / de dire que : je suis professeur. mais si on a jamais travaillé comme professeur on peut pas vraiment dire qu'on est professeur.
> (Per, sta 5)
> ('still, I will / I will work eh / a year in Sweden / (I:mm) before I go to France because I think that it's *already* good to have an education / to say that: I'm a teacher, but if you have never worked as a teacher you can't really say you are a teacher.')

Interestingly, in the corpus there are some cases of *déjà* in the argumentative use placed at the end of the utterance, a position we will discuss in Section 4.4 below.

> (6) non ça me plaisait bien. les cours étaient en anglais *déjà*. / (I:mm) et ensuite c'est pour voir quelque chose de complètement différent. (Isa, NS)
> ('no I liked it. The seminars were in English *already*. And then it's to see something completely different.')

In example (7) of interactive *déjà*, the speaker says that his family in Sweden (Göteborg) told him not to go outdoors when the riots in the suburbs were going on in Paris 2005, and that things always look worse from the outside.

> (7) et moi j'avais j'avais j'avais fait exactement la même chose avec me:s mes amis à Göteborg (I:ouais) quand il y avait les émeutes (I: ah) pour # c'était quoi *déjà*? c'était le sommet. (Pat, NNS P)

('and I did exactly the same thing with my friends in Göteborg when there were the riots for # what was it *again*? It was the summit.')

4.1.2 *Encore*

Textual *encore* appears with four principal functions: *additive, scalar, concessive*, and *interactive*. It could be debated whether the first function really is textual (Hansen 2002 considers it neither temporal nor clearly textual), but it will be counted as textual, since it is not clearly temporal. In a sentence such as *Paul boit encore un café, encore* could be interpreted as 'another' and would thus be additive (*cf.* Benazzo 2000), which is what Nølke (1983: 141) calls *cumulative*.

In its *scalar* use (*cf. déjà* above), *encore* modifies an adverb with the notion of gradation, or an adjective in comparative form. It could be rendered in English by 'even' (example 8).

(8) Luc est *encore* plus beau qu'Adrien (Hansen 2002).
('Luc is *even* more beautiful than Adrien.')

Concessive encore is often used in a conjunctive phrase with *et* or *que* (Hansen 2002). In English, paraphrases are 'still', 'yet', 'even so' (example 9).

(9) …[L]es responsables de la stratégie des grands opérateurs nous annoncent 19 à 20 millions d'abonnés pour décembre de cette année. Et 60 % des Français, en comptant les nourrissons, équipés en 2002. *Et encore*, assure Yves Goblet, responsable de la stratégie et du développement chez Bouygues Télécom, notre rythme de croissance reste modeste par rapport à d'autres pays européens, comme l'Italie ou l'Espagne (Hansen 2002).
('… The marketing directors of the large operators announce that they are expecting 19 to 20 million subscribers by December of this year. And that 60 % of the inhabitants, including infants, will be equipped by 2002. *Yet*, Yves Goblet, in charge of the strategy and of the development at Bouygues Telecom, assures, our growth rate, while certainly stable, remains modest compared to that of other European countries, such as Italy or Spain.')

The *interactive* function is very close to that shown for *déjà* (see above): It is interrogative and shows that the speaker has forgotten the information s/he asks for (Hansen & Strudsholm 2008: 214). However, while *encore* signals impatience from the speaker, there is no such nuance in interactive *déjà*. Example (10) of interactive *encore* is from a NNS, who tells about a course in literature attended in Montreal.

(10) mais ensuite j'ai suivi un cours sur / / comment ça s'appelait encore ? « sexuation et écriture ». mais en fait c'était sur l'écrivaine. (Mat, sta 6)
('but then I went to lectures on // what was the name again? "sexuation et écriture" but in fact it was about the author.')

The additive use in the corpus is illustrated in example (11) by a native speaker who is talking about discovering Stockholm.

> (11) c'est c'est mignon et c'est c'est pittoresque enfin c'est assez joli. c'est vrai que sinon (SOUFFLE) c'est pas. mais bon je crois aussi qu'il faut *encore* du temps et que j'ai j'ai vraiment pas tout découvert quoi. (Ann, NS E)
> ('it's pretty and it's picturesque well it's rather beautiful. Really otherwise it's not. But well I think also you need *more* time and that I haven't really discovered all.')

The scalar use of *encore* is not used very frequently by the NNSs of the corpus. Example (12) is from a stage 4 (low advanced) informant and could be part of a *chunk* (*encore pire*). It is used with the comparative form of the adjective *mal*.

> (12) mais les gens étaient très eh très difficiles à / de parler avec / de parler avec eux mais / à Lausanne. mais ici c'est *encore* pire / (I:mm). j'ai X moi je trouve que c'est (I:mhm mm). (Jes, sta 4)
> ('but the people were eh very difficult / to talk with / to talk with them but / in Lausanne . but here it's *even* worse.')

Concessive *encore* (*et encore/encore que*) is used only by the NS in the corpus (six examples). The speaker in example (13) says that the French exchange students feel they are different from the inhabitants in Stockholm.

> (13) que ce soit aussi parfois par notre (SOUPIRE) notre façon de nous habiller. et *encore* je trouve qu'on est bien bien sages mais euh. (Ann, NS E)
> ('it may sometimes also be because of the way we dress. and *yet* I think we are very prudent but euh.')

4.1.3 *Toujours*

There are two categories of textual *toujours*: *scalar* and *connective*. The connective use comprises three subcategories (*concessive*, *thematic* and the expression *toujours est-il que*) that will be presented here below.

The scalar use (*cf. au moins*) could be rendered in English by 'always', 'at least' (example 14).

> (14) Elle va empoisonner ton existence! ELLE: Peut-être!… mais crois-tu que je sois capable de vivre sans luxe? JEAN: tu peux *toujours* essayer. (Buchi 2007a)
> ('She will poison your existence! SHE: Maybe!…but do you think that I'm able to live without the luxury? JEAN: you could *at least* try.')

Toujours as a connective is either *concessive* or *thematic*. It also includes the fixed expression *toujours est-il que*.

The concessive use (*cf. toutefois, de toute façon*) is equivalent to 'however' or 'anyway' in English. It is usually in a detached position at the end of a phrase. Its scope is often a negative phrase (Buchi 2007a), as in (15).

(15) Je ne sais absolument pas où il peut être… Pas ici, *toujours*. (Hansen 2004)
('I definitely don't know where he could be… Not here *anyway*.')

In the thematic use, *toujours* marks thematic continuity in an enumeration of arguments (*cf. de même*). Possible correspondances are 'still' or 'yet' in English (16).

(16) Dans un autre ordre d'idées, pour lutter contre l'usure des pistons et des cylindres, particulièrement sensible au moment du lancement du moteur, Delahaye réalise un dispositif spécial assurant un graissage supplémentaire au début de la mise en mouvement de la machine. *Toujours* pour réduire l'usure, l'emploi d'organes doués d'une haute dureté superficielle se développe. (Buchi 2007a)
('In another order of ideas, to fight against the wear of the pistons and the cylinders, particularly sensitive at the time of the launching of the engine, Delahaye carries out a special device ensuring an additional greasing at the beginning of the actuation of the machine. *Still* (?) to reduce wear, the use of bodies with a high surface hardness develops'.)

The fixed expression *toujours est-il que* (*cf.* Eng: 'still') introduces a firm statement and signals the return to the main theme after a digression (Buchi 2007a: 121).

The *scalar* use appears at stage 6 (high advanced level, example 17).

(17) si par exemple on veut expliquer la grammaire. / (I:oui) et dE faire ça en français (I:oui) c'e:st ça je trouve euh extrêmement difficile. (I:mm) // on peut *toujours* essayer. j'essaye. (Ker, sta 6)
('if for example you want to explain grammar. / (I:yes) and to do that in French (I:yes) that's what I find extremely difficult. (I:mm) // you can *at least* try. I try.')

The first connective use (*concessive*) is found in the corpus only at the highest level (NNS P) (example 18).

(18) je voulais pas me trompe:r et tout (I:mhm). c'est quand même compli- # une langue compliquée donc. en plus on se fait # les Français ont quand même ten- tendance à reprendre tout ce qu'on dit (I:mhm mhm) corrige:r sans arrêt. ils sont pas # c'est pas très fin (I:mhm mhm) *toujours* mais en même temps les copains que j'ai rencontrés (I:ouais) qui étaient adorables. (Moa, NNS P)
('I didn't want to make mistakes and all (I:mhm). It is complicated nevertheless — # a complicated language so. also you make yourself # the

French have a tendency to repeat everything you say (I:mhm mhm) always correcting. they are not # it isn't nice (I:mhm mhm) *anyway* but at the same time the friends I have met (I:yeah) who were very nice.')

Finally the fixed expression *toujours est-il que* is used by one NS (example 19).

(19)   et eu:h / ben ç:a s'est fait je sais plus dans quelles circonstances (I:mm) mais / *toujours est-il que* / on est venus habiter tous ici. voilà. (Jas, NS P)
('and euh well it happend I don't remember any longer what was the situation (I:mm) but / *still* / we all came to live here. that's how it was.')

Both *scalar* and *concessive* uses are found in the corpus (together with one example that could be interpreted as *thematic toujours*).

4.1.4   *Alors*

The main categories of textual *alors* are *inferential*, *reorienting* and *comparative* (*cf.* Hybertie 1996; Hansen 1998). The inferential use of *alors* marks a consequence or inference (20) between two events or states (English 'so').

(20)   Les volets sont fermés, *alors* ils sont partis (*cf. si...dans ce cas*). (Hybertie 1996)
('The shutters are closed, *so* they must have left.')

A special case of the inferential *alors* is the *interactive* use, when *alors* marks a confirmation request (feedback uptaker) or a question (*cf.* Hansen 1998). While the inferential *alors* refers to a former state in the discourse and could thus be considered as anaphoric, *reorienting alors* is non-anaphoric (or very weekly anaphoric) and signals a shift to a new topic or subtopic (*topic change marker*), but also introduces digressions in the discourse and resumption of the main theme. It is thus not surprising that reorienting *alors* also could mark the shift between different planes of talk and introduce frame-shifts (e.g. to reported speech, change of speaker's perspective). In (21) *alors* introduces the opening of a lecture by a teacher.

(21)   bon *alors* aujourd'hui nous allons parler de... (Hansen 1998)
('right *so* today we will talk about...')

The non-anaphoric *alors* is frequently used in storytelling and simply marks the introduction of a new circumstance or new phase in the course of events (example 22).

(22)   on avait de l'eau, mais on n'avait pas de verre, c'était idiot, *alors* Lise m'a demandé à boire, *alors* j'ai voulu lui faire boire au goulot [...]. (Hybertie 1996)
('we had water, but we didn't have any glasses, it was silly, *then* Lise asked me to give her something to drink, *so* I tried to make her drink from the bottle...')

The comparative *connective alors que* is used to oppose mutually excluding circumstances or properties.

All three categories of *alors* are found in the corpus, the inferential use appears already at stage 4 (low advanced) and the reorienting at stage 5 (medium advanced), while comparative *alors que* appears at stage 6. Interestingly, NSs prefer non-anaphoric to anaphoric *alors*, while the NNSs use mainly anaphoric *alors*, which points to a lower degree of pragmaticalization in the NNS group.

Examples from the corpus of the three categories of *alors* are shown in (23–25).

Inferential use

(23) e:t j'ai aussi de:s des amis à Paris *alors* je faisais le / le trajet chaque week-end. (Ani, sta 5)
('and I also have friends in Paris, *so* I went there every weekend.')

Reorienting/topic change marker

(24) lorsque j'ai : j'ai parlé de ça à ma mère / (I:mhm) parce que ma mère est un petit ah elle est un p un petit (HESITATION) peu raciste quoi un pi peu (I:mm mm) un peu comme tous les Français enfin bon (I:mhm) / *alors* quand je lui dit que moi je me retrouvais dans cette situation… (Pie, NS E)
('when I talked about that with my mother / (I:mhm) because my mother is a little bit racist a little like all French well / *so* when I said to her that I found myself in that situation…')

Comparative connective

(25) c'est une ville étudiante mais ça bouge pas du tout. / *alors que* à Rennes c'est une ville beaucoup plus petite / qui est un peu plus euh / un peu plus au sud. et ça bouge beaucoup plus. (Dor, NS E)
('it's a student city but not so much alive / *while* in Rennes it's a much smaller city a little further south and it's much more alive.')

4.1.5 *Après*

Textual *après* has not been extensively studied until now, to our knowledge. The inferences about its function are thus mainly based on data drawn from our corpus. By textual *après* we mean the *argumentative* marker. We exclude the adverbial expressions *après coup* and *après tout*, though they have discourse functions. Argumentative *après* introduces a new aspect of the subject or a new argument (*cf. et puis*). The marker shows an inter-individual semantic variation, between *concession* and *addition* (*cf. mais c'est vrai que, après tout; et puis; en plus*) and is only used by six speakers. It is systematically (at least twice) used by two NNSs P and by two NSs. The concessive use is shown in (26) and the additive in (27).

> (26) lui aussi mais / il comprend tout (I:oui) / pratiquement. *après* / il a de:s / de:s / forcément des trous / dans le vocabulaire. (I:ouais) mais sinon euh / il se débrouille très bien. (Moa, NNS P)
> ('he too but he understands everything / almost. *Then* / he has of course some gaps in his vocabulary. But otherwise he is getting on well.')

The speaker in (27) is talking about his yet indecisive plans to go to Iceland. *Après* introduces a second argument for not going there.

> (27) I: non mais / # et tu as # pourquoi tu n'essaierais pas ?
> E: euh / / parce que je connais pas / tout bêtement et / / et voilà . *après* il y a encore une fois l'obstacle de la langue / et /. (Ghi, NS P)
> ('I: no but / and you have / why shouldn't you try? E: because I don't know the place / stupid enough / and / and *that's it*. And then there is again the obstacle with the language.')

4.1.6 *Maintenant*

Similarly to *après*, textual *maintenant* and its relation to temporal deictic *maintenant* has not been extensively studied according to Mellet (2005). The author describes *maintenant* as marking a metadiscursive comment of the speaker's own previous statement: A new (or adversative) circumstance is introduced and changes the view on what was just said. The marker could be paraphrased by 'after all' in English.

The number of tokens is low in the corpus, and is found only in the NNS P (28) and NS P groups (29).

> (28) E: j'aime beacoup le franc-parle:r la simplicité : (I:ouais) st.
> I: l'optimisme peut-être (RIRE).
> E: voilà. l'optimisme me plaît. bon / maintenant ma / ma famille sont dans les # sont dans la production des choses. c'est pas évident hein de produire non plus (I:mhm). (Cam, NNS P)
> ('E: I like very much the straightforwardness the simplicity (I:yeah) I: the optimism perhaps (laugh) E: that's it. I like the optimism. Well /*now*/ my family is in the # in the production. It's not evident to produce either.')

In (29) *maintenant* could be paraphrased by *mais* ('but') and is the transition point between the two adversative situations: going to the ballet and, on the other hand, reluctantly taking ballet classes.

(29) I : / et la danse classique / est-ce que tu aimes eu:h ... / pas du tout ? + les bal-
E : non.
I : le ballet ?
E : euh j'aime aller voir euh / des ballets. (I:mm mm) / ça c'est sûr. (RIRE) / maintenant euh / ma mère a essayé de me faire faire de la danse classique euh ...
I : (RIRE)
E : j'ai pleuré pendant six mois. elle a / abandonné. (Ari, NS P)
('I: and classical dance / do you like that /not at all ? bal- E: no. I: ballet? E: I like going to the ballet / that's for sure. (laugh) / *now* / my mother tried to make me take ballet-classes. I cried for six months. She gave up.')

Altogether there are seven tokens used by four speakers, two NNSs P and two NSs, and could thus be considered as a very advanced feature but with an important inter-individual variation.

In summary, as for the three scalar markers, the scalar function emerges from stages 4 to 6, and the argumentative functions are found only at the highest acquisitional level (NNS P). The interactive functions of *encore* and *déjà* emerge at stage 6 and at the highest level, respectively. As for *après* and *maintenant*, textual argumentative functions are found only in the NNS P group. Argumentative/inferential *alors* appears at stage 4, while the *topic change* function emerges at stage 5. An inferred order of acquisition of the textual functions can be summarized in the following way (*cf.* Hancock & Sanell 2010), although the order has to be confirmed using a larger amount of data: Scalar > Argumentative > Interactive/Text organizing (*topic change*). This order indicates that there are parallels between historic development of discourse markers and L2 development of markers, broadly speaking.

4.2 Distribution of temporal (TM) and textual (TX) markers across the different speaker groups: The degree of pragmatic use

In this section, we look at how the temporal and textual markers are quantitatively distributed across the speaker groups. Our initial hypothesis was that the different textual functions could be a relevant feature that characterizes the general development through the stages, and thus contributes to the elaboration of discourse properties that could describe the different levels of acquisition. Tables 3a and 3b show the proportion of textual markers in relation to the overall presence of markers, called Index of Pragmatic Use (IPU, *cf.* Romero Trillo 2002), which is obtained by dividing the number of a textual marker with the total number of each item. It appears that this index reflects the progress of acquisition, in that there is an increase in the IPU, although not to the same extent for all markers.

Table 3a & 3b. The Index of Pragmatic Use (NNS and NS)

N of tokens	Sta4 TX	TM+ TX	IPU Sta4	Sta5 TX	TM+ TX	IPU Sta5	Sta6 TX	TM+ TX	IPU Sta6	NNS P TX	TM+ TX	IPU NNSP
déjà	0	5	0	0	6	0	0	10	0	16	41	39%
encore	1	15	7%	0	6	0	2	14	14%	4	21	19%
toujours	0	7	0	2	18	11%	4	29	14%	1	65	2%
alors	6	12	50%	51	56	91%	18	18	100%	19	20	95%
après*	0	14	0	0	21	0	0	17	0	8	66	12%
maintenant	0	38	0	0	29	0	0	40	0	3	42	7%
Total	7	91		53	136		24	128		51	255	

N of tokens	NS E TX	TM+ TX	IPU NS E	NS P TX	TM+ TX	IPU NS P
déjà	9	30	30%	5	16	31%
encore	5	26	19%	7	28	25%
toujours	1	25	4%	1	34	3%
alors	49	49	100%	42	42	100%
après*	0	8	0	19	40	48%
maintenant	0	12	0	4	26	15%
Total	66	150		78	186	

* Tokens of *après coup* and *après tout* are excluded.

So, which markers are of interest to look at and what does the IPU say? The IPU of *alors* at stage 6 seems to attain that of NSs. In contrast, the use of *déjà* and *encore* are not fully developed at this same stage. Thus, *alors* is a useful indicator of development up to stage 6, while textual *déjà* could be used as an indicator from stage 6 and above. Textual *maintenant* and *après* seem to be relevant features for the highly advanced learner, but both show important inter-individual variation (one speaker provides 75% of the tokens of *après*, which cannot be seen from Table 3) and *maintenant* is, in addition, quite infrequent. For the same reason, i.e. low frequency, textual *toujours* is of less interest. Consequently, the markers that will be discussed in more detail in the following sections are *alors*, *déjà* and *encore*.

In summary, this quantitative IPU provides a rough measurement of development, and follows, at least in the material investigated here, the progress of the stages, with two markers pragmaticalized at stage 5, three at stage 6 and all markers in the NNS P group. However, the IPU should be followed by a finer qualitative analysis, which has been discussed above and to which we will return in the next section. As mentioned above, it is also important to look at the inter-individual quantitative variation and the number of users when group IPU is assessed as in Table 3. We will come back to this discussion in Section 4.5.

4.3 Positions of the markers

The placement of the different markers in the information structure will be scrutinized below. As we mentioned above, we expect that the progressing L2 pragmaticalization entails a syntactic detachment of the markers from the inner clause (or rheme) of the utterance, and that they are placed in outer positions, the pre-front field or post-end field. In spoken French, connectives, modalizing and interpersonal expressions are detached from the rheme (Morel & Danon-Boileau 1998) and sometimes form long sequences in the pre-front field (as illustrated in example 1). We ask whether this expectation is met for the NSs as well as for the NNSs.

The five positions we consider for the temporal and textual markers are the following (I–V):

I. Initial position (pre-front field)
mais **maintenant** plus récemment / il y a / les les Libanais. (Mat, Sta 6)
('but **now** more recently / there are / the the Lebanese.')
et **encore** je dirai que j'habite vraiment dans un quartier protégé. (Ann, NS E)
('**still**, I would say I live really in a safe area.')

II. Integrated position (in the inner clause/rheme)
oui . bien sûr j'ai **déjà** beaucoup oublié mais … (Ker, Sta 6)
('yes. of course I have **already** forgotten a lot but…')
c'était **après** donc la première année en # au lycée. (Liv, NNS P)
('that was **after** then the first year of high school.')

III. Final position (end field or post-end field)
comment on appelle ça en France **déjà** ? (Pat, NNS P)
(what do you call that in France **again** ?)
et j'espère de: m'apprendre / mieux / **maintenant**. (Mon, Sta 4)
('and I hope to : learn / better / **now**.')

IV. 'Autonomous' rheme: (independent intonation)
Pas encore.
('**not yet.**')
I : avant ? E: **et après**. (Mon, Sta 4)

('I: before? E: and **after**.')
non **pas maintenant**. (Jes, Sta 4)
('no not **now**.')

V. Not possible to classify syntactically (or otherwise syntactically incomplete utterances)
In Table 4a and 4b the quantitative results from the analysis of marker positions are shown.

Starting with the temporal markers (in their prototypical, temporal use), the tendencies in Table 4a (NSs) are roughly the same as those found in Table 4b (NNSs): Temporal *déjà*, *encore* and *toujours* are mainly found in the rheme (position 2), with the addition that NNSs are more frequent users of *pas encore* and *pas toujours* (position 4). *Alors*, *après* and *maintenant* are placed mainly in position 1, and to a lesser extent in position 2 or 3. The absence of *alors* in the NS group reflects the pragmatic shifting in relation to the NNSs. The NNSs are more 'conservative' and use temporal *alors* in position 1 and 3 (see also Table 3a above).

Although the total number of tokens is small, some tendencies can be observed in Table 5a and 5b. While the positions of the temporal markers were similar in the NS and NNS groups, the textual markers show some differences regarding positions (Table 5a & 5b): The first observation is that the NNSs have fewer tokens

Table 4a & 4b. Positions of *temporal* markers (NS and NNS)

NS (Exchange+Paris)	Pos 1	Pos 2	Pos 3	Pos 4	Total N (100%)
déjà	–	31 (100%)	–	–	31
encore	1	38 (93%)	–	2	41
toujours	–	56 (98%)	–	1	57
alors	–	–	–	–	–
après	28 (88%)	3	1	–	32
maintenant	21 (64%)	9	3	–	33

NNS (all groups)	Pos 1	Pos 2	Pos 3	Pos 4	Total N (100%)
déjà	–	74 (97%)	–	–	76
encore	1	79 (88%)	–	10	90
toujours	5	152 (90%)	1	9	168
alors	4	–	3	–	7
après	96 (72%)	27	5	5	133
maintenant	101 (57%)	46	24	5	176

Table 5a & 5b. Positions of *textual* markers (NS and NNS)

NS (Exchange+Paris)	Pos 1	Pos 2	Pos 3	Pos 4	Total N (100%)
déjà	8 (57%)	–	6 (43%)	–	14
encore	8	2	2	–	12
toujours	1	1	–	–	2
alors	86 (98%)	–	2 (2%)	–	88
après	20	1	–	–	21
maintenant	4	–	–	–	4

NNS (all groups)	Pos 1	Pos 2	Pos 3	Pos 4	Total N (100%)
déjà	9 (64%)	3	2 (14%)	–	14
encore	–	4	2	–	6
toujours	1	3	1	1	6
alors	86 (91%)	–	8 (9%)	–	94
après	11	1	–	–	12
maintenant	4	–	–	–	4

of *déjà* in position 3. Another tendency is that NNSs have no tokens of *encore* in position 1 (Table 5b), and seem to prefer it in position 2. A third observation is that *alors* in position 3 is more frequent in the NNS group than in the NS group (9% vs. 2%). A relevant question is whether these tendencies are reflected in the use of different subcategories of textual functions. This is the question what we will try to answer in the next section, where we consider positions in relation to the functions and compare the L1 and L2 speakers.

4.4 Positions and functions

In this section we try to show to which extent some functions are over- or underused by NNSs in relation to NS, by looking at the various positions of *déjà*, *encore* and *alors*.

Déjà

We observed that NNSs use a small number of tokens of *déjà* in 3rd position. The most frequent function in position 3 in the NS group is the argumentative one (see also example 6 above), but this function is absent in 3rd position in the NNS group (30).

(30) euh le # enfin le le cliché SIM # y a des clichés physiques *déjà*. c'est comme # c'est ce que tu viens de dire des images qui sont évoquées avec un béret une baguette et du fromage quoi. (Del, NS P)
('euh well the cliché # there are physical clichés *first of all*. It's like # it's what you just said about the pictures evoked with a beret a baguette and cheese, like that.')

Encore
The second observation above, viz. absence of *encore* in position 1, reflects the absence of concessive *encore* (*encore que* and *encore*) in the NNS group (see example 12 above). Five tokens are found in the NS group.

(31) (theme: the interlocutors talk about travelling and E's children)
I: oui les grands partent sans vous. (RIRE) / ils partent de leur côté.
E: ils sont grands / il faut / se plier (I:mm) *encore que*: on a des surprises hein. (Mau, NS P)
('I: yes the older go away without you/ (laugh) / they go away on their own.
E: they are adult you have to comply / *still* you are surprised, really.')

Alors
The number of tokens in position 3 is low in general, but there is a tendency by NNSs to use this position more frequently than NSs. This reflects the fact that all tokens of *alors* in position 3 are *inferential* and that is the preferred function of NNSs (35 Inferential/14 Reorienting, all groups counted), while NS prefer to use *alors* as reorienting/topic change marker (11 Inferential/60 Reorienting). The speaker in example (32) resides in Paris.

(32) I: et la nature / te manque?
E: mm: non.
I: non? / à Paris / Xoù (RIRE)$
E: non parce que souvent on va dans le Jura. / + et
I: ah oui d'accord oui. SIM
E: là (I:mm) SIM il y a …
I: très bien.
E: c'est le même paysage plus ou moins *alors*. (Per, Sta 5)
('I: and you miss the nature? E: no. I: no? in Paris or (laugh)? E: no because we often go to the Jura I: ah oh yes ok. E: there there is… I: very good E: *so* it's the same type of nature more or less.')

In summary, the observed tendencies concerning the preference of positions and functions of the highly advanced speaker (NNS P) are the following: As regards the NNSs, the item *déjà* is absent in position 3 as argumentative marker. *Encore* is absent in position 1 as an argumentative marker in the NNS group (*encore que, et encore*). As for *alors* in position 3, the NNSs prefer an inferential use while NSs use *alors* mainly as reorientation/topic change marker.

4.5 Textual markers: A feature of the highly advanced speaker?

One of the questions posed for this study was whether the use of pragmatic markers derived from temporal adverbs characterizes the highly advanced L2 speaker, i.e. speakers above stage 6 on the Bartning and Schlyter (2004) scale. Table 3a shows that the IPU of *déjà, après* and *maintenant* in the highly advanced group differs from stage 6, where we found no evidence of pragmatic use. When we consider the number of users of each marker, the picture is somewhat modified (Table 6).

Table 6. Number of users of textual markers (of eight speakers/group)

Item	Sta 4	Sta 5	Sta 6	NNS P	NS E	NS P
déjà	–	1	–	5	4	3
encore	1	–	2	3	3	4
toujours	–	1	3	1	1	1
alors	2	7	5	7	8	6
après	–	(1)	–	3	–	4
maintenant	–	–	–	2	–	2

Although *après* and *maintenant* differ between stage 6 and NNS P at group level, a minority of the speakers use these markers (3 vs. 2 in NNS P). On the other hand, one could conclude that the presence of textual *après* or *maintenant* seems to indicate a highly advanced speaker. Textual *déjà* (argumentative function in position 1) seems to be the best candidate to distinguish stages above stage 6, as it is used by 5 speakers out of 8 (and 7 out of 16 in the NS group).

As for explanations for the late emerging textual *déjà* (argumentative/interactive) and *encore* (argumentative), one factor could be the difficulty in identifying functional equivalents in French and Swedish. The Swedish formal equivalents to temporal *déjà* and *encore* (*redan* and *ännu*) do not have argumentative functions. In addition, the Swedish V2 constraint (the finite verb in second position in declarative clauses) allows for the placement of an adverb in the prefield (preverbal position), and the detached/pre-front field position is not preferred in standard Swedish. This could explain the late acquired detachment of *déjà* and *encore*. Further contrastive studies might shed light on this question.

5. Summary of results and conclusion

The results can be summarized in the following way: Pragmaticalization is parallel to syntactic detachment for *déjà*, *encore*, *après* and *maintenant*. *Alors* is already detached as a temporal marker (Table 4). As regards the NNSs: *encore* was not pragmaticalized nor detached from the rheme to position 1 (Table 5b). The NNSs preferred *inferential* marking by *alors*, while the NSs prefer *topic change*.

Is, then, the highly advanced user variety characterized by the use of textual markers? Two features that indicate the advanced user (above stage 6) are the presence of argumentative *déjà* in position 1 and argumentative *après* in position 1.

In this study, where we compare the use of textual functions of six temporal adverbs between NNSs and NSs, we have asked the following questions: Are the markers equally pragmaticalized in both groups? And is it possible to see a development in the degree of pragmatic use across the stages? If there is development, could the textual use of markers be an indication of discourse progress or level of acquisition? Does the progress in pragmatic use entail a syntactic isolation of the markers (to outer positions in the utterance) and is this true for both NSs and NNSs? We also asked to what extent an analysis of the positions could contribute to a finer description of the markers and to a better understanding of their pragmatic function. By pragmaticalization, we mean a general evaluation of the process of pragmatic development and by degree of pragmatic use, a quantitative way to consider polysemy on a pragmatic scale. Although the number of tokens is limited in this study, we have found both these measures fruitful for comparing the spontaneous speech of NNSs and NSs (Table 3). Broadly speaking, the order of emergence of the textual functions indicates parallels between the diachronic/historical development and L2 development of pragmatic uses (Section 4.1). These similarities are not surprising, as language change in general is affected by factors such as input frequency of the items and the inferences speakers make using the language (Traugott 1995). However, other factors, such as contrastive explanations may also contribute to the late emergence of some markers (see 4.5).

A more specific question is which markers might be candidates for characterizing levels above stage 6 in L2 French. *Déjà* was the textual marker that most clearly differed in use between stage 6 and (the more native-like) NNS P. This marker is, next to *alors*, the most frequent (in percentage and regarding the number of speakers). A qualitative analysis of the use of *alors* showed that the distribution of subcategories differed between native speakers and (all groups of) NNSs: NSs prefer (quantitatively) the *reorienting* function and the NNSs the *inferential* use. This could be due to the highly polysemous nature of *alors*, and is interpreted as a more 'conservative' or 'secure' form-function matching by the NNSs. In addition, a factor such as the high inter-individual variation of *alors* in the input might play a decisive role for the late pragmaticalization in the L2 production.

Acknowledgements

I would like to thank the anonymous reviewers and the editors for their careful reading and suggestions for improvements.

References

Bartning, I. (this volume). Synthèse rétrospective et nouvelles perspectives développementales — les recherches acquisitionnelles en français L2 à l'université de Stockholm.
Bartning, I. & Schlyter, S. (2004). Itinéraires acquisitionnels et stades de développement en français L2. *Journal of French Language Studies* 14, 281–299.
Beeching, K. (2009). Sociolinguistic factors and the pragmaticalization of *bon* in contemporary spoken French. In K. Beeching, N. Armstrong & F. Gadet (Eds.), *Sociolinguistic variation in contemporary French*, 215–230. Amsterdam/Philadelphia: John Benjamins Publishing Company.
Benazzo, S. (2000). *L'acquisition de particules de portée en français, anglais et allemand L2. Études longitudinales comparées*. PhD thesis. Université de Paris VIII/Freie Universität Berlin.
Buchi, É. (2007a). Sur la trace de la pragmaticalisation de l'adverbe toujours («Voyons toujours l'apport de la linguistique historique»). *Langue française* 154, 110–125.
Buchi, É. (2007b). Approche diachronique de la (poly)pragmaticalisation de français *déjà* («Quand le grammème est-il devenu pragmatème, déjà ?»). In D. Trotter (Ed.), *Actes du XXIVe Congrès International de Linguistique et de Philologie Romanes* (Aberystwyth 2004), 251–264 [vol. III]. Tübingen: Niemeyer.
Defour, T., D'Hondt, U., Simon-Vanderbergen, A.-M. & Willems, D. (2010). Degrees of pragmaticalization: the divergent histories of 'actually' and *actuellement*. In P. Lauwers, G. Vanderbauwhede & S. Verleyen (Eds.), *Pragmatic markers and pragmaticalization: lessons from False friends*. Special Issue of *Languages in Contrast*, Vol 10 (2), 166–193.
Dostie, G. (2004). *Pragmaticalisation et marqueurs discursifs. Analyse sémantique et traitement lexicographique*. Bruxelles: De Boeck, Duculot.
Dostie, G. & Pusch, C.D. (2007). Les marqueurs discursifs. Sens et variation. *Langue Française* 154, 3–12.
Erman, B. & Kotsinas, U.-B. (1993). Pragmaticalisation: the case of *ba'* and you know. *Studier i Modern Språkvetenskap* 10, 76–93.
Fischer, K. (2006). *Approaches to discourse particles*. Amsterdam: Elsevier.
Giacalone Ramat, A. (2000). Typological considerations on second language acquisition. Special Issue of *Studia Linguistica* 54, 123–135.
Hancock, V. & Sanell, A. (2010). Pragmaticalisation des adverbes temporels dans le français parlé L1 et L2: étude développementale de *alors, après, maintenant, déjà, encore* et *toujours*. In L. Roberts, M. Howard, M. Ó Laoire & D. Singleton (Eds.), *EUROSLA Yearbook*, Vol 10, 62–91. Amsterdam: Benjamins.

Hansen, M.-B.M. (1998). *The function of discourse particles: a study with special reference to spoken standard French*. Amsterdam: Benjamins.
Hansen, M.-B.M. (2002). La polysémie de l'adverbe *encore*. *Travaux de Linguistique* 44, 143–165.
Hansen, M.-B.M. (2004). La polysémie de l'adverbe *toujours*. *Travaux de Linguistique* 49, 39–55.
Hansen, M.-B.M. (2008). *Particles at the semantics/pragmatics interface: synchronic and diachronic issues: a study with special reference to the French phasal adverbs*. Amsterdam: Elsevier.
Hansen, M.-B. M. & Rossari, C. (2005). The evolution of pragmatic markers. *Journal of Historical Pragmatics* 6, 177–187.
Hansen, M.-B. M. & Strudsholm, E. (2008). The semantics of particles: advantages of a contrastive and panchronic approach. A study of the polysemy of French *déjà* and Italian *già*. *Linguistics* 46, 471–505.
Hybertie, C. (1996). *La conséquence en français*. Paris: Ophrys.
Mellet, S. (2005). Réflexions énonciatives autour de *maintenant argumentatif*. Colloque de Linguistique, nov 25, Université Nice Sophia Antipolis.
Morel, M.-A. & Danon-Boileau, L. (1998). *Grammaire de l'intonation. L'exemple du français*. Paris: Ophrys.
Nølke, H. (1983). Les adverbes paradigmatisants: fonction et analyse. *Revue Romane* numéro spécial 23. Copenhague: Akademisk forlag.
Petit Robert. (2001). Dictionnaire alphabétique et analogique de la langue française. Paris: dictionnaires Le Robert. CD-rom, V.2.1.
Romero Trillo, J. (2002). The pragmatic fossilization of discourse markers in non-native speakers of English. *Journal of Pragmatics* 34, 769–784.
Sanell, A. (2007). *Parcours acquisitionnel de la négation et quelques particules de portée en français L2 chez des apprenants suédophones*. PhD thesis. Stockholm University: *Cahiers de la recherche* 35.
Schlyter, S. (2005). Adverbs and functional categories in L1 and L2 acquisition of French. In J.-M. Dewaele (Ed.), *Focus on French as a foreign language: multidisciplinary approaches*, 36–55. Clevedon: Multilingual Matters.
Traugott, E.C. (1995). Subjectification in grammaticalisation. In D. Stein & S.Wright (Eds.), *Subjectivity and subjectivisation*, 31–54. Cambridge: Cambridge University Press.

Résumé

Nous partons dans cette étude de la polysémie d'un certain nombre d'adverbes temporels récurrents en français L1. Cette polysémie serait le résultat d'un développement diachronique (Hansen & Rossari 2005 ; Dostie 2004). Nous nous intéressons ici à l'usage des adverbes *encore*, *déjà*, *toujours*, *alors*, *après*, et *maintenant* dans le français parlé L1 et L2. Nous avons fait l'hypothèse que ces adverbes, à mesure que la L2 se développe, sont de plus en plus pragmaticalisés. Par pragmaticalisation, nous entendons ici le développement des fonctions discursives/textuelles (non-temporelles) des adverbes en français L2. Nous avons pu dégager un ordre de développement des fonctions non-temporelles dans une étude récente (Hancock & Sanell 2010). Dans la présente étude, nous considérerons les fonctions et l'emplacement des adverbes dans la structure informationnelle. Nous nous attendons à ce que la pragmaticalisation des adverbes entraîne leur détachement syntaxique.

L'analyse des positions montre que certaines fonctions argumentatives en position détachée sont absentes, pour deux des adverbes à l'étude, même dans le groupe des locuteurs non-natifs le plus avancé.

Appendix. Transcription conventions

E:	Student (étudiant)
I:	Interviewer (enquêteur)
/, //, ///	Short, medium, long pause (pause courte, moyenne, longue)
.	End of macrophrase (marque fin d'un macrosyntagme)
+ SIM	Beginning and end of overlapping utterances (marques respectives du début et de la fin d'énoncés chevauchant)
#	Interruption or restructuring (interruption ou restructuration)
(RIRE)	Non-verbal sound — in capital letters and in parentheses (bruit non-verbal — en majuscules entre parenthèses)
st	Tongue snapping (clappement de la langue)
eh euh	Hesitation (hésitation)
X	non comprehensible or uncertain syllable (syllabe incompréhensible ou interprétation incertaine)
…	Suspended end of a macrophrase = trois points (fin suspendue d'un macrosyntagme)
:	Vowel lengthening (allongement de voyelle)
friGidaire	Caps — deviant pronunciation (majuscules — prononciation déviante)

La dislocation dans le français oral d'apprenants suédophones
Emploi et développement

Hugues Engel
Université d'Uppsala

Les dislocations sont très fréquentes en français parlé et jouent un rôle essentiel dans la construction des énoncés. C'est pourquoi il est important pour les apprenants du français d'acquérir les moyens grammaticaux et les principes pragmatiques qui sous-tendent l'emploi de cette structure. La présente étude est empirique et se fonde sur un corpus de productions orales de locuteurs non natifs (LNN) : des lycéens apprenants du français, des étudiants de français de l'Université de Stockholm et des LNN ayant vécu de nombreuses années en France. Le corpus comprend également des productions d'un groupe contrôle composé de locuteurs natifs (LN). L'étude examine la question du développement formel et fonctionnel de la dislocation en français langue seconde (L2). Nous nous intéressons également à la façon dont le type de tâche influence l'emploi de la dislocation. Pour étudier cette question, nous analyserons deux tâches, des entretiens et des récits, qui imposent aux locuteurs des efforts cognitifs très différents.

1. Introduction

La dislocation est une construction typique de l'oral (Blanche Benveniste 2000:67–68 ; Gadet 2007:17), très fréquente en français et en suédois. Cette structure présente des propriétés formelles, syntaxiques, sémantiques et pragmatiques comparables dans les deux langues (Larsson Ringqvist 2003). Ces quelques constats conduisent à se demander si l'acquisition de la dislocation par des apprenants suédophones du français est pour autant immédiate et non problématique. Nous montrerons dans ce chapitre que l'acquisition de la dislocation suit plusieurs étapes en nous appuyant sur un corpus semi-longitudinal d'apprenants suédophones du français. Nous constaterons par ailleurs des différences d'emploi de la dislocation entre LN et LNN. Nous verrons en particulier que le changement de tâche communicative affecte différemment l'emploi de la dislocation chez les LN et les LNN.

2. Études antérieures sur la dislocation en français L2

Dans le cadre du projet ESF (*European Science Foundation*), Perdue et al. (1992) ont étudié le développement du français de travailleurs immigrés arabophones et hispanophones. Chez ces apprenants, l'emploi de la dislocation est motivé par le besoin de rendre saillant le syntagme nominal en topique : la structure est utilisée soit pour réintroduire une entité en topique, soit pour sélectionner un référent en cas de compétition entre plusieurs entités pour le rôle de topique. Perdue et al. (1992) remarquent que les apprenants hispanophones développent les dislocations à gauche et à droite à peu près simultanément, tandis que les apprenants arabophones emploient dans un premier temps seulement la dislocation à droite.

Hendriks (2000) s'est intéressée au marquage du topique dans les récits d'apprenants du français L2[1] ayant le chinois pour langue maternelle. Ces apprenants, qui appartiennent à la variété post-basique[2], emploient les dislocations dans quatre fonctions principales : (i) pour réintroduire dans le discours un référent mentionné précédemment, (ii) pour effectuer une désambiguïsation en cas de compétition entre plusieurs référents, (iii) pour rendre ancienne une information nouvelle et (iv) dans quelques cas limités, pour introduire un référent nouveau dans le discours. Hendriks souligne que cette dernière fonction est en principe incompatible avec les contraintes pragmatiques et discursives de la dislocation, dans la mesure où le référent visé par le constituant détaché doit normalement être cognitivement accessible (Lambrecht 1994 : 183 ; *cf.* Larsson Ringqvist 2003 : 122). Et, de fait, la dislocation n'est pas mise en œuvre dans la fonction d'introduction de référent nouveau par les LN de son étude. Néanmoins, la rareté de cet emploi dans les productions des apprenants (4 % du total des dislocations) conduit Hendriks à conclure que les apprenants comprennent globalement le fonctionnement pragmatique et discursif de la dislocation en français. Notons que Lambert (2003 : 110) relève, elle aussi, des cas d'emploi de la dislocation dans des récits d'apprenants polonophones avancés du français avec cette même fonction d'introduction des référents.

---

1. L2 désigne, dans la présente étude, toute langue apprise après la langue maternelle. Ainsi, un locuteur peut avoir plusieurs L2.

2. La variété post-basique est une étape du développement de la L2 succédant à la variété basique (Klein & Perdue 1997). Elle se caractérise notamment par la mise en place de la morphologie flexionnelle.

Outre les fonctions de structuration des contenus informationnels, les dislocations jouent un rôle dans l'organisation socio-interactive des activités de discours (Pekarek Doehler 2004:123): elles permettent, par exemple, d'assurer le maintien de l'organisation préférentielle et de gérer l'intercompréhension. Pekarek Doehler constate que les apprenants germanophones avancés du français de son étude emploient les dislocations dans des fonctions discursives comparables à celles que présentent les dislocations relevées dans les productions de LN, avec toutefois quelques différences. Par exemple, la structure *moi je*, si elle est employée de manière régulière et automatique par les LN, fait l'objet d'un emploi plus spécialisé chez les apprenants : elle est utilisée pour marquer une prise de position ou pour prendre le tour de parole.

Rappelons également que la dislocation est un moyen grammatical permettant de faire référence aux entités. À ce titre, la question de son emploi a également été traitée dans un grand nombre d'études portant sur la référence aux personnes en français L2 (voir, entre bien d'autres, Lambert 2003 ; Chini & Lenart 2008).

Les études antérieures sur la dislocation en français L2 n'ont pas abordé, à notre connaissance, la question de l'appropriation graduelle de cette structure, ni celle de la variation de son emploi selon la tâche. C'est à ces deux questions que nous proposons de nous attacher dans cette étude.

3. Cadre théorique

3.1 Dislocation et acquisition L2

Un certain nombre de travaux en acquisition L2 ont cherché à décrire les différentes étapes du développement grammatical (Ellis 2008:96–98). Il s'agit par exemple des recherches qui ont été menées au sein des projets ZISA (*Zweitspracherwerb italienischer, portugiesischer und spanischer Arbeiter*; Meisel *et al.* 1981) et ESF (Klein & Perdue 1992), ou encore des recherches visant la théorisation du concept de *processabilité* (Pienemann 1998). Elles ont montré que certains éléments d'une L2 s'acquièrent selon un ordre déterminé, valable pour tous les apprenants, que ceux-ci soient guidés ou non (Bartning & Schlyter 2004:281). Dans cette étude, nous nous servirons de l'hypothèse des stades de développement formulée par Bartning et Schlyter (2004). Ces stades sont caractérisés par des faisceaux de traits grammaticaux apparaissant à peu près simultanément dans la langue des apprenants. Ils ont été établis sur la base de données empiriques provenant de deux corpus constitués de productions orales de locuteurs suédophones adultes apprenants du français : le corpus InterFra (de l'Université de Stockholm ; voir Bartning, présent volume) et le corpus d'apprenants suédophones du français de l'Université de

Lund. Les traits étudiés sont, entre autres, la structuration de l'énoncé (nominale, verbale à verbe non fini, verbale à verbe fléchi), le système temporel et modal, la forme et la place de la négation, la forme et la place des pronoms, l'acquisition du genre, l'accord au sein du syntagme nominal, la subordination.

3.2 Formes et fonctions de la dislocation

Blasco-Dulbecco (1999:9) décrit la dislocation comme une structure tripartite composée (i) d'une construction verbale, (ii) d'un constituant détaché et (iii) dans la plupart des cas, d'un pronom de reprise en relation de coréférence avec le constituant détaché. Blasco-Dulbecco souligne qu'il est difficile d'attribuer au constituant détaché une fonction syntaxique traditionnelle. La relation syntaxique avec la construction verbale est prise en charge par le pronom de reprise. Voici quelques exemples de dislocations, tirés du corpus de la présente étude[3].

(1) *les ados i:ls* ne savent pas beaucoup sur la littérature. (Mona, LNN)

(2) *c'*était sensiblement plus aigu *les problèmes* en France / il me semble qu'en Suède. (Olivier, LN)

(3) parce que *lui* / *il* parle pas français avec elle. (Ursula, LNN)

(4) *c'*est où *ça*? (Yvonne, LNN)

Les exemples (1) à (4) montrent que le constituant détaché peut être un syntagme nominal de type soit lexical (*les ados, les problèmes*), soit pronominal (*lui, ça*), et qu'il peut se situer à droite ou à gauche de la proposition dont il dépend. Comme nous le verrons, ces différents types de dislocations apparaissent dans la langue des LNN par étapes successives.

Du point de vue fonctionnel, les dislocations jouent un rôle dans la structuration informationnelle des énoncés. Lambrecht (1994:182–184) décrit la dislocation comme une structure permettant (i) d'activer un référent cognitivement accessible et (ii) de le promouvoir au statut de topique d'un énoncé[4]. Prenons un exemple en anglais[5] (exemple 5) de Lambrecht (1994:177, italiques de l'auteur).

---

3. Dans tous les exemples du chapitre, nous indiquons le constituant détaché et le pronom de reprise en italiques.

4. Blasco-Dulbecco (1999:58–59) a constaté la grande dispersion terminologique qui caractérise les descriptions théoriques de la dislocation. Par souci de simplicité, nous ne présentons ici que le modèle de Lambrecht (1994), que nous utilisons dans notre étude.

5. L'explication donnée par l'auteur, si elle porte sur un exemple en anglais, vaut également pour le français.

(5) Once there was a *wizard*. *He* was very wise, rich, and was married to a beautiful witch. They had two sons. The first was tall and brooding, he spent his days in the forest hunting snails, and his mother was afraid of him. The second was short and vivacious, a bit crazy but always game. Now *the wizard, he* lived in Africa.

Le personnage du sorcier est introduit dans la première phrase du texte. Le référent est alors 'entièrement nouveau' (*brand new*). Dans la suite du texte, d'autres référents sont mentionnés : *a beautiful witch, two sons, the first, the second*. Ceci a pour effet de désactiver le référent SORCIER. Ce dernier reste néanmoins cognitivement accessible. Dans la dernière phrase de l'extrait, la dislocation [*the wizard, he* SV] a pour fonction de réintroduire le référent dans le discours — c'est-à-dire de le réactiver — et de l'établir en topique.

Si l'activation d'un référent et sa promotion au statut de topique sont les deux fonctions discursives de base de la dislocation, celles-ci ne permettent cependant pas de rendre compte de la totalité des emplois de la structure. Lambrecht mentionne entre autres sa fonction contrastive : la dislocation à gauche peut être employée pour marquer un déplacement de l'attention entre plusieurs référents topicaux actifs ; ce n'est pas alors le statut informationnel du référent qui détermine l'emploi de la dislocation, mais le besoin de désigner sans ambiguïté un référent parmi plusieurs référents actifs.

3.3 Emploi des dislocations et type de tâche

Un autre aspect auquel nous nous intéressons dans la présente étude est l'impact de la tâche sur l'emploi de la dislocation. Le type de tâche peut influer sur les performances des LNN et, ainsi, modifier l'image que les résultats donnent du développement et de l'acquisition des structures linguistiques chez les LNN. C'est ce que certains chercheurs appellent la 'variation induite par le type de tâche' (*task-based variation* ; voir Ellis 2008 : 148–149). Pour illustrer cette notion, Romaine (2003 : 426) cite une étude réalisée par Dickerson (1975), dans laquelle des apprenants japonais de l'anglais produisent plus de formes conformes à la langue cible dans des tâches leur laissant la possibilité de contrôler leur production que dans des situations où un tel contrôle ne peut s'exercer. D'autres études ont montré, par exemple, que la familiarité avec l'information traitée et la nature dialogique ou monologique de la tâche ont une influence sur la fluidité de l'énoncé (Tavakoli & Skehan 2005 : 240).

4. Méthodologie et données

La présente étude est empirique, descriptive et exploratoire : elle analyse un corpus de productions orales de LNN de français L2 ayant le suédois pour langue maternelle.

4.1 Informateurs

Pour étudier le développement de la dislocation, nous avons eu recours à un corpus semi-longitudinal se composant de productions orales de 50 LNN : des lycéens apprenants du français et des étudiants de français de l'Université de Stockholm (débutants, étudiants de première et deuxième années, futurs professeurs de français et doctorants) ainsi que des LNN vivant en France depuis plusieurs années.

L'étude comprend également un corpus contrôle de productions orales de 18 LN. Ceux-ci se répartissent en deux groupes : le premier est composé d'étudiants français en échange Erasmus à l'Université de Stockholm ; le second, de LN vivant à Paris. Les étudiants Erasmus ont à peu près le même profil que les apprenants universitaires du français ; et les LN de Paris le même profil que celui des LNN de Paris[6]. L'ensemble de ces données est issu du corpus InterFra du Département de français, d'italien et de langues classiques de l'Université de Stockholm (voir le site du projet InterFra <http://www.fraita.su.se/interfra/> ainsi que Bartning, présent volume).

Les productions des informateurs non natifs ont été classées selon les stades de développement proposés par Bartning et Schlyter (2004) mentionnés en 3.1. Le nombre d'entretiens et de récits classés à chaque stade est précisé dans le Tableau 1[7].

Notons que les productions orales des LNN de Paris présentent un certain nombre de traits morphosyntaxiques et discursifs comparables à ceux des productions des LN (Bartning 2009), c'est-à-dire : des énoncés complexes (gérondif, discours rapporté, préambules comportant un nombre élevé de constituants[8]), un répertoire de marqueurs de discours comparable à celui des LN (*donc, du coup, en fait*), une parole fluide et un large emploi d'expressions idiomatiques. Or ces traits morphosyntaxiques et discursifs sont absents des productions des apprenants aux stades avancés moyen et supérieur. C'est pourquoi nous avons classé les LNN de

---

[6]. Le corpus de l'étude est présenté de manière détaillée dans Engel (2010), qui peut être téléchargé à l'adresse suivante : <http://su.diva-portal.org/smash/get/diva2:313617/FULLTEXT02>.

[7]. Certains apprenants ont effectué les tâches à plusieurs reprises.

[8]. Sur la notion de *préambule*, voir Morel et Danon-Boileau (1998).

Tableau 1. Nombre d'entretiens et de récits classés aux différents stades de développement proposés par Bartning et Schlyter (2004)

	Stade initial	Stade post-initial	Stade intermédiaire	Stade avancé inférieur	Stade avancé moyen	Stade avancé supérieur	LNN de Paris (au-delà du stade avancé supérieur)
Nombre d'entretiens	10	24	6	8	11	11	10
Nombre de récits	4	19	6	11	15	13	10

Paris à un stade de développement situé 'au-delà' de ceux proposés par Bartning et Schlyter (2004 ; voir la dernière colonne du Tableau 1).

4.2 Tâches et types de discours

Tous les informateurs ont participé à des entretiens et ont produit des récits à partir d'un film vidéo muet. Les entretiens étaient semi-guidés : l'enquêteur les dirigeait à partir d'une liste de questions. Il posait donc des questions comparables à tous les locuteurs d'un même groupe. Soulignons cependant que les questions adressées aux lycéens, débutants, étudiants de première et deuxième années et aux futurs professeurs ont porté, entre autres, sur la vie lycéenne ou estudiantine ainsi que sur leurs études de français, tandis que l'entretien du groupe de LNN vivant à Paris était principalement orienté sur la vie en France et sur les différences culturelles entre la France et la Suède. Les récits, quant à eux, ont tous été réalisés à partir d'un même film vidéo muet intitulé *Le bac à sable*. Les narrations des différents locuteurs présentent donc un fort degré de comparabilité. L'histoire du film comporte quatre personnages : une femme, son enfant, un homme et un vendeur de ballons. L'homme et l'enfant sont les deux protagonistes principaux. Le récit enchaîne tour à tour des séries d'actions de l'homme et de l'enfant : en résumé, l'homme, voulant séduire la femme, fait plusieurs tentatives pour amadouer l'enfant, par exemple en lui offrant des bonbons ; mais l'enfant, à chaque fois, se rebiffe. Ce récit est une tâche cognitivement plus astreignante que l'entretien réalisé par les informateurs du corpus (*cf.* Bartning 1990). Dans les entretiens, les locuteurs ont en effet une grande liberté dans le choix des sujets qu'ils abordent, du vocabulaire utilisé, des moyens grammaticaux mis en œuvre, alors que, dans les récits, un cadre strict leur est imposé : les apprenants regardent une vidéo et doivent ensuite en raconter l'histoire. Cet exercice impose donc des contraintes de type lexical : certains mots de vocabulaire — *bac à sable*, *pelle*, etc. — sont requis pour la description de l'action. Le récit exige en outre un effort mnésique particulier, pour se souvenir des différentes étapes du récit.

5. La dislocation dans les récits et les entretiens : analyse des données

Après avoir présenté nos questions de recherche (5.1) et notre méthode d'analyse (5.2), nous étudierons la question du développement de la dislocation (5.3) et l'impact du type de tâche sur l'emploi des dislocations (5.4).

5.1 Questions de recherche et hypothèses

Nous chercherons à répondre aux deux questions de recherche suivantes.

(Q1) La dislocation connaît-elle un développement en français L2 ?
(Q2) Dans quelle mesure le type de tâche influence-t-il l'emploi de la dislocation en français L2 ?

Pour ces deux questions de recherche, nous formulons les hypothèses suivantes.

(H1) L'emploi de certains types de dislocations exige la maîtrise de ressources grammaticales relativement avancées (comme le système pronominal, les pronoms complément d'objet en particulier). Les dislocations nécessitant la mise en œuvre de ces ressources ne sont donc probablement pas employées par les apprenants en début d'acquisition. Nous émettons par conséquent l'hypothèse que les différents types de dislocations se développent par étapes en français L2. En ce qui concerne les fonctions des dislocations, plusieurs études antérieures (présentées en 2) ont montré que certains apprenants du français utilisent les dislocations pour introduire des référents nouveaux dans le discours. Notre hypothèse est que cette fonction, qui n'est pas mise en œuvre par les LN, finit par disparaître des productions des apprenants, c'est-à-dire que l'on assiste à un développement fonctionnel en deux temps : (i) une première étape où cette fonction est employée par certains LNN et (ii) une étape ultérieure où cette fonction cesse d'être mise en œuvre par les LNN.

(H2) Pour examiner la manière dont l'emploi de la dislocation varie selon les tâches auxquelles sont soumis les LNN, nous analyserons un entretien et un récit, qui, comme nous l'avons vu, imposent des contraintes de différentes natures aux locuteurs. Ces deux tâches se distinguent notamment par la latitude laissée aux locuteurs dans leur discours. Pour les raisons énoncées en

4.2, nous émettons l'hypothèse que le récit impose un effort cognitif plus important que l'entretien. La charge cognitive supplémentaire induite par le récit pourrait ainsi avoir une incidence sur la fluidité et sur la manière dont les LNN construisent leurs énoncés, et, ainsi, sur l'emploi des dislocations.

5.2 Méthode d'analyse

Dans l'analyse du développement des dislocations chez les locuteurs du français L2, nous avons distingué développement formel et développement fonctionnel. Nous avons d'abord voulu examiner à quel moment dans l'acquisition apparaissent les différents types de dislocations, c'est-à-dire les dislocations à gauche et à droite, les dislocations lexicales et pronominales, les dislocations dont le référent visé par la séquence détachée est une entité tierce (du type [SN *il* SV] ou [SN *c'est* X]) et celles se référant au locuteur ([*moi je* SV]). Nous avons procédé à l'analyse du développement fonctionnel des dislocations dans un second temps, en nous inspirant du modèle de Lambrecht (1994) présenté en 3.2. Pour l'analyse de l'impact de la tâche sur l'emploi des dislocations, nous avons calculé la fréquence d'emploi des dislocations (c'est-à-dire le nombre de dislocations pour 100 mots) dans les entretiens et dans les récits du corpus.

5.3 Développement de la dislocation en français L2

5.3.1 *Développement formel*

Nous distinguons dans cette section les dislocations se référant à des entités tierces ([SN *il* SV], [SN *c'est* X] et leurs variantes syntaxiques) et celles qui réfèrent au locuteur ([*moi je* SV] et ses variantes syntaxiques). Concernant les dislocations se référant à des entités tierces, nous pouvons d'abord constater que les dislocations nominales — c'est-à-dire les dislocations dont le constituant détaché est de nature lexicale — sont employées[9] avant les dislocations pronominales. Les dislocations nominales [SN$_{lexical}$ *il* SV] (exemple 6) sont mises en œuvre par les apprenants dès le stade initial.

---

9. Par *emploi*, nous entendons *emploi systématique*, pour lequel nous avons défini les critères suivants: au moins deux occurrences chez deux locuteurs différents. Nous n'avons pas pris en compte les occurrences isolées dans la mesure où elles peuvent être le produit d'une expérimentation: l'apprenant emploie la structure dans un premier temps sans lui attribuer encore de fonction bien définie (*cf.* Pallotti 2007:366); on ne peut pas alors encore véritablement parler d'acquisition.

(6) *ma frère il* travaille à l'école. (Heidi, lycéens, entretien 1[10], stade initial)

Les dislocations pronominales commencent à être employées systématiquement à partir du stade avancé moyen. Le premier type relevé dans le corpus de l'étude est [*ça c'est* X] (exemple 7).

(7) mais *ça c'est* aussi / un problème / e:h politique évidemment / de de : la pauvreté dans le pays. (Lena, étudiants de 1ère et 2ème années, entretien 4, stade avancé moyen)

L'autre tendance remarquable est que les dislocations à gauche apparaissent plus précocement que les dislocations à droite : les premières sont employées systématiquement dès le stade initial ; on voit apparaître les dislocations à droite de type [*c'est* X / SN] au stade avancé inférieur (exemple 8).

(8) c'est+ énervant vraiment *le silence*. (Pernilla, étudiants de 1ère et 2ème années, entretien 4, stade avancé inférieur)

Troisième constat : les dislocations dont le pronom de reprise occupe la fonction de complément d'objet (exemple 9) apparaissent plus tard que celles dont le pronom a la fonction sujet.

(9) et *les anglophones* (I:RIRE) il faut pas *les* oublier (Matilda, doctorants, entretien 1 stade avancé supérieur)

Les dislocations de type [*moi je* SV], quant à elles, sont employées de manière systématique à partir du stade post-initial (exemple 10).

(10) eh *moi* eh *je* m'appelle ***. (Anne, débutants, entretien 4, stade post-initial)

L'emploi de ce type de dislocations demeure néanmoins relativement limité au début de l'acquisition, comme le suggèrent les résultats présentés dans le Tableau 2[11].

Comme le montre le Tableau 2, les fréquences moyennes de [*moi je* SV] (et ses variantes syntaxiques) sont situées entre 0,01 et 0,02 dislocations pour 100 mots aux stades initial, post-initial et intermédiaire. La fréquence augmente sensiblement à partir des stades avancés (entre 0,07 et 0,12 dislocations pour 100 mots) pour atteindre un pic dans le groupe des LNN de Paris (fréquence moyenne de 0,37 dislocations pour 100 mots, soit un taux supérieur à celui des deux groupes

---

10. Nous conservons dans tout le chapitre la numérotation originale des tâches du corpus InterFra.

11. Les dislocations de type [*moi je* SV] n'ont été relevées que dans les entretiens. Ceci tient au fait que les locuteurs n'ont en principe pas besoin de faire référence à eux-mêmes pour effectuer la tâche du récit, puisque celui-ci met en jeu quatre personnages, c'est-à-dire des entités tierces.

Tableau 2. Fréquences moyennes des dislocations [*moi je* SV] (et leurs variantes syntaxiques) dans les entretiens (nombre de dislocations / 100 mots)

	Stade initial	Stade post-initial	Stade intermédiaire	Stade avancé inférieur	Stade avancé moyen	Stade avancé supérieur	LNN de Paris (au-delà du stade avancé supérieur)	LN Erasmus	LN Paris
Fréquences moyennes	0,02	0,02	0,01	0,07	0,12	0,12	0,37	0,15	0,13

de LN : 0,15 pour les LN Erasmus et 0,13 pour les LN de Paris[12]). Nous avons pu constater l'existence d'une corrélation forte entre la fréquence d'emploi de ce type de dislocations et les stades de développement (corrélation de Pearson $r = 0,612$, $p < 0,001$)[13]. La corrélation est manifeste dans la Figure 1.

Pour comparaison, nous avons voulu voir s'il existait une corrélation entre la fréquence d'emploi des dislocations se référant à des entités tierces (tous types confondus : nominales et pronominales, à gauche et à droite) et les stades de développement. Le calcul donne une corrélation faible ($r = 0,199$) non significative ($p > 0,05$; voir la Figure 2).

La fréquence d'emploi de [*moi je* SV] augmente donc au fil de l'acquisition, tandis que celle des dislocations se référant à des entités tierces ne semble pas corrélée aux stades de développement.

5.3.2 *Développement fonctionnel*

L'analyse du corpus montre que les apprenants, dès les premiers stades de l'acquisition, emploient la dislocation avec les fonctions de base identifiées par Lambrecht (1994), à savoir (i) l'activation d'un référent cognitivement accessible et (ii) sa promotion au statut de topique d'un énoncé (voir 3.2). C'est le cas de la dislocation [*ma mère elle* SV] dans l'exemple (11).

(11) I : alors tes parents que font tes parents ? quelle est la profession ?
E : <vad mina föräldrar jobbar med ?> [traduction du suédois : 'Ce que mes parents font ?'] eh ma pr ma p ma père est eh // eh (SOUPIR) eh eh

---

12. Cette différence entre LNN de Paris et LN pourrait s'expliquer par le fait que ces derniers jugent la situation de discours comme plus formelle que les LNN de Paris.

13. Dans le calcul de corrélation, nous n'avons pris en compte que le premier entretien des informateurs pour éviter de surpondérer ceux qui ont été enregistrés à plusieurs reprises.

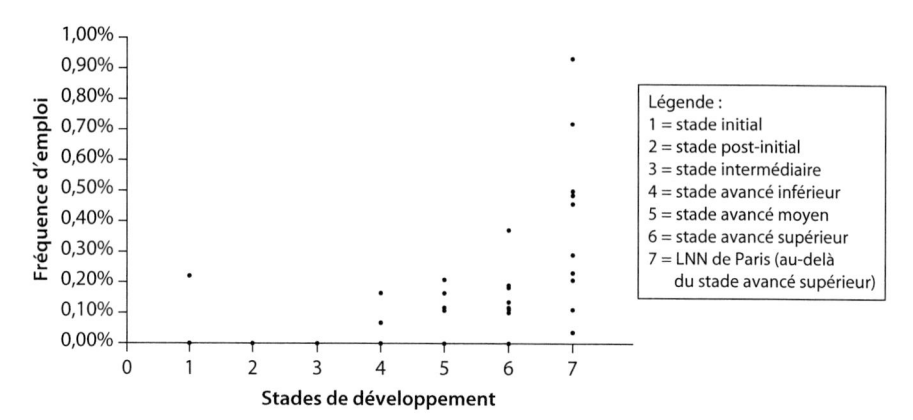

Figure 1. Relation entre la fréquence des dislocations [moi je SV] (et leurs variantes syntaxiques) et les stades de développement

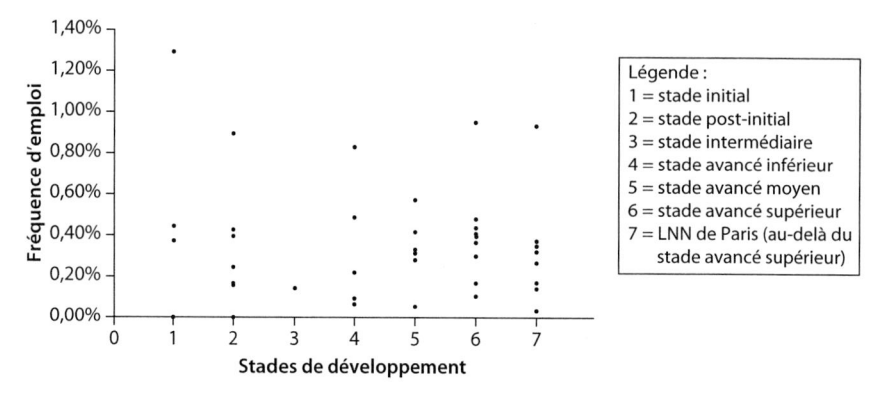

Figure 2. Relation entre la fréquence des dislocations se référant à des entités tierces et les stades de développement

> I : c'est difficile ?
> E : oui. <antikhandlare> ['antiquaire'].
> [...]
> E : hm. et *ma mère elle* est <gemmolog> ['gemmologue']. (Heidi, lycéens, entretien 1, stade initial)

La dislocation à la dernière ligne de l'exemple permet de réactiver et de promouvoir en topique le référent de la MÈRE, qui avait été activé plus tôt, au moment où l'enquêteur (I) demande à l'informatrice (E) quelle profession ses parents exercent (1ère ligne).

Nous avons toutefois identifié deux cas où l'emploi de la dislocation ne met pas en jeu les deux fonctions de base du modèle de Lambrecht. La dislocation est parfois employée pour maintenir de topique en topique un référent déjà actif, et dans d'autres cas pour introduire dans le discours un référent nouveau non cognitivement accessible. Le premier des deux cas de figure est illustré par l'exemple (12) ; le second sera examiné un peu plus loin.

(12) et le garçon ne l'aime pas du tout. // e:t (BRUIT) // qu'est-ce qu'il fait d'abord ? d'ab euh *le garçon il lance la pelle*. / et puis il donne un coup d'pied au: monsieur // qui essaie de lui offrir des bonbons. (Kerstin, futurs professeurs, vidéo 3, stade avancé supérieur)

Dans cet exemple, la dislocation [*le garçon il* SV] (2ème ligne) vise un référent déjà actif et en topique dans les deux propositions précédentes : « et *le garçon*$_{\text{ACTIF, TOPIQUE}}$ ne l'aime pas du tout » et « e:t (BRUIT) // qu'est-ce qu'*il*$_{\text{ACTIF, TOPIQUE}}$ fait d'abord ? ». La dislocation assure, du point de vue de la gestion des topiques, le maintien de topique en topique d'un référent actif. L'emploi de la dislocation s'explique ici par le fait que, après une première pause (//), l'hésitation sur *e:t*, une seconde pause (//) et le commentaire « qu'est-ce qu'il fait d'abord ? », l'informatrice entame un nouvel épisode de son récit, c'est-à-dire la relation d'une nouvelle série d'actions (*cf.* Perdue *et al.* 1992 : 234). Cette fonction de la dislocation n'est cependant pas propre à la L2 ; on la trouve également dans le discours des LN.

Dans les productions de l'étude, les dislocations sont employées pour maintenir de topique en topique un référent actif dans deux autres cas : (i) lorsqu'elles ont une fonction contrastive ou d'emphase (exemple 13) ou (ii) lorsqu'elles sont construites autour de la séquence *c'est* (exemple 14).

(13) [Dans l'extrait suivant, l'informatrice évoque les différentes nationalités et communautés linguistiques que l'on rencontre à Montréal.]
E : et les Espagnols et les Portugais aussi. mais maintenant plus récemment / il y a / les les Libanais / (I:mm). les gens de de de l'Indonésie aussi (I:oui). eh / ben de tout. et *les anglophones* (I:RIRE) il faut pas *les* oublier parce que *eux ils* sont vraiment exi- exilés là. (Matilda, doctorants, entretien 1, stade avancé supérieur)

La séquence détachée *eux* de la dislocation [*eux ils* SV] (3ème ligne) vise LES ANGLOPHONES, référent déjà actif et en topique dans la proposition précédente. L'emploi de la dislocation s'explique ici par un besoin d'attirer l'attention de l'interlocuteur sur ce groupe de population.

Dans l'extrait suivant, l'emploi de la dislocation [*la conversation c'est* X], qui, ici également, vise un référent déjà actif et en topique, s'explique par le caractère quasiment obligatoire de la séquence *c'est*.

(14) I: *la conversation c'*est bien ?
E: mais non *la conversation c'*était très bien. (Eva, étudiants de 1ère et 2ème années, entretien 4, stade avancé inférieur)

La « conversation » dont il est ici question est le cours de conversation que l'informatrice a suivi à l'université. La construction alternative non disloquée « mais non la conversation était très bien » changerait le sens de l'énoncé : *conversation* semblerait viser une conservation en particulier, et pas le cours de conversation. La dislocation [*la conversation c'est* X] est donc une structure obligatoire. Ce n'est pas la gestion des topiques qui détermine ici l'emploi de cette structure, mais une contrainte de nature sémantique.

Soulignons que ces différents emplois de la dislocation se rencontrent également dans les productions des LN. Ceci n'est en revanche pas le cas des dislocations utilisées par certains LNN du corpus pour introduire dans le discours un référent nouveau cognitivement non accessible. Nous trouvons de tels exemples aussi bien dans les récits (exemple 15) que dans les entretiens des LNN (exemple 16).

(15) alors *un petit euh petit garçon et sa et sa mère* / *ils* étaient dans un jardin. / e:t / soudain *un homme* / *il* vient. (Eva, étudiants de 1ère et 2ème années, vidéo 2, stade avancé inférieur)

Dans l'extrait de récit de l'exemple (15), trois personnages sont mentionnés pour la première fois au moyen de dislocations : [*un petit euh petit garçon et sa et sa mère* / *ils* SV] et [*un homme* / *il* SV]. De tels emplois ont également été relevés dans les entretiens de LNN, même aux niveaux les plus avancés, comme dans l'exemple (16), où une dislocation est mise en œuvre pour introduire un référent nouveau dans le discours (« *une copine* / *à moi* / je *l'*avais invitée »).

(16) E: oui (EN RIANT). et je me souviens j'avais un une fête anniversaire une fois / (I:mm) / et *une copine* / *à moi* / je *l'*avais invitée. et je pense que peut-être une semaine à l'avance ou quelque chose comme ça. ensuite je l'avais pas rappelée (I:mhm) pour dire que oui en fait je vais avoir ma fête. (Viveka, doctorants, entretien 1, stade avancé supérieur)

Ces emplois de la dislocation, en principe impossibles en français (*cf.* Lambrecht 1994 : 183 ; Hendriks 2000 ; Larsson Ringqvist 2003), ne sont pas attestés dans les productions des LN. Notons cependant qu'ils sont relativement rares dans les productions des LNN du corpus de l'étude (7 occurrences sur un total de 690 dislocations, soit 1 % des cas).

5.4 L'impact de la tâche sur l'emploi des dislocations

Nous allons à présent comparer le taux d'emploi des dislocations dans les entretiens d'une part et dans les récits d'autre part, pour vérifier notre hypothèse selon laquelle le type de tâche a une incidence sur l'emploi des dislocations. Nous ne nous intéressons dans cette section qu'aux dislocations se référant aux entités tierces, qui sont le seul type commun aux deux tâches : comme nous l'avons indiqué en 5.3.1, les dislocations [*moi je* SV] sont absentes des récits.

Les fréquences d'emploi des dislocations se référant à des entités tierces dans les deux tâches sont présentées dans les Tableaux 3 et 4.

La comparaison de la fréquence des dislocations dans les productions des LN et des LNN permet de constater que les LNN font varier leur emploi des dislocations entre les deux types de tâches plus fortement que les LN (voir la dernière ligne des Tableaux 3 et 4). En effet, entre les entretiens et les récits, la fréquence reste à peu près stable pour les LN Erasmus (+0,08 dislocations pour 100 mots) et baisse même légèrement pour les LN de Paris (-0,22), tandis que la fréquence moyenne est systématiquement plus élevée dans les récits des LNN que dans leurs

Tableau 3. Fréquences des dislocations se référant à des entités tierces dans les entretiens et les récits des LNN (nombre de dislocations / 100 mots)

	Stade initial	Stade post-initial	Stade intermédiaire	Stade avancé inférieur	Stade avancé moyen	Stade avancé supérieur	LNN de Paris (au-delà du stade avancé supérieur)
(1) Fréquence moyenne dans les entretiens	0,21	0,20	0,13	0,37	0,27	0,35	0,34
(2) Fréquence moyenne dans les récits	1,28	0,91	0,83	1,32	1,15	1,11	1,04
(3) = Différence : (2)–(1)	1,07	0,71	0,70	0,95	0,88	0,76	0,70

Tableau 4. Fréquences des dislocations se référant à des entités tierces dans les entretiens et les récits des LN (nombre de dislocations / 100 mots)

	LN Erasmus	LN Paris
(1) Fréquence moyenne dans les entretiens	0,25	0,22
(2) Fréquence moyenne dans les récits	0,33	0
(3) = Différence : (2)–(1)	0,08	−0,22

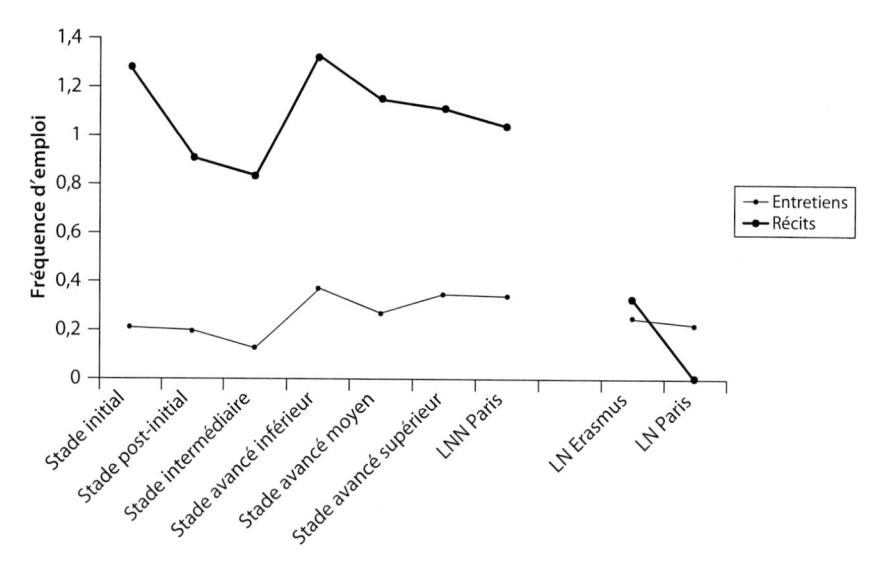

Figure 3. Fréquences moyennes des dislocations dans les entretiens et dans les récits des LN et des LNN (nombre de dislocations / 100 mots)

entretiens : la différence de fréquences se situe entre +0,70 (stade intermédiaire et LNN de Paris) et +1,07 dislocation pour 100 mots (stade initial). Cette différence entre LN et LNN apparaît clairement dans la Figure 3.

La Figure 3 montre que LNN et LN emploient des dislocations à un taux de fréquence à peu près comparable dans les entretiens (entre 0,1 et 0,4 dislocations pour 100 mots). En revanche, la fréquence moyenne des dislocations augmente fortement dans les récits des LNN, mais pas dans ceux des LN. Pour vérifier la significativité statistique de ce résultat, nous avons regroupé l'ensemble des LNN d'une part et les LN d'autre part, pour appliquer à ces deux groupes le test t de Student à deux échantillons indépendants. Le calcul montre que l'écart constaté entre les fréquences dans les deux tâches des LNN est significativement plus grand que celui observé dans les productions des LN ($p < 0,001$). Ainsi, la fréquence d'emploi des dislocations varie significativement plus dans les productions des LNN que dans celles des LN. En d'autres termes, la fréquence d'emploi des dislocations est plus sensible à la tâche chez les LNN que chez les LN.

6. Discussion et conclusion

La dislocation connaît un développement en français L2. C'est ce qu'a permis de constater l'analyse formelle, qui a donné les résultats suivants : (i) les dislocations lexicales se développent avant les dislocations pronominales ; (ii) les dislocations à gauche apparaissent avant les dislocations à droite ; (iii) les dislocations dont le pronom de reprise occupe la fonction de complément d'objet se développent après celles dont le pronom a la fonction sujet. Notons cependant que, en français, les dislocations à droite sont d'un emploi plus rare que les dislocations à gauche. Leur apparition dans notre corpus à un stade plus tardif que les dislocations à gauche pourrait donc être l'effet de leur faible fréquence. Les deux autres grandes tendances du développement de la dislocation (i et iii), pour leur part, pourraient s'expliquer par le fait que l'emploi des dislocations pronominales et des dislocations dont le pronom de reprise occupe la fonction objet nécessite une maîtrise relativement avancée du système pronominal du français. L'emploi des dislocations pronominales implique l'acquisition préalable du double système de pronoms du français, c'est-à-dire à la fois les formes conjointes (*je*, *tu*, *il*, etc.) et les formes disjointes (*moi*, *toi*, *lui*, etc.) des pronoms. Les dislocations dont le pronom de reprise occupe la fonction objet sont mises en œuvre aux niveaux avancés. Ceci est le fait de l'acquisition relativement tardive du pronom objet, qui, chez les apprenants suédophones du français, est employé conformément à la langue cible à partir des stades avancés (Bartning & Schlyter 2004 ; Granfeldt & Schlyter 2004). Nous avons par ailleurs observé que l'emploi de la dislocation [*moi je* SV] est fortement corrélé aux stades de développement. En cela, [*moi je* SV] se distingue des dislocations se référant à des entités tierces. Cette différence pourrait s'expliquer par le fait que, contrairement aux dislocations se référant aux entités tierces, la dislocation pronominale de la première personne du singulier n'a pas réellement d'équivalent en suédois. L'équivalent formel [*jag jag* SV] est d'un emploi rare en suédois, à la différence de [*moi je* SV] en français parlé. En suédois, d'autres ressources que les dislocations sont mises en œuvre pour assumer les fonctions que jouent [*moi je* SV], par exemple l'accentuation du pronom (« *JAG vet* », 'JE sais' = 'MOI je sais').

En ce qui concerne le développement fonctionnel de la dislocation, nous avons vu que les LNN emploient très précocement les dislocations avec des fonctions de gestion des topiques comparables à celles des dislocations relevées dans les productions des LN, à une exception notable près : l'introduction de référents nouveaux dans le discours. Hendriks (2000) a également relevé quelques cas de dislocations employées pour introduire un référent nouveau dans le discours, comme dans l'exemple 17 (issu d'un récit de Hendriks 2000 : 388).

(17)   Un jour *un cheval il* est venu dans un pré où il y a des fleurs.

Comme nous l'avons mentionné en 2, ces cas d'introduction de référents nouveaux sont cependant rares, ce qui conduit Hendriks (2000 : 389) à conclure que les apprenants adultes L2 de la variété post-basique de son étude n'éprouvent pas de difficulté à comprendre les règles pragmatiques et discursives qui sous-tendent l'emploi des dislocations en français. Rappelons néanmoins que ce phénomène a été également noté dans d'autres études (voir par exemple Lambert 2003, citée en 2). Autrement dit, si l'emploi des dislocations pour introduire des référents nouveaux est assez peu courant dans les productions des LNN, il n'en présente pas moins une certaine constance. Nous pouvons conclure que la plupart des apprenants mettent en œuvre les règles pragmatiques et discursives de l'emploi de la dislocation en français, même si nous pouvons constater, dans les productions de certains apprenants, des emplois déviants qui persistent même aux stades les plus avancés. Ces déviances suggèrent que les dislocations sont utilisées par les LNN pour répondre à d'autres besoins que la gestion des topiques, par exemple pour construire des énoncés en plusieurs étapes: les locuteurs mentionnent dans un premier temps le référent, pour, dans un second temps — éventuellement après une pause —, affirmer quelque chose à propos de ce référent au moyen d'un SV précédé d'un pronom. Certains LNN semblent avoir recours à ce mode de construction de l'énoncé même pour les référents nouveaux.

Soulignons que certains chercheurs font une analyse des séquences [SN *il* V] qui diffère de la nôtre. C'est par exemple le cas de Sornicola (2003), qui considère que l'on ne peut systématiquement considérer ces séquences comme des dislocations ; il est en effet possible que, chez certains apprenants, la séquence [pronom + verbe] joue le rôle de verbe: le pronom serait agglutiné au verbe (*cf.* Gadet 1989: 170). Cette hypothèse permettrait d'expliquer l'emploi des séquences [$SN_{indéfini}$ *il* V] : n'étant pas des dislocations — puisque le pronom est agglutiné au verbe —, elles ne sont donc pas soumises aux règles pragmatiques qui imposent que le référent visé soit cognitivement accessible. Ce type d'analyse n'est cependant pas celui que nous avons retenu dans le présent travail, en raison notamment de la difficulté à distinguer dans un corpus les dislocations et les cas d'agglutination du pronom au verbe. En effet, il est difficile de trouver des critères opérationnels qui permettraient de réaliser cette distinction.

Enfin, en ce qui concerne la variation induite par le type de tâche, nous avons constaté que les différences de fréquences entre entretiens et récits sont significativement plus grandes dans les productions des LNN que dans celles des LN. Il est possible d'expliquer cette différence de comportement linguistique entre LNN et LN de plusieurs façons. Tout d'abord, elle pourrait tenir au fait que les LNN tendent à être plus explicites que les LN (voir Hendriks 2003 ; Lambert 2003 ; Ahrenholz 2005 ; Chini 2005). Ainsi, les LNN emploieraient des dislocations là où les LN mettent en œuvre des moyens grammaticaux plus 'légers', par exemple des SN définis non disloqués ou des pronoms. L'emploi par les LNN des dislocations à des taux de fréquence plus élevés que les LN pourrait constituer une stratégie des LNN pour établir des références claires et non ambiguës dans leurs récits.

Une autre explication possible des différences d'emplois des dislocations entre LN et LNN pourrait tenir à la nature de la tâche du récit et à l'effort d'attention qu'elle nécessite. Les recherches en psychologie cognitive montrent en effet que la capacité d'attention est limitée, si bien qu'une forte concentration du locuteur sur certaines activités réduit les ressources attentionnelles disponibles pour d'autres activités et peut avoir une incidence sur la production orale, par exemple sur son exactitude, sa complexité ou sa fluidité (Tavakoli & Skehan 2005). Or une tâche de type narratif telle que le récit de notre étude exige des efforts d'attention particuliers — pour se souvenir de la succession des événements, pour assurer une certaine cohérence au récit, pour s'assurer que l'interlocuteur identifie correctement les personnages —, alors que, dans les entretiens, les locuteurs conservent une grande marge de manœuvre dans le choix du lexique et des sujets abordés. L'effort cognitif induit par le récit viendrait donc s'ajouter à ceux nécessités par la production du discours en français, qui sont plus importants pour les LNN que pour les LN. L'effort cognitif supplémentaire induit par le récit serait en somme pour les LNN la 'goutte d'eau' provoquant l'augmentation de la fréquence d'emploi des dislocations. L'emploi relativement élevé des dislocations dans les récits pourrait ainsi constituer une stratégie des LNN permettant de compenser cet effort d'attention accru : les dislocations leur serviraient de jalons dans la production de leurs récits, constitueraient des sortes de supports permettant aux LNN de construire leur récit en différentes étapes.

En conclusion, la différence constatée entre LNN et LN dans les fréquences d'emploi des dislocations entre entretiens et récits permet donc de confirmer, pour la structure particulière de la dislocation, que le type de tâche a une incidence sur la performance des LNN.

Références

Ahrenholz, B. (2005). Reference to persons and objects in the function of subject in learner varieties. In H. Hendriks (Ed.), *The structure of learner varieties*, 19–64. Berlin/New York: Mouton de Gruyter.
Bartning, I. (1990). L'interlangue française des apprenants universitaires suédois. Aspects de l'accord du verbe. In O. Halmøy, A. Halvorsen & L. Lorentzen (Eds.), *Actes du XIème congrès des romanistes scandinaves* (Trondheim, 13–17 août 1990), 29–38.
Bartning, I. (2009). The advanced learner variety : 10 years later. In E. Labeau & F. Myles (Eds.), *The advanced learner variety : the case of French*, 11–40. Berne : Peter Lang.
Bartning, I. (présent volume). Synthèse rétrospective et nouvelles perspectives développementales. Les recherches en acquisition du français L2 à l'Université de Stockholm (1990–2010). *Langage, Interaction et Acquisition* 3:1.
Bartning, I. & Schlyter, S. (2004). Itinéraires acquisitionnels et stades de développement en français L2. *Journal of French Language Studies* 14, 281–299.
Blanche Benveniste, C. (2000). *Approche de la langue parlée en français*. Paris : Ophrys.

Blasco-Dulbecco, M. (1999). *Les dislocations en français contemporain. Étude syntaxique*. Paris: Honoré Champion.

Chini, M. (2005). Reference to person in learner discourse. In H. Hendriks (Ed.), *The structure of learner varieties*, 65–110. Berlin: Walter de Gruyter.

Chini, M. & Lenart, E. (2008). Identifier le topique dans une tâche narrative en italien et en français chez les natifs (L1) et les apprenants (L2). *Acquisition et Interaction en Langue Étrangère* 26, 129–148.

Dickerson, L. (1975). The learner's interlanguage as a system of variable rules. *TESOL Quaterly* 9, 401–407.

Ellis, R. (2008). *The study of second language acquisition*. Oxford/New York: Oxford University Press.

Engel, H. (2010). *Dislocation et référence aux entités en français L2. Développement, interaction, variation*. Cahiers de la Recherche 43, Université de Stockholm.

Gadet, F. (1989). *Le français ordinaire*. Paris: Armand Colin.

Gadet, F. (2007). *La variation sociale en français*. Paris: Ophrys.

Granfeldt, J. & Schlyter, S. (2004). Clitisation in the acquisition of French as L1 and L2. In P. Prevost & J. Paradis (Eds.), *Acquisition of French: focus on functional categories*, 333–370. Amsterdam: John Benjamins.

Hendriks, H. (2000). The acquisition of topic marking in L1 Chinese and L1 and L2 French. *Studies in Second Language Acquisition* 22, 369–397.

Hendriks, H. (2003). Using nouns for reference maintenance: a seeming contradiction in L2 discourse. In A. Giacalone Ramat (Ed.), *Typology and second language acquisition*, 291–326. Berlin/New York: Mouton de Gruyter.

Klein, W. & Perdue, C. (Eds.) (1992). *Utterance structure: developing grammars again*. Amsterdam: John Benjamins.

Klein, W. & Perdue, C. (1997). The basic variety (or: Could not languages be much simpler?). *Second Language Research* 13, 301–347.

Lambert, M. (2003). Cohésion et connexité dans des récits d'enfants et d'apprenants polonophones du français. *Marges linguistiques* 5, 106–121.

Lambrecht, K. (1994). *Information structure and sentence form: topic, focus, and the mental representations of discourse referents*. Cambridge/New York/Melbourne: Cambridge University Press.

Larsson Ringqvist, E. (2003). Dislokation i franska och svenska. In E. Larsson Ringqvist (Ed.), *Ordföljd och informationsstruktur i franska och svenska*, 121–146. Växjö: Växjö University Press.

Meisel, J., Clahsen, H. & Pienemann, M. (1981). On determining developmental stages in natural second language acquisition. *Studies in Second Language Acquisition* 3, 109–135.

Morel, M.-A, & Danon-Boileau, L. (1998). *La grammaire de l'intonation: l'exemple du français*. Paris: Ophrys.

Pallotti, G. (2007). An operational definition of the emergence criterion. *Applied Linguistics* 28, 361–382.

Pekarek Doehler, S. (2004). Une approche interactionniste de la grammaire: réflexions autour du codage grammatical de la référence et des topics chez l'apprenant avancé d'une L2. *Acquisition et Interaction en Langue Étrangère* 21, 123–166.

Perdue, C., Deulofeu, J. & Trévise, A. (1992). The acquisition of French. In W. Klein & C. Perdue (Eds.), *Utterance structure: developing grammars again*, 225–300. Amsterdam: John Benjamins.

Pienemann, M. (1998). *Language processing and second language development: processability theory*. Amsterdam/Philadelphie: John Benjamins.

Romaine, S. (2003). Variation. In C. Doughty & M. Long (Eds.), *The handbook of second language acquisition*, 409–435. Oxford: Blackwell.

Sornicola, R. (2003). Crosslinguistic comparison and second language acquisition: an approach to topic and left-detachment constructions form the perspective of spoken language. In A. Giacalone Ramat (Ed.), *Typology and second language acquisition*, 327–363. Berlin/New York: Mouton de Gruyter.

Tavakoli, P. & Skehan, P. (2005). Strategic planning, task structure, and performance testing. In R. Ellis (Ed.), *Planning and task performance in a second language*, 239–273. Philadelphie: John Benjamins.

Abstract

This chapter investigates the use and development of dislocations in oral productions by Swedish learners of French L2. Dislocations are highly frequent in French oral speech and play an essential role in building utterances. L2 users of French must therefore acquire the grammatical means necessary to build this structure as well as the pragmatic principles underlying its use. The study is empirical, and based on a corpus of oral productions from a wide range of non-native speakers (NNS), from beginners studying at university to L2 users who have spent many years in France. The corpus also includes oral productions from a control group of native speakers (NS). The aim is to determine how the different forms and functions of dislocations develop in French L2. Furthermore, the study examines the influence of tasks on the use of dislocations, by analysing two tasks which place very different demands on the informants in terms of cognitive effort, namely interviews and retellings.

Vocabulary aspects of advanced L2 French
Do lexical formulaic sequences and lexical richness develop at the same rate?

Fanny Forsberg Lundell and Christina Lindqvist
Stockholm University / Uppsala University

In her overview of research on the advanced L2 learner, Bartning (1997) aims at characterizing the advanced learner variety. This characterization is above all based on morphosyntactic traits. The aim of this contribution is to present additional characteristics of the advanced learner as defined by Bartning (1997), as well as to describe even more advanced levels based on recent research concerning spoken L2 French. More specifically, the main issue under investigation is whether two vocabulary measures, viz. lexical richness and lexical formulaic sequences, can be used to distinguish between different advanced levels and thus contribute to the characterization of the advanced learner of French. An additional issue investigated here is whether these two lexical aspects correlate with each other or whether they develop at different rates.

1. Introduction

The present study investigates two aspects of vocabulary acquisition in Swedish advanced learners' oral production of L2 French: lexical richness and lexical formulaic sequences. Lexical richness is here conceived of as the proportion of low-frequency vocabulary in oral production. Lexical formulaic sequences (Lexical FSs) are word combinations (e.g. V + N or Adj. + N), with combinatorial restrictions, which reflect target language idiomaticity. Although there has been a growing interest in research on the acquisition of vocabulary in L2 French (*cf.* Lindqvist 2010; Ovtcharov *et al.* 2006; Tidball & Treffers-Daller 2007, 2008; Treffers-Daller *et al.* 2008), few studies are concerned with the vocabulary of advanced learners. In addition, as pointed out by David *et al.* (2009: 147), morphosyntax has been in focus in studies of the development of French learner language.

In her overview of research on the advanced learner, Bartning (1997) aimed at characterizing the advanced learner variety, but in this case the characterization was above all based on morphosyntactic traits. In a later study, Bartning and Schlyter (2004) presented a proposal for developmental stages in Swedish learners' L2 French (based on the *InterFra* corpus, (http://www.fraitaklass.su.se/english/interfra), and the *Lund* corpus). Again, morphosyntax constituted the basis for the description of developmental paths in L2 French. As no lexical criteria have been taken into account in these earlier studies, we will focus on two lexical traits, namely lexical richness and Lexical FSs, in the present paper. Hopefully, these lexical traits will contribute to the characterization of the advanced learner of French. We will also discuss the use of lexical traits to characterize stages beyond the advanced stages by investigating the oral production of very advanced learners. In fact, Bartning *et al.* (2009) have already discussed the possibility of a stage beyond the most advanced stage (6), based on criteria such as formulaic language and elaboration of the information structure. The collection of new *InterFra* data of learners/users in a second language setting called for a refinement of the concept of the advanced learner. Indeed, the term 'advanced learner' is often used to refer to university students at different levels of advancement, but few researchers investigate learners who are long term residents in the L2 community and thus receive considerably more input than formal learners, enhancing their possibilities to attain nativelike levels of L2 use. In the present paper, we investigate the question of whether lexical richness and Lexical FSs reinforce the proposal of such a stage, preliminarily called stage 7. Moreover, we also include native speaker baseline data, in order to investigate whether it is possible to attain a nativelike level for these specific vocabulary aspects.

Finally, in addition to contributing to a description of aspects of lexical competence along the advanced acquisitional stages, the aim of this paper is to investigate whether there is a relationship between the development of lexical richness and that of Lexical FSs. Both Lexical FSs and lexical richness have proved to be useful measures for describing L2 development (Forsberg 2008; Lindqvist *et al.* 2011), but to our knowledge, no study to date has examined the relationship between these two measures for L2 French. As both aspects seem to be dependent on frequency of input, one could expect that they would develop in a similar way.

2. Background: Formulaic language and lexical richness in advanced L2 French

2.1 L2 Formulaic language and the advanced L2 learner of French

Numerous L2 researchers have taken an interest in these sequences that are not generated by the language grammar, seem arbitrary to the L2 learner, have to be memorized rather than generated, but make language use sound natural and fluent and actually account for language to quite an impressive extent (*cf.* Erman & Warren's, 2000, figures 50–60% of the English language). As Forsberg (2010) suggests, formulaic sequences come in many different shapes, and they are probably acquired and processed differently and used for different functions in discourse. As already mentioned, the present study focuses on the subcategory Lexical FSs.

Few studies exist on L2 French and formulaic language, both as regards beginners and advanced learners. Concerning advanced learning — the topic of this chapter — researchers tend to consider formulaic language either from the perspective of fluency enhancers or from the perspective of idiomaticity and nativelike selection.

One of the first and best known studies is that of Raupach (1984), who studied German university students of L2 French before and after a study-abroad period in France, with special focus on fluency gains. Raupach (1984) found that learners made use of a considerable number of *formulae* (the term used by Raupach) in order to maintain fluency. Raupach divided the formulae into the subcategories of organizers, and fillers/modifiers. The first category are thus textual organizing devices such as *c'est* ('it is') and *il y a* ('there is'). Fillers and modifiers function as 'zones of safety' and as modalizing markers (*je crois* 'I believe' and *je pense* 'I think'). One of the major findings of Raupach's (1984) study is that the learners, especially after their stay in France, overused both types, as compared to the native speaker control group.

The development of second language fluency is also studied in Towell *et al.* (1996). Similar to Raupach (1984), they set out to measure fluency gains in university students of L2 French after a study-abroad period in France. Among other things, they discovered that fluency gains are not due to speed but to longer and more complex utterances characteristic of spoken French, e.g. clefts, pseudo-clefts and the presentation devices *il y a* and *c'est*, the latter being the most frequent chunk in spoken French (L1 and L2) (Forsberg 2008). Furthermore, Towell *et al.* (1996) found a substantial number of 'situational lexicalized phrases', also contributing to the gains in fluency observed after their stay in France. All in all, both of these studies showed that formulaic sequences of certain types contribute to fluency.

Another perspective on formulaic language in French is taken by Edmonds (2010). She investigated whether anglophone learners of L2 French, having resided in France for short (4 months) or long (about 10 years) periods of time make the same judgments as regards naturalness of formulaic sequences (or *conventional expressions*, in her terminology). Surprisingly, she found no differences between learner groups and native speakers, suggesting that as regards judgment, these learners are well on their way towards developing nativelike selection.

Forsberg (2008) studied the use of formulaic sequences from a more general point of view at four different learner levels as compared to native speaker production, from beginner students to very advanced users of L2 French. The aim of the study was to find out whether use of formulaic sequences is indicative of second language development. Evidence strongly suggests that it is. There is an increase in the quantity of formulaic language use as the learner progresses, so that the largest proportion was found in the production of very advanced learners and native speakers. The most difficult category to acquire for L2 learners appears to be that of Lexical FSs (e.g. *poser une question* 'ask a question', *faire attention* 'pay attention') (Forsberg 2008; Lewis 2008). In Forsberg's study, only the very advanced users who had lived in France for at least five years used this category to the same extent as the native speakers.

Bolly (2008) studied the collocations of two high-frequency verbs, *prendre* ('take') and *donner* ('give') (what Forsberg calls Lexical FSs), in the writings of Anglophone French university L2 learners and native speakers of French. Her main findings were that the learners tended to overuse verb + noun collocations with *donner* and underuse verb + noun collocations with *prendre*. Furthermore, she found that deviances affected either the verb or the appropriateness of the entire collocation with respect to the context of use. Bolly suggests that learners' use of collocations might be influenced by the morphosyntax and the semantics of the verbs involved in the collocations.

Furthermore, several recent studies have shown that formulaic language measures succeed at discriminating between learners at different advanced levels, where grammar measures fail (Bartning *et al.* 2009; Forsberg & Bartning 2010). In the first study, three groups of advanced learners of L2 French with different degrees of exposure to French were studied with regard to morphosyntax, information structure and formulaic language. Formulaic language was the only measure that yielded significant differences between learners in a foreign language setting and learners in a second language setting. In the second study, learners placed by the DIALANG test at the six different CEFR-levels (A1-C2) performed two written tasks in French. Their productions were then analyzed in terms of morphosyntactic accuracy and formulaic language. While morphosyntactic measures discriminated between levels up to the B2 level, formulaic language succeeded at discriminating between the most advanced levels, i.e. B2-C2. Taken together, these results indicate that language proficiency in terms of structural development, and that in terms of formulaic language development, do not follow the same rate.

In view of the research presented above, we can draw the conclusion that the production of lexical collocations seems to be a persistent problem, even at advanced or very advanced levels. For this reason it was decided in the present study to investigate the potential of this category to discriminate between different learner groups as well as to compare the development of the category with another lexical measure.

2.2 Lexical richness and the advanced L2 learner of French

According to Read (2000), lexical richness can be used as a superordinate term and covers several aspects of vocabulary acquisition: lexical density (the ratio between function words and content words), lexical diversity (lexical variation), lexical sophistication (the proportion of sophisticated words e.g. low-frequency words), and proportion of errors. There are several measures of lexical richness, depending among other things on what is being analyzed (see below).

Tidball and Treffers-Daller (2007) investigated lexical richness in L2 French using different measures (the D measure, the index of Guiraud, the Advanced Guiraud, and the Limiting Relative Diversity measure). They compared two groups of learners: first-year and third-year students at a British university, and one group of native French speakers. The results showed that there were significant differences between the first-year group and the native speakers, as well as between the third-year group and the native speakers, considering all measures of lexical richness. There were also significant differences between the learner groups for all measures except one. Thus, the most advanced learners in this study did not reach the level of the native speakers regarding lexical richness.

In a later study, Tidball and Treffers-Daller (2008) investigated different ways of measuring lexical sophistication in L2 French. They used the Advanced Guiraud and tested different modifications of this measure. They found that using teachers' judgments was the best way to define a basic vocabulary. That is, instead of using the frequency of words, for example, as an indicator of word difficulty, experienced teachers were asked to judge whether words produced by the learners in a retelling should be considered basic or advanced. The Advanced Guiraud based on teachers' judgments was the measure that best separated two learner groups of French. Again, there were significant differences between the learner groups as well as between the most advanced learners and a group of native speakers, which indicates that the most advanced group did not attain the native speaker level of lexical richness.

Treffers-Daller (2009) investigated lexical diversity in an oral retelling task in French in three groups: Dutch/French bilinguals (Dutch dominant), Flemish learners of French, and French/English bilinguals (French dominant). The results showed that there were significant differences between the three groups: the French dominant bilinguals had a more varied vocabulary than the Dutch dominant bilinguals. In a more detailed analysis of the use of nouns and verbs using the index of Guiraud, Treffers-Daller (2009) could conclude that there were significant differences between the groups and that these differences were of the same magnitude as the analysis of the whole production.

Ovtcharov *et al.* (2006) examined lexical richness in intermediate and advanced learners of French in Quebec. The participants were employed by the Canadian government and French was a requirement for their job position. The data consisted in oral proficiency interviews (test situation) with a native speaker of French. The learners were divided into two proficiency levels, based on the results of the interviews. Ovtcharov *et al.* used the Lexical Frequency Profile method (Laufer & Nation 1995) in order to measure lexical richness from a frequency-based perspective. Within this framework, the general assumption is that a relatively high proportion of low-frequency words is indicative of a rich vocabulary. Ovtcharov *et al.* found that the most advanced group had a significantly higher proportion of low-frequency words than the less advanced group. They also compared the learners' lexical profiles with those of native speakers of French and found that there were no statistically significant differences between the most advanced learners and the native speakers in the use of low-frequency words in oral production. This led the authors to conclude that the most advanced learners actually seemed to reach the lexical richness of native speakers. This result thus runs counter to the ones reported on above, where learners were not found to reach native-like levels of lexical richness. This is perhaps not unexpected, however, as the learners in the Ovtcharov *et al.* study were most likely more advanced learners, having French as a tool in their professional activities.

Lindqvist *et al.* (2011) investigated lexical richness in the oral production of Swedish learners of French and Italian L2. They used a frequency-based method similar to the Lexical Frequency Profile (Laufer & Nation 1995), the Lexical Oral Production Profile (LOPP). For French, they compared the proportion of low-frequency words in two advanced groups of learners and one group of native speakers. The learner groups were divided on the basis of Bartning and Schlyter's (2004) proposal of morphosyntactic stages. The results showed that the most advanced learners had a significantly higher proportion of low-frequency words than the less advanced group. In addition, there were no significant differences between the most advanced group and the native speakers, which suggested that the most advanced learners approached the native speakers with regard to this particular aspect of lexical competence.

In sum, earlier studies on lexical richness have found differences between learner groups at different proficiency levels using different types of measures. Only two studies have seen that advanced learners approach native speakers as regards lexical richness (Ovtcharov *et al.* 2006; Lindqvist *et al.* 2011).

3. Formulaic language, lexical richness and correlations with other linguistic measures

A few recent studies have investigated the relationship between formulaic language, lexical richness and other linguistic measures, but the results are far from conclusive to date. Mizrahi and Laufer (2010) studied the correlation between general vocabulary knowledge (as measured by the Vocabulary Levels Test) and collocational knowledge (a sub-group of formulaic language) in near-native speakers of L2 English (level estimated through self-rating). They found that Israeli near-native speakers of English attained nativelike levels of general vocabulary but failed to reach nativelike levels as regards collocations. Gyllstad (2007), on the other hand, found clear correlations between results on a vocabulary size test and a receptive collocation test, studying advanced learners of L2 English. However, these learners were not nearly as advanced as those in Mizrahi and Laufer's study; they were Swedish L2 high school and university students. One explanation for the diverging results would be that the two aspects develop in parallel up to a certain level, but that collocational knowledge develops slower after some time. It is also important to note that Gyllstad's study tested receptive knowledge whereas Mizrahi and Laufer's tested productive knowledge. It has been suggested that collocations pose far more problems in production than in reception (*cf.* Warren, 2005). In the same vein as Gyllstad (2007), several other studies have also shown a clear correlation between overall language proficiency and mastery of formulaic sequences (Boers *et al.* 2006; Lewis 2008; Stengers *et al.* 2011).

The question concerning correlations between lexical richness and other measures has been investigated in David *et al.* (2009). They examined the relationship between lexical development and morphosyntactic development in British learners of L2 French. Lexical development was measured with the index of Guiraud, which measures lexical diversity. Grammatical development was measured using Mean Length of Utterance (MLU). David *et al.* (2009) found that lexical diversity correlated with MLU in that the more varied the vocabulary of the learner, the greater the MLU. However, in a similar study, Malvern *et al.* (2004) found no correlations between lexical diversity and MLU in L2 French. In David *et al.* (2009), lexical diversity was also compared to the use of grammatical gender. The results showed that there were no correlations between lexical diversity and gender. Thus, it could be concluded that lexical diversity correlated with some of the morphosyntactic measures, but not all. As previously mentioned, Tidball and Treffers-Daller (2007, 2008) investigated different measures of lexical richness. They found that all measures (see above) correlated significantly with a C-test, which measures overall proficiency. Lemmouh (2010) investigated the relationship between different lexical aspects in the written L2 English of Swedish learners. He found that there was a modest correlation between lexical richness, as measured by the Lexical Frequency Profile (Laufer & Nation 1995), and vocabulary depth (knowledge of collocations and derivations). There were no correlations between lexical richness and receptive or productive vocabulary size.

As very few studies have examined exactly what we want to investigate here, it is difficult to know what to expect on the basis of earlier studies. As regards formulaic language, it seems that it rarely develops at the same pace as other linguistic features. Concerning the relationship between lexical richness and other variables, there are no clear results. Some studies have shown correlations with certain measures, while others have not. The studies that have focused exclusively on different aspects of vocabulary do seem to have found a relationship, however. Such was the case in Lemmouh (2010) and Tidball and Treffers-Daller (2007, 2008). However, as previous studies have used tasks different from the one used in this study, we do not expect to obtain similar results. In the present study, in contrast to many of the earlier studies that used tests, it was deemed important to investigate spontaneous spoken data.

4. This study

4.1 Participants and task

Lexical richness and Lexical FSs will be analyzed in L2 French in three groups of Swedish-speaking informants. They will also be compared to a group of native speakers (see Table 1).

All informants were recorded within the *InterFra* project at Stockholm University. Group 1 consists of ten 4th and 5th term university students and doctorate students. They are advanced, semi-formal learners, i.e. they have learned French mostly in Sweden, but some of them have been to a French-speaking country for one–two years (mean Length of Residence, LoR: 1.4 years). They have been classified at stages 5 and 6 — the medium advanced and the superior advanced stages of the developmental continuum presented in Bartning and Schlyter (2004) — on the basis of morphosyntactic traits. Groups 2 and 3 consist of Swedes who have moved to Paris and thus use French as a second language on

Table 1. The participants

Groups	N	Years of French studies	Length of residence in France	Age
Group 1 Stage 5+6	10	6–12	1–3 (mean 1.4)	25–35
Group 2 Juniors	10	2–6	5–15 (mean 6.7)	25–30
Group 3 Seniors	10	2–6	15–40 (mean 23.0)	40–55
Group 4 Natives	10	–	–	25–60

a daily basis. The ten 'Juniors' in Group 2 have lived in Paris for 5–15 years (mean LoR 6.7 years). Their ages on arriving in France were 18–19 years on average, and they were 25–32 years old when they were recorded. The ten 'Seniors' in Group 3 have lived in Paris for 15–40 years (mean LoR: 23 years). They were 40–55 years old at the time of the recordings, and came to France at approximately 21–24 years of age. The control group consists of ten native speakers of French. It is difficult to say whether there exist any differences in terms of linguistic proficiency between the two groups in Paris. A distinction can definitely be made between L2 learners in a foreign language setting (Group 1), L2 users in a second language context (Groups 2 and 3) and native speakers (Group 4, NS). It is quite obvious that both second language groups have been exposed to far more input than the learners in Group 1. If results from Groups 2 and 3 surpass those of Group 1, we find evidence in support for a stage 7, as mentioned in the introduction. This would also indicate that vocabulary measures are better at characterizing very advanced levels, than morphosyntactic criteria, at least as regards these data. Considering length of residence the literature has shown (e.g. Cummins 1981) that its effect tends to diminish after five years of residence in the target language community. However, since we are dealing with frequency-dependent phenomena, lexical richness and formulaic sequences, it is plausible to assume that there will be differences even between the two Paris groups, which is why it was decided to keep these two groups separated.[1] The fact that the learners in group 3 have spent more time in the target language community probably means that they have been exposed to more input generally. Thus, they should have had the possibility to add

---

[1]. In Forsberg Lundell *et al.* (in press), the participants in the two Paris groups are categorized differently, based on a listener test, which groups speakers into those who pass as native speakers of French and those that do not. The first group is labeled as 'near-natives', following Abrahamsson and Hyltenstam's (2009) definition.

new words to their vocabulary to a larger extent than the learners in group 2. The longer time you spend in the TL environment the better the possibilities to encounter low-frequency words and extensive exposure also allows for collocational links to be strengthened.

All the informants performed the same task which was a 15–20 minutes long interview with a native speaker of French on subjects such as work/studies, spare time activities, family, etc. Studying the lexicon, it is important to be somewhat cautious when using such an 'open' task. Each informant's life story has a non-negligible effect on the use of lexis, since the themes brought up might vary considerably. One may speak of ballet and another of advertising, while yet another may mainly talk about his/her family. It should also be noted that such tasks are probably easier than a more controlled task, since they give the speaker more freedom to talk about known topics. For example, when comparing the results from Forsberg (2008) and Forsberg and Fant (2010), it turns out that L2 speakers are more nativelike in their use of formulaic language in an interview than in a pragmatic role-play or a retelling task. The advantage is that we use the same type of interview with all the 40 speakers and we have the possibility to investigate spontaneous language use.

4.2 Methods

4.2.1 *Identification and classification of lexical formulaic sequences*
The issue of how to define and identify formulaic language is complex, probably due to the irregular and intuitive nature of formulaic language on the one hand, and to the large diversity of structures grouped under the label 'formulaic' on the other. The two most commonly used ways of identifying formulaic language in corpora are the statistical method and the phraseological method (*cf.* Granger & Pacquot 2008). Within the phraseological methodology, to be used here, the researcher identifies potentially formulaic/conventional sequences based on linguistic criteria related to syntactic, semantic and pragmatic restrictions.

The present study makes use of Erman and Warren's (2000) original categorisation of *prefabs* (their term), which was slightly modified in Erman *et al.* (in press), a model based on the phraseological tradition. In Erman *et al.* (in press), formulaic sequences can be classified into Lexical and Qualifier FSs. In the present study, only Lexical FSs will be investigated. They incorporate at least one content word and are used for extralinguistic reference and denote actions (such as *faire la fête* 'to party'), states (*avoir peur* 'to be scared'), objects (*année sabbatique* 'sabbatical year') and so on. When it comes to the practical identification of Lexical FSs, Erman and Warren (2000) make use of the criterion *restricted exchangeability*. In order for a sequence to qualify as a prefab in their terminology, an exchange of one of the words for a synonymous word must always result in a change of meaning or a loss of idiomaticity (Erman & Warren 2000: 32).

Forsberg (2008) proposed an operationalization of the *restricted exchangeability criterion*. The first step in identification is to manually identify, in the corpus, the Lexical FSs that meet the criterion based on researcher intuition. This is then complemented by searches on Google.fr. To test the extent to which restricted exchangeability applies to a sequence, an analogous sequence, which has been subject to one of the following modifications, is constructed.

- One of the words is exchanged for a synonymous word.
- One of the words is exchanged for an antonymous word (for example *ça marche mal* 'it works badly' instead of *ça marche bien* 'it works well').
- Change of article (from definite to indefinite or absence of article).
- Change of number (from plural to singular or vice versa).
- Change in word order (for example *égalité femmes/hommes* 'equality women/men' instead of *égalité hommes/femmes* 'equality men/women').

For a sequence to be counted as formulaic, it has to appear at least twice as frequently on Google as any of the modified versions.[2]

4.2.2 *Measuring lexical richness*

Lexical richness is measured using a frequency-based method, the *Lexical Oral Production Profile*, developed in Lindqvist *et al.* (2011).[3] The method is similar to the Lexical Frequency Profile (Laufer & Nation 1995), in that it assumes that frequency plays an important role in vocabulary acquisition, in the sense that the most frequent words of the language are acquired first, and that the less frequent words are acquired later in the acquisition process. However, as the learner data analyzed consisted of oral production, it was deemed necessary to create frequency bands that were also based on oral native speaker data. Thus, for French, the Corpaix corpus of spoken L1 French, which has been compiled at the Université de Provence (Campione *et al.* 2005), was used. The corpus contains 1 million words. For a detailed description of this corpus, see Pallaud and Henry (2004). A frequency list based on the *Corpaix* corpus, compiled by J. Véronis, is available online. The list consists of word forms. Lindqvist *et al.* lemmatized this list using

---

[2] Ideally, frequency bands for (lexical) formulaic sequences should have been used in order to match the lexical richness measure (*cf.* Section 4.2.2.). However, to our knowledge, such frequency bands are not available for French.

[3] The method has been further elaborated, by integrating aspects other than frequency (Bardel *et al.* 2012). However, as the first version of the method has proven to allow for separation between different proficiency levels, it will be used in the present study.

TreeTagger, which resulted in 2 766 lemmas. On the basis of these, three frequency bands were created, each band containing approximately 1 000 lemmas.[4]

In order to calculate the lexical richness of a text, all the lemmas produced in an interview by each informant were compared to the frequency bands, which resulted in a lexical profile showing the proportion of lemmas (tokens) in the frequency bands. The lemmas that do not belong in any of the frequency bands are categorized as "off-list", e.g. Band 1: 90%, Band 2: 2%, Band 3: 3%, Off-list: 5%. The general assumption is that a relatively high proportion of lemmas in Band 3 and Off-list indicates a rich vocabulary.[5]

4.3 Research questions and hypotheses

The following research questions are posed:

1. Is it possible to discern lexical development between stages 5 and 6 (Group 1) and informants in a second language setting (Groups 2 and 3), in terms of lexical richness, on the one hand, and Lexical FSs, on the other? Based on these measures, is it reasonable to propose advanced stages beyond stage 6?

In view of the results of earlier studies (Bartning *et al.* 2009; Forsberg 2010), where similar groups of informants were studied, it is hypothesized that we will find differences between Group 1 and Groups 2 and 3, in terms of Lexical FS use. It is also hypothesized that no differences will be found between the most advanced groups and the NSs, since this was the case for similar groups of learners and NSs in Forsberg (2010). However, more informants are included in the present study and some of the NSs are not the same. In Lindqvist *et al.* (2011) it was found that the most advanced learners (stage 6) reached nativelike levels with respect to lexical richness. However, in that study, the NSs were students with no working

---

[4] A one-million word corpus may seem small. However, it was not possible to have access to a larger corpus. It is difficult to find large corpora of spoken language, especially for French. Lindqvist *et al.* (2011) estimated that *Corpaix* was sufficient for the purposes of creating frequency bands, as it allowed them to create three frequency bands, each containing approximately 1 000 lemmas. This is to compare to the Lexical Frequency Profile (see www.lextutor.ca/vocabprofile), for which each frequency band contains 1 000 word families (for both English and French).

[5] For both the formulas measure and the lexical richness measure, the counts are based on tokens. In future research, it would be interesting to also base the counts on types to see if the results will be different. As for the lexical richness measure for instance, some of the most frequent words are also often used several times in a conversation, which means that words in Band 1 such as *je* ('I') or *et* ('and') may increase the number of tokens in that frequency band, whereas infrequent words normally also have fewer occurrences.

experience. In the present study, the control group consists of NSs with some or many years of professional experience. This leads us to believe that they will have a more developed vocabulary than the NSs in the previous study. Our general assumption is that vocabulary is an aspect that learners constantly have the possibility to develop during the acquisitional process. As for the learner groups in the present study, there are important differences in exposure to the target language, and we expect that this will be reflected in their lexical richness. We hypothesize that Group 1 will have a less developed vocabulary, revealed by the relatively low proportion of low-frequency words in their oral production, than the learners who have moved to Paris and stayed there for several years. Given the differences in length of residence between Groups 2 and 3, we hypothesize that Group 3 will have the more developed vocabulary.

2. Is there a correlation in the development between the two vocabulary measures, i.e. lexical richness and Lexical FSs?

We hypothesize that Lexical FSs will be related to development of lexical richness since they are both dependent on frequency of exposure. In addition, earlier results show that both measures are promising tools for distinguishing between levels.

4.4 Results

4.4.1 *Lexical formulaic sequences*

Table 2 shows the results for Lexical FSs in the different groups. The results refer to total number of tokens of Lexical FSs per 100 words. All differences have been calculated through One Way ANOVA analysis with Tukey-Kramers post-test.

As regards Lexical FSs, significant differences can be found among several groups but not all. Firstly, a difference ($p<0.05$) is found between Groups 1 and 2, which is in line with the results presented in Bartning *et al.* (2009). The least advanced learners (Group 1) also differ significantly from the NSs ($p<0.0001$), which comes as no surprise. However, they do not differ significantly from Group 3, which is rather difficult to interpret. If Lexical FS use should be considered as

Table 2. Results: formulaic sequences (tokens)

Group	LFS/100 words (mean)
1.Stage 5+6	1.9 (SD 0.9)
2.Juniors	3.4 (SD 1.0)
3.Seniors	2.8 (SD 0.8)
4.Natives	4.1 (SD 1.0)

a measure of proficiency, Group 2 (Juniors) would then be more advanced than Group 3 (Seniors), since Group 2 have a significantly higher score than Group 1 but Group 3 does not. In addition, there is no difference between Group 2 and Group 4 (NS), whereas there is a significant difference ($p<0.05$) between Group 3 and 4. However, the differences between Group 2 and 3 are not significant, but there is clear tendency for Group 2 scores to be higher. Since the number of participants is limited, it is possible that individual differences give rise to these somewhat puzzling results. As Table 2 shows, the standard deviations are fairly high in all groups. As will be discussed in Section 4.3, this leads us to view formulaic sequence use as not only a function of frequency of input, but also related to other factors (of socio-psychological orientation, as suggested by Dörnyei et al. 2004). All in all, the results allow us to suggest that formulaic language is a good measure of advanced L2 development. It succeeds in separating stages 5 and 6 from a more advanced stage 7, thus lending support for an elaboration of Bartning and Schlyter's (2004) advanced stages. In addition, it shows that it is possible to approach nativelike performance on this measure (which regards quantity of Lexical FSs), which is the case for Group 2.

4.4.2 *Lexical richness*

Table 3 shows the lexical profiles of the groups, i.e. the mean proportions of lemmas (tokens) in the different frequency bands. What is of interest here is the proportion of low-frequency words used, i.e. the proportion of Band 3 and Off-list, which presumably indicates lexical richness (*cf.* Laufer & Nation 1995).

As Table 3 shows, the proportions of low-frequency words (Band 3+off-list) seem to reflect the proficiency level of the learners in the sense that Group 1 has the lowest proportion (3.86%) and Group 3 the highest proportion of the learner groups (5.25%). The NSs have the highest proportion (7.27%). In order to examine whether these differences were statistically significant we ran an ANOVA. The results showed that there were significant differences between Groups 1 and 3 ($p<0.01$), and between Group 1 and the NSs ($p<0.001$). However, no significant differences were found between Groups 1 and 2. This result does not coincide

Table 3. Results: lexical richness

Group	Band 1	Band 2	Band 3	Off-list	Band 3 + off-list
1.Stage 5+6	94.11	2.02	0.69	3.24	3.86 (SD 0.60)
2.Juniors	93.65	1.84	0.80	3.71	4.52 (SD 1.07)
3.Seniors	92.74	2.01	0.75	4.51	5.25 (SD 1.55)
4.Natives	90.02	2.72	1.12	6.15	7.27 (SD 0.72)

with the results concerning Lexical FSs, where there were significant differences between precisely these two groups. The fact that Group 2 seems to have a vocabulary that is similar to that of Group 1 would indicate that Group 2 has not developed beyond stage 6 with respect to lexical richness.

Significant differences in lexical richness were also found between Group 2 and the NSs ($p < 0.05$). Interestingly, there are no significant differences between Group 3 and the NSs. This would indicate that the lexical richness of this very advanced group is similar to that of the NS group. This issue was also brought up in Lindqvist et al. (2011). They compared learners at stage 6 with NSs and found no significant differences in the proportion of low-frequency words. They interpreted this as suggesting that the learners of that study actually had a lexical richness similar to that of NS. However, in that study, the very advanced Paris-based Groups 2 and 3 were not investigated. As we have seen in the present study, these groups, especially Group 3, display more advanced vocabularies than Group 1. In light of the new data analyzed in the present study, we would argue that the fact that Lindqvist et al. did not find significant differences between stage 6 and NSs is probably because they used a different group of NSs: students at Stockholm University with very limited working experience. In the present study, the NSs all have several years of working experience, which plausibly gives them the opportunity to come into contact with a more varied vocabulary with different kinds of specialized terminology for instance. This is certainly reflected in their lexical richness. Some examples of low-frequency words used by the native speakers in the present study are *électromécanique* 'electromechanical engineering', *interstellaire* 'interstellar', *maquette* 'scale model', which definitely belong to a specialized vocabulary related to their profession. These results bring attention to the difficulties involved in choosing appropriate NS control groups as benchmarks for L2 performance.

The fact that Group 3 has a higher proportion of low-frequency vocabulary than the other learner groups is in line with our hypothesis that vocabulary is an aspect that develops continuously over time. The Seniors have lived in the target language environment for a long time and have consequently received a lot of input, plausibly of words that are not easily encountered in a formal setting. It seems that frequency of exposure actually plays a role in the acquisition of low-frequency words, since Group 3, with a considerably longer mean LoR, has a higher proportion of this category of words, than Group 2. Examples of such words are *entente* 'agreement', *clivage* 'divide', *bourrer* 'cram full', *attache* 'tie', *déclic* 'trigger', *estomper* 'blur', *intoxiquer* 'brainwash', *poireauter* 'hang about'.

4.4.3 Correlation

Our second research question concerns the correlation between lexical richness and Lexical FSs: do they develop at the same rate in the individual learner? It was hypothesized that a measure of Lexical FSs would correlate with that of lexical richness, since both features are dependent on frequency. It has already been shown that the two measures display divergent results in group comparisons, but we also wanted to run a Spearman rank correlation between the two measures. The following result was obtained: (n = 30) $r = 0.34$, $p = 0.06$, suggesting that we are dealing with a weak correlation which is not quite significant. Our hypothesis is consequently not confirmed, but neither can it be completely rejected. Given the low number of participants, it cannot be excluded that we are actually dealing with a positive correlation. If we look at the separate results for the formulaic sequence measure and the lexical richness measure, we see that they both yield group differences, but not necessarily the same ones and whereas the formulaic sequences measure yields differences between Groups 3 and 4, the lexical richness measure does not. This would imply that lexical richness is actually something that develops continuously over time and that the long residence of Group 3 actually has an effect for this measure. But this does not, curiously enough, seem to be the case for formulaic language, since Group 3 does not produce more nativelike results than Group 2. It appears, then, that formulaic sequence use is not only dependent on frequency but also on other factors. It has been proposed that the use of formulaic sequences is dependent on factors such as motivation, aptitude and socio-cultural integration (Dörnyei *et al.* 2004; Kecskes 2002), which suggests that it is not a phenomenon that follows a linear progression but is dependent on individual differences. Given the limited number of participants and the spontaneous nature of the oral task at hand, these results should, however, be interpreted with caution.

5. Conclusions

In the present study we analyzed two aspects of vocabulary in advanced learners of French: lexical richness and Lexical FSs. We compared three learner groups — one group of foreign language learners and two groups of second language learners with different lengths of residence in the target language country — and one group of native speakers. As regards Lexical FSs, the results showed that there were differences between Groups 1 and 2, which suggests that the Group 2 learners have moved beyond stage 6 as regards formulaic sequence use. However, this is not the case for Group 3. Whereas the latter group performed in a nativelike way on the lexical richness measure, as regards Lexical FSs they do not. However, Group 2 does not differ significantly from the NS in terms of Lexical FSs. This means that

Group 3 is to be considered the most advanced group as regards lexical richness, whereas Group 2 is the most advanced with respect to formulaic sequences. The analysis, however, reveals that, for both measures, it is possible to attain nativelike levels (relatively high proportion of low-frequency lemmas vs. tokens of Lexical FSs).

For lexical richness, the proportion of low-frequency lemmas, the results indicate that it develops in the expected way: the less advanced learners had the lowest proportion, while the most advanced learners had the highest proportion. However, there were no statistically significant differences between Groups 1 and 2. This result seems to indicate that Group 2 has not moved beyond stage 6 in terms of lexical richness. In contrast, this seems to be the case for Group 3, which approaches the native speakers as there were no significant differences between these groups. We interpreted this as a possible effect of the amount of exposure to the target language and as a confirmation of our hypothesis that vocabulary is an aspect that constantly develops.

The results for both measures indicate that there seems to be evidence of an additional stage beyond stage 6, since both lexical richness and formulaic sequences continue to develop, albeit differently for the different groups. The new measures used in the present study can consequently describe linguistic development beyond stage 6, which morphosyntactic measures have failed to do (*cf.* Bartning *et al.* 2009). However, the present study does not clearly indicate parallel development between the two aspects of the lexicon investigated. A correlation analysis was conducted and no strong, significant correlation was obtained. The fact that different aspects of vocabulary do not always develop in parallel has also been noted in e.g. Lemmouh (2010) and Mizrahi and Laufer (2010) (*cf.* Section 3).

In future research, we will further investigate the relationship between different aspects of vocabulary in advanced learner French. One of the shortcomings of the present study was the low number of informants in each group. More data has recently been collected from advanced learners performing various vocabulary tasks. These data will hopefully further our understanding of the lexical competence of the advanced learner in L2 French and contribute to the characterization of the advanced learner variety.

Acknowledgements

We would like to thank two anonymous reviewers for their very useful comments on earlier versions of this paper.

References

Abrahamsson, N. & Hyltenstam, K. (2009). Age of onset and nativelikeness in a second language: listener perception vs linguistic scrutiny. *Language Learning* 59, 249–306.
Bardel, C., Gudmundson, A. & Lindqvist, C. (2012). Aspects of lexical sophistication in advanced learners' oral production. Vocabulary acquisition and use in L2 French and Italian. *Studies in Second Language Acquisition* 34, 269–290.
Bartning, I. (this volume). Synthèse rétrospective et nouvelles perspectives développementales — Les recherches acquisitionnelles en français L2 à l'université de Stockholm.
Bartning, I. (1997). L'apprenant dit avancé et son acquisition d'une langue étrangère. Tour d'horizon et esquisse d'une caractérisation de la variété avancée. *Acquisition et Interaction en Langue Étrangère* 9, 9–50.
Bartning, I., Forsberg, F. & Hancock, V. (2009). Resources and obstacles in very advanced L2 French. Formulaic language, information structure and morphosyntax. In L. Roberts, Véronique, G.D., Nilsson, A. & Tellier, M. (Eds.), *EUROSLA Yearbook 9*, 185–211. Amsterdam: Benjamins.
Bartning, I. & Schlyter, S. (2004). Itinéraires acquisitionnels et stades de développement en français L2. *Journal of French Language Studies* 14, 1–19.
Boers, F., Eyckmans, J., Kappel J., Stengers, H. & Demecheleer, M. (2006). Formulaic sequences and perceived oral proficiency: putting a lexical approach to the test. *Language Teaching Research* 10, 245–261.
Bogaards, P. (2000). Testing L2 vocabulary knowledge at a high level: the case of the Euralex French Tests. *Applied Linguistics* 21, 490–516.
Bolly, C. (2008). *Les unités phraséologiques: un phénomène linguistique complexe? Séquences (semi-) figées avec les verbes prendre et donner en français écrit L1 et L2. Approche descriptive et acquisitionnelle*. Doctoral dissertation, Université Catholique de Louvain, Belgium.
Campione, E., Véronis, J. & Deulofeu, J. (2005). 3. The French Corpus. In E. Cresti & M. Moneglia (Eds.), *C-ORAL-ROM, Integrated reference corpora for spoken Romance languages*, 111–133. Amsterdam: John Benjamins.
Cummins, J. (1981). Age on arrival and immigrant second language learning in Canada: a reassessment. *Applied Linguistics* 2, 132–149.
David, A. (2008). Vocabulary breadth in French L2 learners. *Language Learning Journal* 36, 167–180.
David, A., Myles, F., Rogers, V. & Rule, S. (2009). Lexical development in instructed L2 learners of French: is there a relationship with morphosyntactic development? In B. Richards, D. Malvern, P. Meara, J. Milton & J. Treffers-Daller (Eds.), *Vocabulary studies in first and second language acquisition*, 147–163. Basingstoke: Palgrave Macmillan.
Dörnyei, Z., Durow, V., & Khawla, Z. (2004). Individual differences and their effects on formulaic sequence acquisition. In N. Schmitt (Ed.), *Formulaic sequences*, 87–106. Amsterdam: John Benjamins.
Edmonds, A. (2010). On the representation of conventional expressions in L1-English L2-French. Unpublished doctoral dissertation, Indiana University.
Erman, B. & Warren, B. (2000). The idiom principle and the open choice principle. *Text* 20, 29–62.
Erman, B., Denke, A., Fant, L. & Forsberg Lundell, F. (in press). Nativelike selection in long-residency L2 users: a study of multiword structures in the speech of L2 English, French and Spanish. *International Journal of Applied Linguistics*.

Forsberg, F. (2008). *Le langage préfabriqué — formes, fonctions et fréquences en français parlé L2 et L1*. Bern: Peter Lang.
Forsberg, F. (2010). Using conventional sequences in L2 French. *International Review of Applied Linguistics* 48, 25–50.
Forsberg, F. & Bartning, I. (2010). Can linguistic features discriminate between the communicative CEFR-levels? — A pilot study of written L2 French. In I. Bartning, M. Martin & I. Vedder (Eds.), *Communicative proficiency and linguistic development: intersections between SLA and language testing research. Eurosla Monograph Series* 1, 133–158. European Second Language Association.
Forsberg, F. & Fant, L. (2010). Idiomatically speaking — effects of task variation on formulaic language in high proficient users of L2 French and Spanish. In D. Wood, (Ed.), *Perspectives on formulaic language in acquisition and communication*, 47–70. New York: Continuum.
Forsberg Lundell, F., Bartning, I., Engel, H., Hancock, V., Lindqvist, C. & Gudmundson, A. (in press). Beyond advanced stages in high-level spoken L2 French. *Journal of French Language Studies* 24 (2).
Granger, S. & Pacquot, M. (2008). Disentangling the phraseological web. In S. Granger & F. Meunier (Eds.), *Phraseology. An interdisciplinary perspective*, 27–49. Amsterdam: John Benjamins.
Gyllstad, H. (2007). *Testing English collocations. Developing receptive tests for use with advanced Swedish learners*. Doctoral Dissertation, Lund University.
Kecskes, I. (2002). *Situation-bound utterances in L1 and L2*. Berlin: Mouton de Gruyter.
Laufer, B. & Nation, P. (1995). Vocabulary size and use: lexical richness in L2 written production. *Applied Linguistics* 16, 307–322.
Lemmouh, Z. (2010). *The relationship among vocabulary knowledge, academic achievement and the lexical richness in writing in Swedish university students of English*. Doctoral dissertation, Stockholm University.
Lewis, M. (2008). *The Idiom Principle in L2 English*. Doctoral dissertation, Stockholm University.
Lindqvist, C. (2010). La richesse lexicale dans la production orale de l'apprenant avancé de français. *La Revue Canadienne des Langues Vivantes* 66, 393–420.
Lindqvist, C., Bardel, C. & Gudmundson, A. (2011). Lexical richness in the advanced learner's oral production of French and Italian L2. *International Review of Applied Linguistics* 49, 221–240.
Malvern, D., Richards, B., Chipere, N. & Durán, P. (2004). *Lexical diversity and language development. Quantification and assessment*. Basingstoke, New York: Palgrave Macmillan.
Mizrahi, E. & Laufer, B. (2010). Lexical competence of highly advanced L2 users: is their collocation knowledge as good as their productive vocabulary size? Paper presented at Eurosla 20, Reggio Emilia, Italy.
Ovtcharov, V., Cobb, T. & Halter, R. (2006). La richesse lexicale des productions orales: mesure fiable du niveau de compétence langagière. *The Canadian Modern Language Review* 63, 107–125.
Pallaud, B. & Henry, S. (2004). Amorces de mots et répétitions: des hésitations plus que des erreurs en français parlé. In G. Purnelle, C. Fairon & A. Dister (Eds.), *Le poids des mots. Actes des 7es Journées internationales d'Analyse statistique des Données Textuelles*, 848–858. Louvain-la-Neuve: Presses universitaires de Louvain.
Raupach, M. (1984). Formulae in second language speech production. In H.W. Dechert, D. Möhle & M. Raupach (Eds.), *Second language production,* 114–137. Tübingen: Gunter Narr.
Read, J. (2000). *Assessing vocabulary*. Cambridge: Cambridge University Press.

Stengers, H., Boers, F. & Housen, A. & Eyckmans, J. (2011). Formulaic sequences and L2 oral proficiency: does the type of target language influence the association? *International Review of Applied Linguistics* 49, 321–243.
Tidball, F. & Treffers-Daller, J. (2007). Exploring measures of vocabulary richness in semi-spontaneous French speech. A quest for the Holy Grail? In H. Daller, J. Milton & J. Treffers-Daller (Eds.), *Modelling and assessing vocabulary knowledge*, 133–149. Cambridge: Cambridge University Press.
Tidball, F. & Treffers-Daller, J. (2008). Analysing lexical richness in French learner language: what frequency lists and teacher judgement can tell us about basic and advanced words. *Journal of French Language Studies* 18, 299–313.
Towell, R., Hawkins, R. & Bazergui, N. (1996). The development of fluency in advanced learners of French. *Applied Linguistics* 17, 84–119.
Treffers-Daller, J. (2009). Language dominance and lexical diversity: how bilinguals and L2 learners differ in their knowledge and use of French lexical and functional items. In B. Richards, D. Malvern, P. Meara, J. Milton & J. Treffers-Daller (Eds.), *Vocabulary studies in first and second language acquisition*, 74–90. Basingstoke: Palgrave Macmillan.
Treffers-Daller, J., Daller, H., Malvern, D., Richards, B., Meara, P. & Milton, J. (Eds.) (2008). Knowledge and use of the lexicon in French as a second language. *Journal of French Language Studies* 18. Special issue.
Véronis, J. (2000). Fréquence des mots en français parlé. http://sites.univ-provence.fr/veronis/data/freq-oral.txt. Accessed July 17, 2011.
Warren, B. (2005). A model of idiomaticity. *Nordic Journal of English Studies* 4, 35–54.

Résumé

Dans son survol de recherches sur l'apprenant avancé, Bartning (1997) a pour but de caractériser la variété avancée. Cette caractérisation est surtout basée sur des traits morpho-syntaxiques. Notre objectif est d'enrichir la caractérisation des apprenants avancés par la prise en compte de traits supplémentaires, mais aussi de décrire des niveaux supérieurs, à partir des recherches récentes sur le français L2. Plus précisément, nous nous posons la question de savoir si deux dimensions lexicales, à savoir la richesse lexicale et les séquences préfabriquées lexicales, pourraient éventuellement distinguer des niveaux dans cette variété et, ainsi, contribuer à enrichir sa caractérisation. De plus, sera examinée ici la corrélation entre ces deux variables. S'agit-il de deux aspects qui se développent en parallèle ou non ?

Formulaic and proceduralised language in the initial and advanced stages of learning French

Richard Towell
University of Salford

This chapter is based on the model of SLA presented in *Approaches to Second Language Acquisition* (Towell & Hawkins 1994). It begins by presenting that view in summarised form. It then looks at four sets of empirical data drawn from two longitudinal multiple case studies and interprets the evidence in the light of the particular approach. The first two deal with learners in the initial stages of learning and show how they have to store formulaic knowledge in order to be able to extract syntactic information. The second two deal with advanced learners and show how they have to chunk and proceduralise intermediate knowledge in order to be able to develop both their knowledge and their fluency. The study of the advanced learners shows, however, that they do not become either as knowledgeable or as fluent in the L2 as they are in the L1. An interpretation of that evidence within the model offered suggests that this is because their L2 is based on a multiplicity of knowledge sources and that processing this kind of knowledge is more demanding of the memory systems than acquiring knowledge of and the ability to process the L1.

1. Introduction: A model for SLA

This chapter is based on a specific model of SLA first outlined in detail in *Approaches to Second Language Acquisition* (Towell & Hawkins 1994) and will be referred to as the TH model. This model argues for a role for Universal Grammar in providing innate information about syntactic structure but it places that role within an overall acquisitional process which requires a considerable amount of further learning once UG has made its contribution and allows for learning which is not constrained by UG.

The justification for an appeal to UG is quite simply that the surface structure of language does not reveal sufficiently the underlying syntactic regularities of that language (Hawkins 2001; White 2003). Therefore, innate information is required to enable learners to interpret the external evidence base by constraining the syntactic hypotheses which can be entertained. However, the evidence shows that second language learners learning after about the age of seven are influenced by other factors as well (see discussion in Long 1990). They will often prefer to transfer the structure of the L1 and may seek to make use in the L2 of inappropriate structures of the L1 to mimic the structures of the L2. Both of these strategies will enable the learner to produce second language utterances but not on the basis of the same underlying knowledge as is held by an L1 speaker.

Furthermore, this model argues that the knowledge of the syntax which may be acquired with the aid of UG is not immediately 'usable' in the sense of being available for use in comprehension and production of real-time language. One central reason for this is that the actual forms of the language and the constraints associated with specific lexical forms have to be learnt as a rather different kind of knowledge. It is one thing to know with the assistance of UG that a given language has or does not have verb raising as a characteristic; it is another to know which verbs will raise and which will not and which have specific argument structures. This second kind of knowledge has to be acquired on a piecemeal basis. In addition, the learner has to become confident that the knowledge is correct and has to become practised in the correct use of the forms to a level where they can be comprehended or produced unconsciously in real time. This is not a rapid process.

Relying to a large extent on the psychological models provided by J.R. Anderson and colleagues (Anderson 1983, 2000; Anderson & Lebiere 1998; Anderson et al. 2004) in this model it is suggested that all forms of knowledge must be stored in one of two memories. One store is the declarative memory and it is claimed that all knowledge is initially declarative, although some forms of knowledge may pass through the declarative memory very quickly (see discussion in Johnson 1996: 96ff). This memory is mostly for the kinds of knowledge which may be made conscious in the sense that, if a user chooses to do so, the knowledge may be consciously 'inspected'. Knowledge can be swiftly stored in declarative memory but retrieving it may be a slow process and may consume a great deal of working memory. The other store is the procedural memory. This memory is mainly for knowledge which the user is not able to bring to a level of consciousness. It is the kind of knowledge on which all those activities which we come to perform unconsciously rely. The memory is divided into two parts — associative and autonomous. In the associative part of the procedural memory, procedural knowledge can be combined with declarative knowledge in order to build up integrated skills. In this sense, it will still be partly accessible to consciousness. Over time and as practice confirms actions carried out on the basis of associative procedural memories, the actions may be stored in the autonomous part of the procedural memory. At that time, they are not consciously retrievable (although the same knowledge will continue to exist in declarative form). The example which Anderson uses is telephone numbers. When first given a telephone number, it may be noted in a diary and this 'declarative information' referred to when dialing. Over time, by virtue of practice, it becomes normal to dial the number without thinking as the information has been stored procedurally. The number will still be available to you in your diary (declarative information) but normally you will retrieve it swiftly and unconsciously from your autonomous procedural memory. The TH model suggests that second language learning, with its mixture of innate UG constrained knowledge of syntax, learned knowledge of specific language forms and the ability to process interlanguage in real time comprehension and production, relies on these memory systems as knowledge of the language and the ability to use the language is built up over time.

In practical terms, given that second language learners learning the language after the age of seven encounter the difficulties mentioned above associated with transfer and mimicking and that they are usually required to do more complicated things with language than their early learning allows them to do, they usually have to begin by learning words and formulaic utterances which will enable them to communicate at least minimally in expected situations. Fortunately, their well-developed (in relation to children learning their L1) memory capacities will allow them to store such utterances and to recall them as lexicalised units for use in context. They can also learn explicit grammatical rules which describe surface regularities of the language and try to apply them when understanding or producing utterances. The difficulty they have is in extracting from formulaic utterances and from surface descriptions knowledge of the underlying regularities of the language which are inadequately reflected in the surface structures.

The TH model of Second Language Acquisition, the principles of which are set out above, is summarised in Diagram 1 below.

The top box on the diagram indicates that learners are assumed to be equipped with UG knowledge of the universal constraints on syntactic structure. This places a constraint on the hypotheses they can entertain with regard to syntax. This knowledge has been used in the acquisition of their first language. However, having acquired that language they will tend to want to transfer (t) the knowledge of L1 syntax which they now have to the L2 and they may also on occasions make use of that L1 syntax to mimic L2 structures when in fact L1 learners produce them on a different basis. UG, transfer and the ability to mimic (m) provide the learners with a set of internal hypotheses about the syntax of the language, hence the single downward arrow. They are then confronted with the external evidence from the L2 as they are exposed to it — the two upward arrows. That information is largely lexical to begin with. They have to acquire the lexical items of the L2 as they encounter them. These include formulaic utterances as they hear them

```
                    ┌──────────────────┐
                    │ Universal grammar│
                    └────────┬─────────┘
                          (t)│
           ┌──────────────┐  │ (m)
           │ First language│  │
           └──────┬───────┘   │
           ┌──────┴───────────┴────┐
           │  Internal hypotheses   │
           └──┬──────▲──────▲──────┘
              ▼      │      │
```

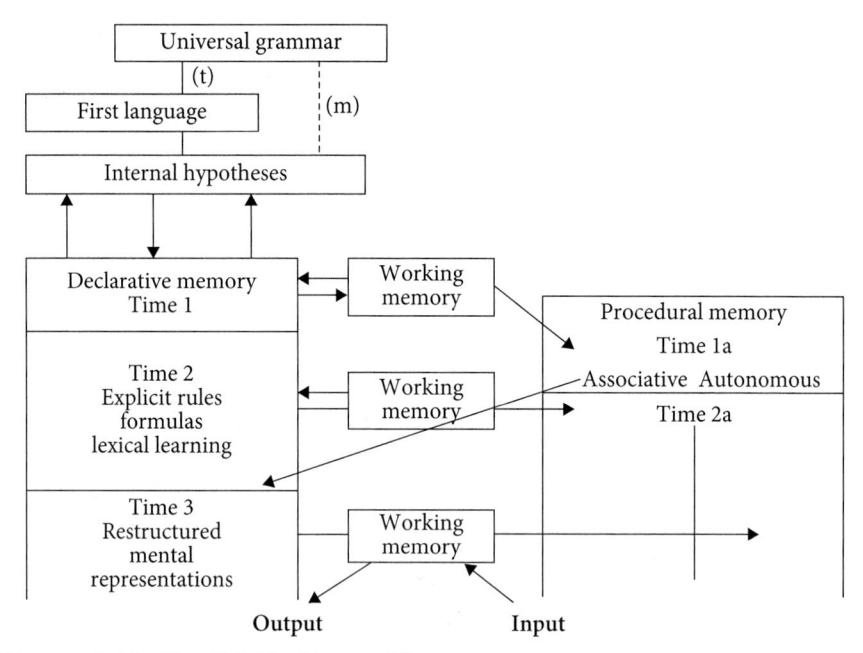

Diagram 1. The Towell & Hawkins model

in context. They may also have learnt explicit rules for the surface structure. All of this information is initially entered in the declarative memory. Within that memory learners interpret and store this information as best they can. However, very quickly, they have to ensure that this knowledge can be used spontaneously in real-time comprehension and production. It is not possible to comprehend or produce language on a purely conscious and item-based basis; the information has to be restructured by identifying regularities and storing them as procedures in procedural memory as quickly as possible. However, as the knowledge is initially necessarily incomplete and unreliable, it will be stored in associative procedural memory until it becomes sufficiently practised and reliable for it to be stored in the autonomous procedural memory — which may take a very long time indeed. Working memory, which is usually thought to be of limited capacity, is an essential conduit for all the information into, out of and between memories and is likely to be constantly overloaded. However, over a long period of time successful learners will build up a stock of stored items in their declarative memory and will have identified regularities and stored them as procedures in procedural memory; they will thus gradually become more at ease in comprehending and producing language accurately and fluently in real time.

A consequence of this view of SLA is that acquisition is a continuous dynamic interplay between the acquisition of new information, the extraction of that which can be generalised and the storage of what has been acquired in suitable form, first in associative procedural memory and then, much later, in the autonomous procedural memory. That information which is lexical in nature (words, formulaic utterances) will be stored in declarative memory. Where regularities are identified (e.g. syntactic, morphological and phonological patterns), they will be created as procedures and stored in procedural memory. Regularities which become so fixed that they are newly created formulas may be stored in declarative memory in restructured form. This interplay is represented in the diagram by arrows indicating transfer of information from one memory to the other and back again.

The process is likely to begin with the learning of chunks or formulaic language because that is how the external data present themselves. The learner then has to extract generalisable information from those chunks with the assistance of the internal and external hypotheses. That generalisable information has then to be integrated within the progressive development of the knowledge of the overall lexis, syntax, and morphology. Lexical and discourse information is likely to be stored as enhanced chunks in the declarative memory. As the knowledge develops and becomes reliable it must be stored in ways that make it widely usable in all contexts, i.e. as generalisable production mechanisms (procedures) in the procedural memory and as revised chunks in the declarative memory. This will translate in different ways at different stages. In the initial stages the first requirement will be the successful 'unpackaging' of information derived from chunks. In so far as that succeeds, the internal and external hypotheses will allow the information to be restructured as knowledge which can be applied to other linguistic forms which pattern in the same way. Once that is completed and numerous procedures have been practised, this now reliable information can be stored in the procedural memory system as newly appropriated procedures which integrate syntactic, morphological and lexical information. This might be called a form of 'repackaging' of the information but in ways which are specific to the particular learner who now 'owns' or controls this information. In turn, such storage will allow new memory space to be freed up to permit further cycles of acquisition as the learning proceeds.

In the rest of this article, I will look at empirical evidence from the initial and advanced stages of the learning of French to see how it can be interpreted within the model. A key element is that both sets of studies are longitudinal case studies which allow access to the development of linguistic knowledge and language processing in individual learners.

2. Formulaic language in the initial stages

We will look first at the way in which learners in the very earliest stages of learning a second language have been seen to deal with formulaic language. Words, chunks and formulas have to be acquired from the very start to give a minimum of communicative interaction. They have to be recognised in context so that utterances can be understood and they have to be available as a production strategy so that a reply can be formulated.

The early learners were studied by Myles (2005), Myles et al. (1998), Myles et al. (1999) in English secondary schools. In this study the learners were asked to undertake a range of activities in each of their first six terms when learning French. The children were asked to participate in activities outside the classroom and to interact either with another pupil in paired activities or to interact with an interviewer. The activities varied and therefore the density of particular linguistic forms in each 'round' varied. In this section we shall look at the evolution of interrogative forms. In the next section we will look at the development of the verb phrase. In both cases we will be relying on data collected from the same learners at different times within this same research project.

Interrogative formulas make up a considerable amount of the forms taught in the first years of language instruction as a means to permit interaction. In French, the formulas are syntactically complex. The usually taught forms are: *comment t'appelles-tu?* ('what are you called?') and *comment s'appelle-t-il?* ('what is he called?') with the possible full noun phrase versions such as *comment s'appelle la fille?* ('what is the girl called?'). These are complex forms involving the use of reflexive pronouns, the use of inverted subject clitic pronouns or full noun phrases and *wh*-fronting of a question word. It could not be expected that learners could control such advanced syntax from the initial stages and it is therefore clear that they have to be learned as chunks or formulas (Myles *et al.* 1999: 50–52 provide a definition of what they mean by that term.). The interesting question is what learners manage to do with such chunks over time and specifically whether they can extract from them the generalisable syntactic information mentioned above. The tasks which the learners were asked to undertake required changes of reference from first person to third person and the use of full noun phrases in the place of the subject pronoun. There was therefore communicative pressure to develop the syntax at least to cope with these communicative needs.

The overall project involved 60 children. Of those 16 were studied in detail with regard to the development of interrogative forms. Myles *et al.* (1999) indicate that the majority of the 16 appear not to have developed very far in the 'creative' use of interrogative forms. In most cases the *comment t'appelles-tu?* formula appeared to be initially learnt but later on most interrogatives were formed by verbless utterances: "...our learners increasingly resort to such V-less utterances over time in order to ask questions, so that these form over two-thirds of all questions in round 6" (1999: 70). However, where subjects did make progress with these forms a 'common general route, at variable rates' could be seen, as follows:

1. Chunk inappropriately used, over-extended; for example *comment t'appelles-tu ?
2. Chunk over-extended, but with lexical NP tagged on; for example *comment t'appelles-tu le garçon ?
3. Chunk starting to break down: subject pronoun omitted or replaced by a NP; for example *comment t'appelles (la fille) ?
4. Further breaking down: reflexive pronoun changes to *s*': subject pronoun is omitted or replaced by a lexical NP; for example, *comment s'appelle ?; comment s'appelle... garç — un garçon ?
5. Third person pronoun is used; for example, *comment s'appelle-t-il ?* (Pupil 09 only) (1999: 67).

Myles *et al.* indicate that the minority of pupils who do make progress realise relatively early on that the *-tu* element contains the reference to outside meaning and that in consequence it may be substitutable (as in 3 above). They struggle, however, to find which other items might fit the available 'slot' and they sometimes ignore the 'slot' completely and add an additional item (as in 2 above). The authors comment that "Until a pronominal system emerges in these learners ... they have to rely on a number of strategies in order to overcome production problems" (1999: 67). There is, however, a pattern to the development:

> In our classroom data, it seems that the learners who are able to memorize formulas successfully, and who were still working on them by the end of the study, are also the learners who were earliest to engage in creative construction and who progressed furthest along the continuum during the course of our two year study (e.g. Pupils 03,09,57) (1999: 76).

Thus, overall, they conclude that "creative construction and chunk breakdown clearly go hand in hand" (1999: 76). Commenting further on those learners who do manage to make progress, Myles *et al.* state: "This first group of learners seems to be able to successfully automatize formulaic routines, thereby enabling them to free up controlled processes to attend to the form of language rather than being constrained by processing limitations to concentrate on the purely semantic and pragmatic constraints that are characteristic of the very early stages" (1999: 77). In terms of the TH model, this is a process whereby the formulaic routines are first stored as associative procedural knowledge. The learners are then able to work on them, consciously and unconsciously, to extract generalisable information about areas such as subject clitic pronouns.

3. Syntactic Learning in the initial stages

In a further article related to these learners, Myles (2005) takes up the issue of whether or not they have managed to acquire the verb phrase and in particular subject clitic pronouns in finite declarative constructions. The French finite verb phrase requires the use of subject clitic pronouns or full noun phrases as overt subjects and agreement between the subject and the verb as expressed by morphological variation. Whilst overt subjects are required in English, there is less visible morphological variation related to agreement. Evidence from French L1 acquisition suggests that learners first make use of non-finite forms in contexts where finite forms would be expected. Subsequently, they acquire the use of finite verbs. A key point is that they learn to make use of morphological variation at the same time as they acquire the use of subject clitic pronouns (Pierce 1992; Herschensohn 2000, 2001).

We have seen in the previous section how learners in these studies began to isolate the subject clitic pronoun in interrogative formulas. The Myles (2005) study tracks the evolution of the verb phrase across 14 learners i.e. a subset of the 16 reported on previously. The relevant recordings were made at the end of the first year of learning (after 141 hours of instruction) and at the end of the second year of learning (after a further 254 hours of instruction). The data are taken from one-to-one interviews in which a researcher first recounted a story based on a set of shared pictures and then asked the learner to provide their own version. The story required third person narrative and did not allow much use of the kinds of chunks which had been taught in the classroom. The events in the narrative required the use of verbs.

Learners initially make use of a large number of NPs but over time the number of verb phrases increases and within the verb phrases the number of finite verbs increases, although this remains at a level of just over half. Specifically, the results show, first, that the number of propositions which include a verb phrase increased considerably between the first and second recordings: "In the first narrative task, learners supplied VPs overtly around 55% of the time and by the second elicitation, they were able to supply VPs 76% of the time. The difference is significant ($Z=-3.15$, $p<0.002$) using a Wilcoxon Signed Ranks test" (2005: 98–99). Second, the proportion of verb phrases containing finite verbs moves from 51.6% on the first occasion to 56.4% on the second occasion. This is again significant ($Z=-2.88$, $p<0.004$). Myles notes that those learners who are most successful "correspond very closely to those we had previously identified as having made the most progress in their development of interrogatives and in their analysis and creative use of chunks in earlier studies" (2005: 101). The study concentrates on the development of subject clitic pronouns. These are not very frequent as learners prefer to make use of full noun phrases but there are 34 examples across all learners and across both elicitation tasks. They are "almost exclusively used with tensed verbs" (2005:103). This is important because, as noted above, this is what happens with L1 learners. Pierce (1992:92–93) cited by Myles, draws the conclusion that "this finding of a contingency between subject pronouns and finiteness is a very strong indication that the early grammar represents and projects Infl". Myles does not feel such a conclusion can be drawn for all the learners but it can be argued that it is true of the most advanced group. Myles points up that the use of *être* as a copula verb increases in the data from 62 examples at Time One to 86 examples at Time Two and that the usage occurs especially amongst those who are the most advanced. They also systematically make use of agreement between subject and verb. Myles (2005:108) suggests that "it might well be the case that these forms of *être* and *avoir* trigger the move from lexical to functional projections, as suggested by Hawkins (2001)."

In terms of the TH model, these examples show how learners are able to extract from the data those elements which will enable them to create the necessary underlying knowledge of the syntax with the help of the constraints of UG. UG specifies in advance the existence of an abstract universal syntactic tree (downward arrow in the diagram) but it cannot populate that tree with the knowledge to be derived from the specific language being learnt. That can only happen in the presence of the relevant evidence — the data arriving via the external evidence (upwards arrows in the diagram). The evidence postulated here suggests that the variation which the learners observe in the form of the free grammatical morpheme *être* and the relationship which is established with the variable subject clitic pronoun provokes the unconscious realisation that this language has an Inflectional Phrase. This is evidence of UG innate knowledge interacting with external evidence to open the door to the full establishment of the verb phrase. It is an illustration of how the extraction of what was called in the introduction generalisable information operates. For those learners who manage to reach this stage, it should prove to be the beginning of an ability to construct probably the most important element of most languages, the verb phrase. We shall now move on to examine what happens in the advanced stages.

4. Syntactic Learning in the advanced stages

The evidence from learners in advanced stages comes from another longitudinal study, this time of learners in higher education (Hawkins *et al.* 1993). These were students who had chosen to study languages at the University of Salford. As such, they can be thought to equate to the good learners in the studies by Myles *et al.*, in the sense that it is on the basis of high achievement in secondary studies that they will have decided to study languages. As was the case for the Myles *et al.* research project, activities were carried out with a whole cohort of students and a small subgroup was studied in more detail. The whole cohort was studied on a cross-sectional basis by taking the second and final year cohorts. The subgroup was made up of a subgroup of 12 learners from the second cohort who were followed over the four years of their study at university. Data were gathered relating to two aspects of their language development: syntax and fluency. Fluency development will be discussed in Section 5. In terms of the earlier discussion, by the time learners have studied the language for a further five years, they have established the notion of subject verb agreement within the verb phrase, most often they can produce correct agreements and they no longer use non-finite verbs in contexts where finite verbs are required. However, in one of the aspects of syntax related to the verb, verb raising, there is still uncertainty. In French both auxiliary and lexical verbs raise whilst in English only auxiliary verbs raise. This changes the position of negatives (*not, pas*), frequency adverbs (*often, souvent*), and floated quantifiers (*all, tous*). These will all come after the lexical verb in French and before the lexical verb in English. To exemplify with examples which are translation equivalents:

> French: *Les garçons (ne) regardent **pas** la télévision le vendredi*
> English: *The boys **don't** watch television on Fridays*
>
> French: *Les garçons regardent **souvent** la télévision le vendredi*
> English: *The body **often** watch television on Fridays*
>
> French: *Les garçons regardent **tous** la télévision le vendredi*
> English: *The boys **all** watch television on Fridays*

The same will not be true of examples with auxiliary verbs where the negators, frequency adverbs and floated quantifiers will all follow the verb in both languages.

It follows therefore that the difficulty for English native speakers learning French will be to realise that there is this difference and apply it in the appropriate cases. The knowledge of this aspect of syntax was repeatedly tested by the use of grammaticality judgement tests. In the tests the students were asked to state to what extent on a scale of 1–5 they found the correct French examples and incorrect versions modelled on the English word order above e.g. **Les garçons souvent regardent la télévision le vendredi* acceptable or not. We will deal only with the results from those parts of the grammaticality judgement tests which dealt with these aspects in relation to lexical verbs. The tests allowed the researchers to measure the extent to which the students accepted sentences which were grammatical as correct (Gramm as Gramm), knew that the ungrammatical sentences were incorrect (Ung as Ung) and whether they thought that sentences which were ungrammatical were grammatical (Ung as Gramm). In the tables below the figures are percentages of the total number of sentences recognised across the whole cohorts as being grammatical or ungrammatical and thought to be ungrammatical when they were grammatical.

As far as negatives were concerned, the results from the whole cohorts showed that the intermediate second year students (n = 75) obtained very high percentage scores for grammatical sentences, high but far from perfect scores on the ungrammatical sentences and accepted a small percentage of ungrammatical sentences as grammatical. The students in the final year (n = 29) performed better in each area and displayed knowledge comparable to native speakers.

Table 1. The acquisition of negation by the whole cohort. Negators

	Gramm as Gramm	Ung as Ung	Ung as Gramm
Intermediate	95.8	79.4	12.7
Advanced	93.1	86.2	9.2

As far as frequency adverbs were concerned, the results showed that whilst students in the second year were good at recognising grammatical sentences as such, they could only recognise that just over half of the ungrammatical sentences were indeed ungrammatical and they accepted more than a third of the ungrammatical sentences as grammatical. By the final year, this situation had improved considerably but there were still just over a fifth of the ungrammatical sentences being classified as grammatical.

Table 2. The acquisition of frequency adverbs by the whole cohort. Frequency adverbs

	Gramm as Gramm	Ung as Ung	Ung as Gramm
Intermediate	86.5	52.6	38
Advanced	94.5	72.4	20.6

As far as floated quantifiers were concerned, the results showed that less than half of the grammatical sentences were recognised as grammatical by both the second year and the final year students, that less than a third of the ungrammatical sentences were recognised by the second years and only just over a half by the final years and that more than a half of the ungrammatical sentences were thought to be grammatical by the second years and more than a third were thought to be so by the final years.

Table 3. The acquisition of floated quantifiers by the whole cohort. Floated quantifiers

	Gramm as Gramm	Ung as Ung	Ung as Gramm
Intermediate	46.3	31.7	60
Advanced	44.8	55.7	36.2

Thus the position of negators, frequency adverbs and floated quantifiers is seen to remain problematic to some degree even after eight years of instruction in French and in the case of the final year students after eleven years including a period of at least six months living and working in France. Of the three items, negators are seen to be best learnt, frequency adverbs next best and, although there is progress in recognising more sentences as ungrammatical and classifying fewer ungrammatical sentences as grammatical, the knowledge of floated quantifiers remains weak.

We will now look at the evidence from the cohort of 12 students. The grammaticality judgement results can be plotted on line graphs for these individuals with the two lines representing their efforts in their second year and their efforts in their fourth and final year (as shown in Figure 1).

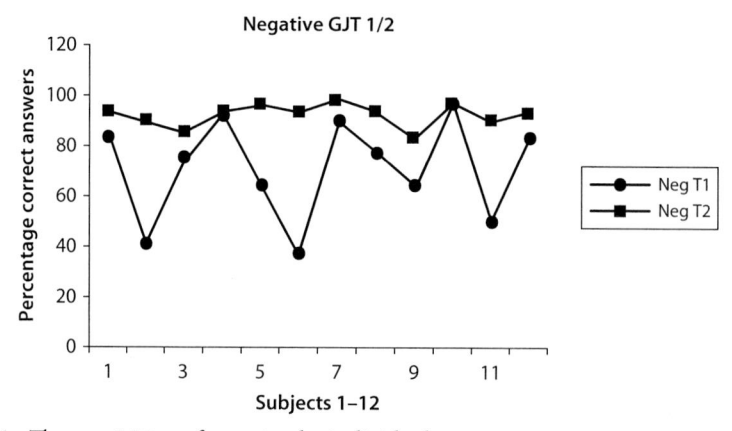

Figure 1. The acquisition of negation by individuals

The negative graphs show consistently high scores in the final year but extremely variable performance across the group in the second year. The difference is significant (t = −3.94, $p < 0.002$). Three students, 2, 6 and 11, can be seen to perform especially badly in year 2.

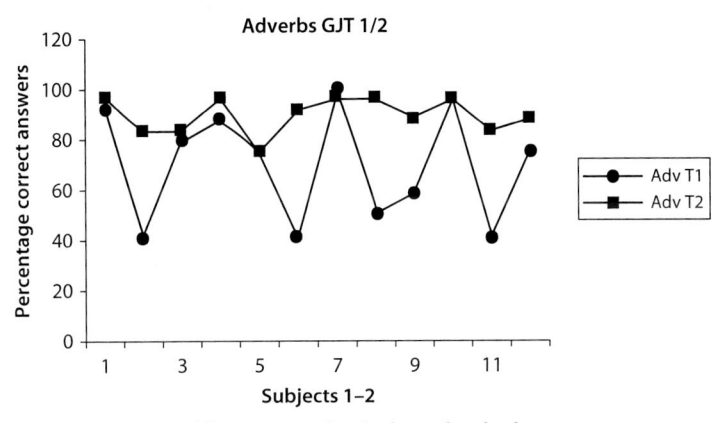

[Figure 2: Adverbs GJT 1/2 chart showing Adv T1 and Adv T2 across subjects 1-12]

Figure 2. The acquisition of frequency adverbs by individuals

The adverb graphs are similar to the negative graphs except that the final year performance is not so high. The differences are significant ($t = -3.2$, $p < 0.008$). In the second year, students 2, 6 and 11 are again seen to perform badly and 8 and 9 are also weak (see Figure 2).

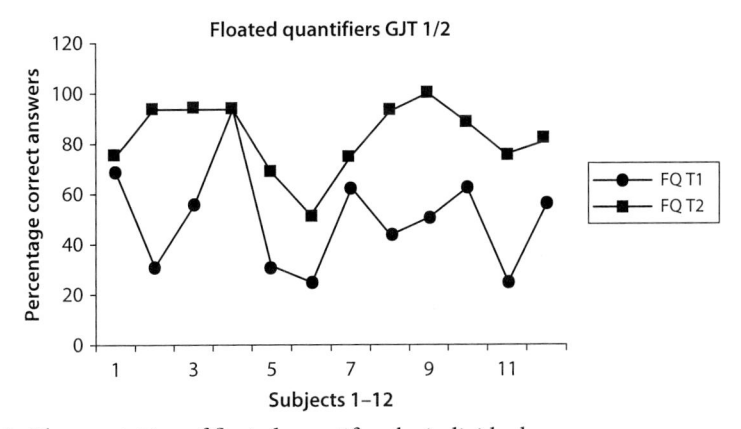

[Figure 3: Floated quantifiers GJT 1/2 chart showing FQ T1 and FQ T2 across subjects 1-12]

Figure 3. The acquisition of floated quantifiers by individuals

The floated quantifier graphs (Figure 3) show that although up to six members of the group were nearing the 100% mark in their final year, the other six were not. The second year performance was very poor with only four students above 60%. The differences are significant ($t = -5.64$, $p < 0.002$). The bottom scorers in the second year were again subjects 2, 6 and 11 this time with subject 5 nearly at the same level.

Overall these data show that some specific aspects of the consequences of verb raising remain problematic for these learners after a period of 11 years learning French, including a period of residence abroad. However, with the exception of floated quantifiers, most learners do finally achieve a level of performance which, whilst not native like, is accurate to some degree most of the time in grammaticality judgement tests. Herschensohn (1997) carried out the same test with even more advanced learners and showed that higher and more consistent scores can be achieved by learners with PhDs in French and/or lengthier periods of residence in France.

In terms of the TH model, the most likely explanation of what is happening is that this is an area where UG constraints were enough to establish the principle of verb raising but not enough to overcome the influence of the L1 (the influence of the box at the top of the diagram) with regard to how it works in all aspects of the language. Instead, learners are slowly building their knowledge of the grammar by recognising surface patterns from exposure to data and possibly by having the surface patterns pointed up by instruction and corrective feedback. The Herschensohn results suggest that more of that can produce effective outcomes. As represented in the diagram, this is declarative knowledge which they then store in the associative procedural memory as procedures which they can recognise and reproduce. The use of such knowledge is likely to slow down their rate of language processing and is likely not to be as consistently accurate and reliable as L1 knowledge, hence the relative inconsistencies still present at the advanced stage. The data also reveal the individual variation amongst the learners. Whilst in the final year there is less variation amongst the group, as can be seen from the relative grouping of the scores, it is clear that some learners, notably 2, 6 and 11, were consistently weaker in each area in year 2. That may require some explanation.

5. Proceduralised language and the advanced stages

The TH model seeks not only to show how knowledge of a second language is initially acquired but also how it is progressively stored in memory. The way knowledge is stored is critical for aspects of language use such as fluency. Only when knowledge is stored in the procedural memory will it be possible to use it fluently in real-time language production and comprehension. Levelt (1989, 1999) has persuasively argued that linguistic knowledge must be stored in productions for fluent use. Although the model does not show this, it may also be true that there is a relationship between the ability to process language and the ability to acquire syntactic and lexical knowledge. The reasoning is that if language processing is effortful for whatever reason, it is likely to consume more of the available memory space and this may mean that there is less memory space available for the acquisition of linguistic knowledge. Establishing how memory works and the respective roles of declarative, procedural and working memory is very difficult but it seems not unreasonable to suspect a relationship between processing and knowledge acquisition. Myles has already hinted at this with her suggestion that it is when beginning learners are able to free up controlled processes that they can attend to the form of language. If processing is slow and possibly difficult then attention to the form of language may have to be sacrificed until a point is reached when sufficient of the new knowledge has been proceduralised for memory space to be available: this would mean a slower pace of learning for those whose processing is slow. There is insufficient space in this article to allow textual illustration of how students' fluency increased (see Towell *et al.*1993; Towell *et al.* 1996, Towell 2002; Towell & Dewaele 2005) and therefore we will limit the investigation to statistically based indications of what changes took place between Year Two — prior to a period of residence abroad — and Year Three — post residence abroad. Of particular interest, however, is whether there are any indications of differential processing abilities between those subjects who were seen to be weak in terms of grammatical knowledge in the second year, i.e. subjects 2, 6 and 11, compared with those who were stronger at that stage.

We will look briefly at two measures: Speaking Rate and Mean Length of Run. Speaking Rate (SR) is calculated by dividing the total number of syllables produced in a given speech sample by the amount of total time (including pause time), expressed in seconds, required to produce the speech sample. The resulting figure is normally then multiplied by sixty to give a figure expressed as syllables per minute. It gives an indication of the speed at which the whole process of producing speech happens including whatever time speakers devote to thinking of what to say and planning speech. Mean length of run (MLR) is calculated as the mean number of syllables produced in utterances between pauses of .28 secs and above. (see Towell *et al.*1996 for discussion of this limit). MLR gives an indication of how much speech the learner is able to encode at a given time without pausing: it can be seen as a proxy for having proceduralised speech forms. Figures 4 and 5 show how the SR and the MLR evolved for the 12 speakers of the subgroup between the second term of the second year and the third term of the third year, i.e. the period during which they spent six months living and working in a French speaking country. The graphs also display the levels attained when the speakers were asked to tell the story of Balablok in English. This was done right at the end of their fourth year.

The SR graph (Figure 4) provides us with four pieces of potentially significant information:

a. the learners scored significantly higher on SR in Y3 than in Y2 ($t = -3.65$ $p = < 0.002$) (with the exception of S10 who scored higher in Y2)

b. there is a significant difference between the learners' SR score in French and in English (t = −4.8 p = < 0.0002) (with the odd exception of S5 who scored higher in Bal Y3 than in English)
c. the rank order correlation between all three recordings is high which is an indication that the pattern of scoring relative to the individual learner remained very similar (Pearson Correlation Y2/Y3 = 0 .86; Y3/Eng = 0.73)
d. three learners — S1,6 and 11 scored much lower than others with S2 not far behind.

The MLR graph (Figure 5) presents much the same picture:

a. the learners score significantly higher in Y3 than Y2 (t = −3.24, p = < 0.003)
b. there is a significant difference between the learners' MLR score in French at Y3 and in English (t = −3.33, p = < 0.003) (with the odd exceptions of S5 who attained a higher score in French Y3 than in English and S10 whose score was actually 0.07 higher in Y2 than in English)
c. the rank order correlations show that the pattern of scoring relative to the individual remained very similar (Pearson correlations Y2/Y3 0.72; Y3/Eng 0.70)
d. some learners had much lower MLRs than others in the early stages of French, — S2, S6 and S11 with S1 not far behind — and in the case of S2, S6 and S11 these were reflected in relatively low MLRs in the L1.

Speaking Rate Balablok

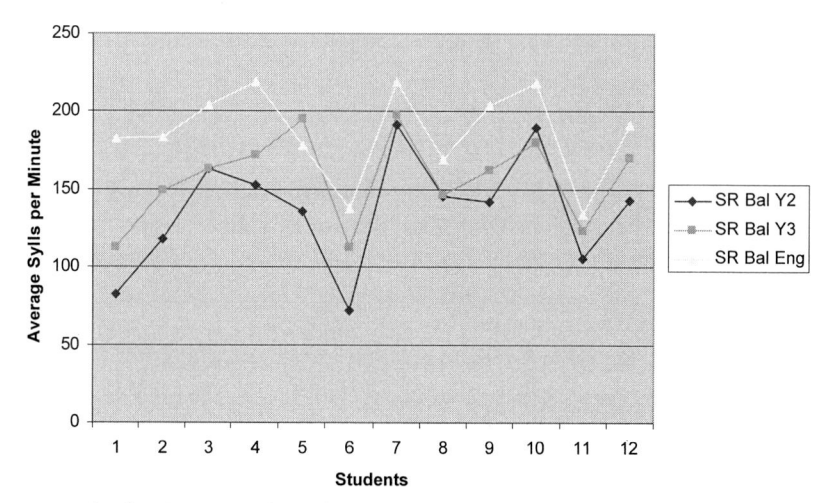

Figure 4. The development of Speaking Rate by individuals

Balablok MLR

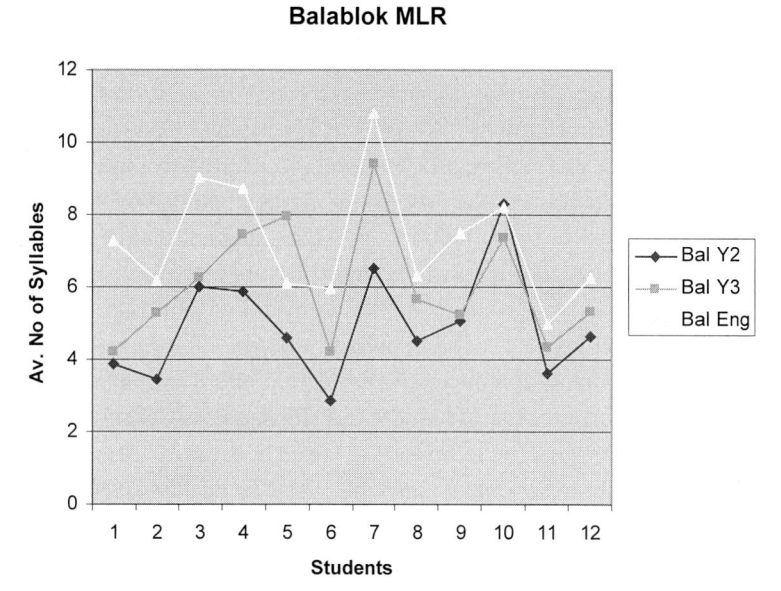

Figure 5. The development of Mean Length of Run by individuals

In terms of the TH model, this is interpreted as evidence that over time the knowledge of the second language becomes proceduralised. But there are three important observations to be made, each of which gives rise to potentially important questions. First, the process of proceduralisation seems to be relative to the individual and therefore might be determined by some individual physiological capability which influences both the L1 and the L2. What might that be? Second, with the exception of S5 (whose performance remains unexplained), the learners do not reach the same levels as they attain in their L1. Whilst this may be explained simply by the fact that the learners have spent less time on task than they have with the L1, there may be other factors as well, such as the nature of the L2 knowledge. Is this knowledge the same as that of the L1, guided by UG and integrated within the memory systems, or is it a different kind of knowledge, such as speeded-up declarative knowledge which is unlikely ever to become as 'autonomous' as the L1? Third, the learners who scored low in Year Two on the grammaticality judgement tests also scored low in Year Two on the SR and MLR measures. Is this a coincidence or might there be explanations which link the two?

6. Discussion

We now have the opportunity to look at the different sets of evidence presented and to try and tease out what lessons we may learn overall. The first set showed us learners struggling to deal with an overload of information from the data with which they were presented. Myles *et al.* (1999) suggested that only those learners who were able to store formulas effectively were able to work on them in order to analyse their syntactic content. Within the TH model it was argued that this showed the importance of storing information in the declarative memory to allow analytical work to take place in the procedural memory, guided by the constraints of UG. The second set of information from Myles showed that at least some of the learners did manage to unpackage information about subject clitic pronouns and did so as a consequence of realising that morphological variation on the free grammatical morpheme *être* went hand in hand with the variation of the pronoun. In UG terms, such a realisation meant the projection of Infl and the opening up of the verb phrase. In terms of the TH model this showed how UG constraints assist in the unpackaging of syntactic information. Given that the learners who did best at unpackaging this information were also the ones who dealt most effectively with the storage of formulas, it may be further argued that the ability to store information in the memory systems is critical for further acquisition. Our third set of information suggests, however, that even if the verb phrase can be opened up in the early stages in the way described, it is not fully acquired even in advanced stages. Although the advanced learners, who were already a self-selecting group of good learners, were able to use negators, frequency adverbs and floated quantifiers with a reasonable level of accuracy after eleven years of study and a period of intensive residence abroad, they were not as consistent or accurate as native speakers in their L1. The interpretation for this within the TH model would be that the L1 is learnt in a way in which UG constrains the learning so as to maximise efficiency in the acquisition of syntactic knowledge. That knowledge, once learnt, is integrated in an ultra efficient way within the memory systems as the declarative knowledge is almost instantaneously proceduralised at the associative level: everyday consistent practice then reinforces and confirms the reliability of that knowledge which rapidly becomes autonomous. When it comes to the L2, however, the settings for the L1 compete and interfere with the information coming in about the L2 and make the constraining role of UG less efficient. As a consequence learners have to rely on other kinds of information, such as surface regularities or instruction to derive the required information. This diversity of sources of rather uncertain knowledge does not allow proceduralisation to take place in the same way and as a result learning is less efficient. This lack of efficiency puts considerable strain on the memory systems and this strain is revealed in our fourth set of evidence. When measures such as Speaking Rate and Mean Length of Run are used, it becomes clear that in the L2 the rate at which advanced L2 learners speak is slower than their speaking rate in their L1 and that they use smaller runs, although they do increase their scores over time. These measures also produce great individual variation. Looking at our third and fourth sets of evidence from the same subgroup of learners, we also noted that, even if the differences in grammatical knowledge had lessened by the end of the learning process, those who scored low on SR and MLR in the second year were also those who scored low on the knowledge of syntax at that point. As for the evidence from the initial stages of learning, this suggests that a lower ability to process and store language goes hand in hand with an inability swiftly to acquire the syntax. Within the TH model, there are two possible complementary reasons for this. First, if it is a matter of letting UG do its work, then as Myles has suggested, it may be that storage of formulas is necessary to free up the necessary memory space. For advanced learners, it may be storage of their own formulas which is important, i.e. the knowledge which they have already acquired needs to be stored in declarative memory to allow the knowledge to be restructured in the procedural memory (consciously in the associative and unconsciously in the autonomous). Second, if, as suggested above, UG cannot suffice because the interference of the L1 is too great, then learners need to make full use of the observation of surface derived regularities and also instructionally and feedback derived information. This again may be conscious and/or unconscious but either way it will take up considerable memory space and more than that required for the learning of the L1. This again suggests that storage of information in memory systems is a critical factor in second language acquisition. Overall, the picture which emerges at the initial and advanced stages of the second language acquisition of French is one in which the acquisition of linguistic knowledge and of the ability to process the language are tied together in a dynamic interplay.

However, it was noted in the introduction that the evidence relied on here is derived from longitudinal case studies. It should further be noted that within the studies, many of the conclusions relied on small subgroups of the cohorts studied. It has to be accepted that this potentially greatly limits the generalisation of the conclusions which can be drawn. Although statistical means have been used to establish levels of significance for the observations introduced, the actual sample sizes are very small. This is often the case where an attempt is made to study different aspects of the behaviour of the same learners. Yet it is only by looking in detail at these different aspects of the behaviour of individual learners and recognising their similarities and differences and the way their individual interlanguage evolves over time, that it becomes possible even to talk about inter-relationships between linguistic knowledge and language processing. This is an argument that language processing is the key to the development of linguistic knowledge. After all, UG is static, it can only be acted upon by external factors and that must take place through language processing. What is needed is larger scale longitudinal studies which would enable us to move beyond the preliminary observations offered here.

References

Anderson, J.R. (1983). *The architecture of cognition.* Cambridge, MA: Harvard University Press.
Anderson, J.R. (2000). *Cognitive psychology and its implications* (5th Edition). New York: Worth.
Anderson, J.R. & Lebiere, C. (1998). *The atomic components of thought.* Mahwah, NJ.: Erlbaum.
Anderson, J.R, Bothell, D., Byrne, M.D., Douglass, S., Lebiere, C. & Qin, Y. (2004). An integrated theory of the mind. *Psychological Review* 111, 1036–1060.
Hawkins, R. (2001). *Second language syntax.* Oxford: Blackwell.
Hawkins, R., Towell, R. & Bazergui, N. (1993). Universal grammar and the acquisition of French verb movement by native speakers of French. *Second Language Research* 9, 189–233.
Herschensohn, J. (1997). Parametric variation in L2 speakers. In E.M. Huges & Greenhill, A. (Eds.), *Proceedings of the 21st annual Boston university conference on language development*, 281–292. Somerville, MA: Cascadilla Press.
Herschensohn, J. (2000). *The second time around: Minimalism and L2 acquisition.* Amsterdam: Benjamins.
Herschensohn, J. (2001). Missing inflection in second language French: accidental infinitives and other verbal deficits. *Second Language Research* 17, 273–305.
Johnson, K. (1996). *Language teaching and skill learning.* Oxford: Blackwell.
Levelt, W.J. (1989). *Speaking. From intention to articulation.* Cambridge, MA: MIT Press.
Levelt, W.J. (1999). Producing spoken language: A blueprint of the speaker. In C. Brown & P. Hagoort (Eds.), *The neurocognition of language*, 83–122. Oxford: Oxford University Press.
Long, M. (1990). Maturational constraints on language development. *Studies in Second Language Acquisition* 12, 251–285.
Myles, F. (2005). The Emergence of Morpho-Syntactic Structure in French L2. In J.-M. Dewaele (Ed.), *Focus on French as a foreign language*, 88–113. Clevedon and Philadelphia: Multilingual Matters.
Myles, F., Hooper, J. & Mitchell, R. (1998). Rote or rule? Exploring the role of formulaic language in classroom foreign language learning. *Language Learning* 48, 323–363.
Myles, F., Mitchell, R. & Hooper, J. (1999). Interrogative chunks in French L2: a basis for creative construction? *Studies in Second Language Acquisition* 21, 49–81.
Pierce, A. (1992). *Language acquisition and syntactic theory: a comparative analysis of French and English child grammars.* London: Kluwer.
Towell, R. (2002). Relative degrees of fluency: A comparative case study of advanced learners of French. *International Review of Applied Linguistics in Language Teaching* 40, 117–150.
Towell, R. & Dewaele, J.-M. (2005). The role of psycholinguistic factors in the development of fluency amongst advanced learners of French. In J.-M. Dewaele (Ed.), *Focus on French as a foreign language*, 210–239. Clevedon and Philadelphia: Multilingual Matters.
Towell, R. & Hawkins, R. (1994). *Approaches to second language acquisition.* Clevedon and Philadelphia: Multilingual Matters.
Towell, R., Hawkins, R. & Bazergui, N. (1993). Systematic and nonsystematic variability in advanced language learning. *Studies in Second Language Acquisition* 15, 439–460.
Towell, R., Hawkins, R. & Bazergui, N. (1996). The development of fluency in advanced learners of French. *Applied Linguistics* 17, 84–120.
White, L. (2003). *Second language acquisition and universal grammar.* Cambridge: Cambridge University Press.

Résumé

Ce chapitre s'inscrit dans l'approche proposée par Towell & Hawkins (1994) : « Approaches to Second language Acquisition ». Après son exposé liminaire, le chapitre rend compte de quatre analyses empiriques basées sur deux études de cas longitudinales dont les résultats sont interprétés dans le cadre de l'approche exposée au préalable. Les deux premières analyses portent sur des apprenants en début d'apprentissage. Elles mettent en évidence la nécessité de stocker en mémoire les connaissances formulaiques avant de pouvoir en extraire les connaissances syntaxiques. Les deux autres analyses sur des apprenants de niveau avancé montrent comment les connaissances existantes doivent être automatisées afin de permettre d'une part d'autres acquisitions linguistiques et d'autre part la fluidité de la parole. Les études au niveau avancé montrent aussi que ni les connaissances de la langue étrangère ni la fluidité de parole en langue étrangère n'atteignent le même niveau qu'en langue maternelle. Ces résultats envisagés dans le cadre de la même approche trouvent des éléments d'explication dans la multiplicité des sources de connaissances où les apprenants puisent pour acquérir une deuxième langue et au poids de leur traitement sur la mémoire par rapport aux procédures d'acquisition et de traitement en première langue.

The acquisition of additive scope particles by Moroccan Arabic L1 learners of French

Georges Daniel Véronique
Aix-Marseille University

The study analyzes the acquisition of the additive particles *aussi* ('also'), *même* ('even') and *encore* ('still') by five Moroccan Arabic L1 adult learners of French, participants in the ESF project (Perdue 1984). On the basis of a comparison between the French scope particles and their Moroccan Arabic equivalents, it is hypothesised that transfer from L1 plays an indirect role in the acquisition of French scope particles because of major semantic and syntactic differences between the two languages. The study sets out to describe the emergence and use of additive scope particles in a sample of texts spanning circa three years. It is shown that *aussi* is used quite early in the longitudinal data collected. *Même* is differently used in various learner varieties and *encore* is acquired late. The study compares the findings about the acquisition of additive particles in Moroccan Arabic learner varieties with previous work.

1. Introduction

The chapter studies the acquisition of the three additive particles *aussi*, *même* and *encore* in French as a second language (henceforth FSL) by Moroccan Arabic (henceforth MA) L1 speakers. It investigates the properties of these scope particles in MA FSL learner varieties at the *pre-basic variety* (Perdue 1996), at the *basic variety* (Klein & Perdue 1997) and at *post-basic variety* stages and assesses the influence of L1 in their acquisition. In order to describe the properties of *aussi*, *même* and *encore*, thetic and categorical (Sasse 1987) learner varieties' utterances, which include scope-bearing particles, are parsed at the structural and informational levels. The paper is based on data collected in the course of the ESF project (Perdue 1984). Section 2 of the paper provides a theoretical framework for the corpus study. Section 3 compares additive particles in French and in MA. Section 4 summarises previous work on the acquisition of French scope particles in L2. Section 5 provides the rationale for the study, the research questions and the method of analysis. Section 6 describes the informants and the database investigated. Sections 7, 8 and 9 describe the main findings on the use and acquisition of *aussi, même* and *encore*. These findings are discussed in Section 10.

2. A framework for the study of the acquisition of scope particles

This section spells out the theoretical underpinnings of the corpus study and defines information organisation and scope.

2.1 The *quæstio* model and information organisation

Following the *quæstio* model (von Stutterheim & Klein 1989), discourse and text may be viewed as a response based on the linguistic means available to the speaker to a set of underlying *quaestiones* (and *sub-quaestiones*). These questions shape reference to the semantic domains of entities (persons/objects), of actions, of properties and states, of time and space and of modal values in discourse. They select the initial topic situation (Klein 2008), the domains to be placed in focus, referential movements and the unfolding of information in text, in terms of main and side structures for instance, and in terms of thetic and categorical utterances.

Following Sasse (1987), thetic constructions are defined as expressions that state the existence of an entity or an event. According to Erteschik-Shir (2007) and Klein (2008), thetic constructions may contain stage topics and permanently available topics, which enable the hearer to identify the topic time, the topic place and the topic entity of the state of affairs depicted. Thetic constructions include presentational clauses, existentials and identificational sentences. Lambrecht (1994: 138) describes thetic constructions as sentence-focus or argument-focus structures. Categorical utterances ascribe a property to an entity, i.e. assert and predicate (Sasse 1987). Lambrecht (1994) classifies categorical utterances as predicate-focus structures, with a topic-comment structure. Categorical utterances may contain individual topics (Erteschick-Shir 2007).

In the *quæstio* model, underlying questions and sub-questions organise both the text and its utterances. These questions provide a means to identify presupposed or given topics and elements that are in focus chosen out of a set of potential alternatives. Along the same line of thought, Lee (2003) defines a contrastive topic as an item that provides an answer to a conjunctive question (one element of a set: the contrastive topic is singled out in the answer). A contrastive focus is produced in answer to a disjunctive question requiring an 'either or' answer (one element of a set of two must be specified).

2.2 Defining scope

Scope has been the subject of much controversy in linguistics for the past 40 years, especially in the study of negation and of quantifiers (see Lyons 1977: 143–150 *inter alia*). Since Quine's analysis of quantifiers *any* and *every* (Quine 1960: 138–141, 1977: 202), the issue of wide and narrow scope has been disputed (McCawley 1981: 100–101 *inter alia*). When various scope-bearing particles (negation, sentence adverbials, quantifiers etc.) co-occur, the question of relative scope arises. König (1991: 48–53) describes the role of markers such as linear order, and intonation in the identification of relative scope. The syntax and semantics of scope particles in relation to focus are extensively discussed by König (1991) *inter alia.*

Following Nølke (1980), Dimroth and Klein (1996), and Dimroth and Watorek (2000), scope will be defined as the structural relation that holds between the position of a scope bearing particle and its domain of application (henceforth DA). The DA of a particle "refers to the part of the utterance affected by the basic meaning of the scope particle" (Dimroth & Watorek 2000: 311). The basic meaning of a scope particle (Nølke 1980; Dimroth & Klein 1996) is defined as the way it applies to a set of alternatives. It may add a specific item to a list of alternatives — it is then an additive particle — or else, state that a specific item is the only one that applies within a set of available alternatives — in this case, it is a restrictive particle. Besides, the particles may also "induce an order for the set of values under consideration" (König 1991: 68) — these are scalar particles. König (1991) posits that in "fully-fledged" languages, scope — bearing particles are focus particles that include the element in focus within their DA. Sanell (2007: 24) provides the examples in (1a), (1b) and (1c), where the DA of *seulement* ('only') is always *trois chaises* ('three chairs') but the element in focus proper varies, with different entailments. Additive particles may also have a contrastive topic within their scope (see for instance Watorek & Perdue 1999).

(1) a. J'ai *seulement* [**trois chaises**].
    ('I have only three chairs', i.e. I have no other furniture.)
  b. J'ai *seulement* [**trois** chaises].
    (i.e. I do not have five chairs.)
  c. J'ai *seulement* [trois **chaises**].
    (i.e. I have no armchairs.)

In this study devoted to the analysis of 'unstable' learner varieties, the identification of the scope of the particles studied and the analysis of their interaction with the organization of information will constitute major empirical issues.

3. Additive scope particles in French and Moroccan Arabic

3.1 French additive scope particles

French *aussi*, *encore* and *même* are additive particles, with scalar meaning in the case of *même* and *encore*. Following Perrin-Naffakh (1996), Fuchs (1993) and Gayraud (2004), the placement of *aussi*, *même* and *encore* in an assertion follows the pattern described in Table 1 below.

Table 1. The placement of *aussi*, *même* and *encore*

	Position A Sentence Initial	Position B Preverbal (adjacent to subject)	Position C Embedded (between Aux and V)	Position D Postverbal	Position E Sentence Final
aussi	−	+ (except if a clitic pronoun)	+	+	+
même	+	+	+	+	+
encore	−	−	+	+	+

+ means that the particle may be present in that position; − implies that the placement of the particle is ungrammatical in that position

Même has the widest distribution compared to *aussi* and *encore*. As often noted, *aussi* is usually adjacent to the constituent which is within its DA,[1] as in (2).

(2) a. [Marie] aussi mange une orange.
('Marie also eats an orange', i.e. Besides Paul, Marie eats an orange too.)

However, *aussi* may also exhibit relative scope as in (2b) and (2c). In (2b),

(2) b. [Marie] mange aussi une orange.
('Marie also eats an orange.') (Perrin-Naffakh 1996: 144.)

the scope of *aussi* goes to the left. It bears on distant *Marie* which is within its DA, with the same meaning as in (2a).

(2) c. [Marie mange aussi [une orange]].
('Marie also eats an orange.') (Perrin-Naffakh 1996: 144.)

---

1. Watorek and Perdue (1999) provide an example of *aussi* in initial position, *aussi dans la rue il y a un bus* ('also in the street there is a bus') but this example is ungrammatical for many French informants, at least if *aussi* is to be understood as an additive particle. Gayraud (2004: 177) points out that *aussi* in sentence-initial position is interpreted by her informants as a causal connector.

In (2c), the scope goes to the right on adjacent *une orange* which is within its DA (an orange and not an apple) — narrow scope — or on the whole predicate ('Marie eats an orange, besides indulging in other activities'). Thus, although the scope of *aussi* usually extends to the left, it may also go to the right when *aussi* is in postverbal position.[2] In clefted sentences, *aussi* with narrow scope, may be placed to the right or to the left of the item within its DA as in (3).

(3) C'est *aussi* [Marie] qui travaille / C'est [Marie] *aussi* qui travaille.[3]
('It is also Marie who works / It is Marie also who works'.) (Perrin-Naffakh 1996: 145.)

Même has an additive scalar meaning and exerts its scope on the constituents which are on its right, except when it occupies sentence final position. However as shown by Anscombre (1973: 48), the scope of *même* may be narrow or wide as in (4a) and (4b):

(4) a. A Paris, même [les travailleurs] ont réussi à réaliser l'unité contre les attaques du gouvernement.
('In Paris, even the workers have succeeded in realizing unity against government's attacks'.)
b. A Paris, même, [les travailleurs ont réussi à réaliser l'unité contre les attaques du gouvernement].
('In Paris even, the workers have succeeded in realizing unity against government's attacks, i.e. In Paris, this is the case of workers, besides other social categories which have accomplished other activities'.)

Encore as a scalar additive particle has at least three different meanings: addition (*more*), continuation (*still*) and iteration (*again*) (Gayraud 2004: 179). It has both a temporal (Fuchs 1993) and a non-temporal reading, as in the following examples from Benazzo (2003: 186):

(5) a. Il boit *encore*.
('He *still* drinks / He drinks *again*'.)
b. Il boit *encore* un café
('He drinks *another/one more* coffee'.)

---

2. I am grateful to one reviewer whose comments helped me clarify this point.

3. In the absence of wider context, (3) may be analysed either as "a categorical utterance where the element in focus is highlighted by a particular focus construction" (comment from one reviewer) or as a thetic construction. In the latter case, (3) should be analysed as an argument-focus construction, awaiting an upcoming constituent.

3.2 Moroccan Arabic additive particles

MA *ḥətta* ('even', 'also')[4] and *bāqi/mā-zāl*[5] ('still', 'not yet') are the translational counterparts of French *aussi, même* and *encore*. However, they are not the exact equivalents of the French scope particles, as it will be shown below.

Ḥətta is classified both as a preposition and a conjunction by Harrell (1962). It spans the semantic space covered by French *aussi* and *même*. The scalar additive particle *ḥətta* conveys the meaning of identity, of equality, of increase and of addition. Its scalarity is used to express temporal values such as "*until, as far as, up to, even*" (König 1991: 163–165). *Ḥətta* is frequently associated with *wahəd* ('one'), *ʃi* ('thing') or *haʒa* ('thing') to form a negative polarity item (Adila 1996). As a rule, the direction of the scope of *ḥətta* extends to the right, like French *même*. It may be in sentence initial (6) or sentence internal positions (7). Units in its scope are usually adjacent to the particle. Hence:

(6) hətta wāhəd ma ʒa
    even one   NEG come:PERFECTIVE:3.SG:M[6]
    ('Nobody came.') (Caubet 1993.)

(7) ma ka-tʕaṛf-i   həttа wāhed ?
    NEG PRES-3-know:IMPERFECTIVE-F even one
    ('Do you know anybody?'.) (Caubet 1993.)

NPs and clauses may lie within the DA of *ḥətta*.

Bāqi and *mā-zāl* (*encore*, 'still' / 'not yet') are also scalar additive particles and negative polarity items. The syntax and the semantics of these units differ from French *encore* since they are both verbs: an active past participle for *bāqi* and a negated inflected verb for *mā-zāl* (NEG-3.SG.cease:PERFECTIVE).[7] The scope of *bāqi*

---

4. One reviewer signals that Classical Arabic *ʔayḍan*, a translational equivalent of French *aussi*, is not mentioned in this paper. Although Harrell and Sobelman (eds.) (2004) provide the following example for MA: *ʕandu sijaṛa u-walaladu ʔayḍan ʕāndhom sijaṛa l–l-wāhed* ('he has a car, and his sons also each have a car'), this item has not been obtained spontaneously from consultants for MA. Hence, it has not been included in the study.

5. *Mā-zāl* refers to Classical Arabic (one reviewer referred the author to *A dictionary of modern written Arabic*, Harrassowitz Verlag, 4th edition, 1979, authored by Hans Wehr and edited by J. Milton Cowan). Negators in MA include *ma-*, hence *ma-zāl* in the examples taken from Caubet (1993). Harrell (1962) uses rather *mā-zāl* in examples of MA.

6. I am grateful to one reviewer who introduced me to the *Leipzig Glossing rules* and provided glosses for the MA examples.

7. This analysis was provided by one reviewer.

and *māzāl* also extends to the right. *Mā-zāl* and *bāqi* may occur in sentence initial or sentence internal positions.

(8) bāqi yum-in (Mostari, p.c).
still day-DUAL
('[It remains] two days (more)'.)

(9) huwa bāqi ka-ixdem   mʕa-na
he   still PRES-3.SG.M-work:IMPERFECTIVE with-1.PL
('He is still working with us'.) (Caubet 1993.)

Bāqi is usually associated with imperfective verb forms.

(10) ma-zāl ka-itiq   bi-k.
still PRES-3.SG.M-believe:IMPERFECTIVE with-2.SG
('He still believes you'.) (Caubet 1993.)

Mā-zāl and *bāqi* may co-occur in the same clause as in 11.

(11) mā-zāl bāqi   j-əskən   fi-dāṛ   wāldī-h
still staying 3.SG.M-live:IMPERFECTIVE in-house parents-3.SG.M
('He still lives in his parents' house'.) (Harrell 1962.)

The MA particles *ħətta*, *bāqi* and *mā-zāl* closely interact with the MA negator. In the context of *ma-zāl* and *bāqi*, the use of *ʃ* in the negator is optional, hence:

(12) ma-zāl ma-mʃit-(ʃ)
still NEG-come:PERFECTIVE-1.SG
('I have not yet gone'.) (Adila 1996.)

Ħətta introduces various lexical items *in lieu of ʃ*, the usual second component of the negator *ma... ʃ*.

(13) ana ma- gelt   ħətta ħaʒa
me NEG- say:PERFECTIVE-1.SG until thing
('Me, I said nothing'.) (Adila 1996.)

3.3 French and MA scope particles contrasted

French particles *aussi*, *encore* and *même* differ from MA *ħətta*, *bāqi*, *mā-zāl* on various counts. The MA scope particles have different syntactic statuses from their French counterparts as exemplified by the fact that *bāqi* and *mā-zāl* are verbs and by the combinatorial capacities of *ħətta*. The lexical nature of the three MA items also stand in sharp contrast with their French adverbial counterparts as illustrated above, especially their negative polarity. Besides, there is some overlap between the three MA scope particles in the expression of temporality.

4. The acquisition of scope particles in French as a second language

The acquisition of scope particles and of negation in L2 has been extensively studied during the past years, especially within the ESF project (1981–1988) (Perdue 1984) and its successors (see Hendriks 2005; Dimroth & Starren 2003 *inter alia*), but also by Andorno (2005) and Sanell (2007). Development in the placement of scope particles both in Romance and Germanic languages is related to the acquisition of finiteness. However, the path and the rhythm of development of these items differ in the acquisition of Dutch, German, French and Italian as L2. In the acquisition of Germanic languages as L2, scope particles which act as linking words in early learner varieties may block the marking of finiteness on the verb at later stages (Dimroth *et al.* 2003).

Dimroth and Watorek (2000) studied *inter alia* the use of the additive particle *aussi* in the data produced by three Spanish and three MA learners of French. They examined six tokens of *aussi* obtained during seven recordings of Spanish learners of FSL and 13 tokens of *aussi* from eight recordings of MA learners in narrative discourse. They showed that in the data:

a. Scope particles are adjacent to the item in their DA, and that the direction of scope is variable, with a dominant left orientation, contrary to their initial hypothesis that scope would be oriented to the right in early learner varieties.
b. The placement of scope particles was sensitive to certain aspects of the management of topic and focus, namely to the existence of contrastive topics.

Benazzo and Giuliano (1998) and Benazzo (2005) showed that in the course of acquisition, the scope of the particles analyzed narrows down from wide scope over the whole utterance to adjacency to DA. After integration in the finite utterance, wide scope developed again. Sanell (2007: 121) partly confirmed Benazzo's results for *aussi* in pre-*basic* and *basic varieties* (*stade initial* and *post-initial*) for Swedish learners of French L2, especially in terms of adjacency. *Aussi* in utterance-internal position was rare in the Swedish data despite the development of verbal inflection. Gayraud (2004) for L1 and Benazzo (2005) for L2 insisted on the fact that additive particles are acquired before iterative particles. This is also reported by Sanell (2007: 128–129).

According to Sanell (2007), the main differences between the development of scope particles in early FSL learner varieties and in more advanced varieties are:

- an extension of the use of *aussi* in sentence-internal position marked by adjacency and scope to the right;
- the use of *aussi* as a one-word utterance;
- the use of *encore* in sentence-internal position with scope to the right to mark continuity and later iteration.

5. Rationale, hypotheses and method

5.1 Rationale

The present study is prompted by two main reasons. Firstly, the acquisition of scope by MA L1 learners has been little studied, except for Giacomi *et al.* (2000), Dimroth & Watorek (2000), and Starren (2001) who provides an extensive analysis of temporal adverbs, including *encore*. The present paper aims at extending previous analyses and at discussing some of their results. Secondly, the additive scope particles of MA and French stand in sharp contrast because: (i) the semantics of *ħǝtta, bāqi* and *mā-zāl* which are negative polarity elements differ partly from that of *aussi, encore,* and *même*; (ii) the word classes of *ħǝtta, bāqi* and *mā-zāl* in MA are heterogeneous *vis à vis* French adverbials *aussi, encore,* and *même*; (iii) the syntax of *bāqi, mā-zāl* and *ħǝtta* is different from that of their French counterparts (see Section 3 above). It is expected that these contrasts will shape the acquisition of FSL by MA learners in the domain of scope particles.

5.2 Hypotheses

The corpus study of the scope bearing particles *aussi, même* and *encore* attempts to check the following hypotheses:

i. Given the semantic and syntactic differences between *ħǝtta, bāqi* and *mā-zāl* and their French counterparts, and the partial semantic overlap of MA additive scope particles, especially in the domain of temporality (see 3 above), it may be hypothesised that the MA L1 learner of French will find no direct one to one relation between the MA particles and their French equivalents. Hence, there will be no direct transfer from L1 to L2. However, the partial equivalence between *ħǝtta* and *aussi* for instance — as a scope particle, *aussi* is not found in initial utterance position in French — may be a source of difficulty.
ii. Because of the partial equivalence between both sets of scope particles, the properties of the target language (TL) are expected to play a major role in shaping the acquisition of scope particles in MA learner varieties.

iii. French scalar items are expected to emerge late in FSL MA learner varieties because of their meaning and of the partial overlap between scope particles in L1 and L2.

5.3 Method

The tokens of scope particles and their DA in the sample of data (see footnote 11 below) produced by three informants (Zahra, Abdelmalek and Abdessamad)[8] were coded according to their position:

- Position A: Utterance-initial.
- Position B: Adjacent to the item within its DA. Position B may be observed either with elliptical utterances, in two words sequences, and in thetic or categorical utterances.
- Position C: Internal, in preverbal position. The verb is not necessarily inflected.
- Position D: Internal, in post-verbal position. The verb is not necessarily inflected.
- Position E: Utterance-final.

The items within the DA of *aussi*, *même* and *encore* have been coded as:

- NP:[9] NP in a two word sequence, or in an utterance, whether elliptical or not,
- Utterance: the whole utterance,
- Other: items other than NP or the whole utterance.

Three contexts have been singled out for the detailed analysis of scope particles[10] because they represent the different types of utterances observed in learner varieties and because of their frequency: with an NP, within a presentational thetic construction *se/ja/jāna* X ('there is X') and within a categorical clause containing a verb.

---

8. The sample of data produced by three informants out of five has been coded *in toto*.

9. The NP within the DA of a scope particle may be adjacent to the particle (see Position B) or distant from it. It may be distant when the particle is in one of the following positions A, C, D, E. The difference between adjacent and distant NP within the DA of a particle has not been directly coded.

10. Because of lack of space, only a limited number of examples will be provided.

6. Informants and database[11]

Data have been collected from the following Moroccan L1 speaking informants, Zahra (Z), Abderrahim (B), Abdelmalek (A), Abdessamad (H) and Malika (M), who participated in the ESF project for ca. three years (for sociobiographical details, see Giacomi *et al.* 2000).

During the data collection period, the MA learner varieties under analysis evolved from a *pre-basic/basic variety* to a *post-basic variety* (Klein & Perdue 1987; Bartning 2009). 19 activities *in toto*, pertaining to the three cycles of data collected from Zahra, Abdelmalek, Abderrahim, Abdessamed and Abderrahim, have been analyzed (see footnote 11).

179 tokens of *aussi*,[12] 212 tokens of *même* and 74 tokens of *encore* have been parsed in the database (*cf.* Table 2). Different informants use scope particles with different frequencies. Abdessamad uses the three scope markers with a high frequency whereas most other informants tend to use *encore* less frequently than the other markers.

7. *Aussi* in MA learner varieties

7.1 Position and DA of *aussi*

Table 3 below provides a survey of the positions of *aussi* in the data of three out of the five informants of the study.

---

11. Data collection with the MA learners was based on three cycles of nine sessions of data collection or encounters. Each session or encounter is coded as Cycle X Encounter X, i.e. 1.1 = cycle 1 encounter 1, etc. Each encounter comprised a range of tasks. Thus, 1.7a means conversation held during the seventh encounter of cycle 1.

The data analysed for this paper were based on the following activities: a (conversation), c (playlet), d (image description), i ('Modern Times' retellings), j (role play), r (commenting role play), s (narrative) produced by each informant, per cycle and per encounter. The sample of activities analysed comprises six activities from encounters 1.1, 1.2, 1.5, 1.6, 1.7, 1.9 of Cycle 1, seven activities from encounters 2.1, 2.2, 2.5, 2.7, 2.9 from Cycle 2 and six activities from encounters 3.1, 3.2, 3.5, 3.7, 3.9.

12. A survey of all the recordings of Zahra yielded 116 tokens of *aussi* and 23 tokens of *même*. Starren (2001:137) has counted 66 tokens of *encore / toujours* in the whole of Zahra's data and 46 tokens of the same item in Abdessamad's recordings.

Table 2. Tokens of *aussi* (also), *même* (even), *encore* (still) in the sample analyzed

Particles	Zahra (Z) aussi	même	encore	Abderrahim (B) aussi	même	encore	Abdelmalek (A) aussi	même	encore	Abdessamad (H) aussi	même	encore	Malika (M) aussi	même	encore
Cycle 1	12	0	0	7	0	1	1	20	1	17	29	2	13	0	3
Cycle 2	5	0	0	0	0	1	27	71	1	25	45	2	0	2	16
Cycle 3	20	5	20	0	0	3	10	8	0	11	20	10	31	12	14
Total	37	5	20	7	0	5	38	99	2	53	94	14	44	14	33

Table 3. Position of *aussi* in data from Zahra, Abdelmalek and Abdessamad

Informants	Position A Utterance Initial	Position B Adjacent to item in its DA	Position C Internal Preverbal (in utterance with verb)	Position D Internal Postverbal (in utterance with verb)	Position E Utterance Final
Zahra	3	31	0	0	3
Abdelmalek	2	24	0	0	12
Abdessamad	3	33	0	2	15
Total	8	88	0	2	30

As Table 3 shows, and as it will become clear in the detailed context analysis below (see 7.2), *aussi* is mainly adjacent to the item in its DA, with scope going to the left. *Aussi* is more frequently used with narrow scope, which bears mainly on the first NP in the utterance[13] (see Table 4).

Table 4. Items within the DA of *aussi* in data from Zahra, Abdelmalek and Abdessamad

	Zahra	Abdelmalek	Abdessamad
NP	32	32	42
Utterance	4	6	10
Other	1	0	1
Total	37	38	53

Cases of wide scope over the utterance or NP2 have a lower frequency than adjacent narrow scope on NP1.

7.2 Context analysis of *aussi*

The three contexts in which *aussi* is analyzed — with an NP, with presentational *ja/jāna* ('there is') and with a clause — have been collected throughout the database. *aussi* + *presentational* and *aussi* + *clause* occur more frequently in the data collected in Cycles 2 and 3.

7.2.1 *Aussi* + NP
A. In *pre-basic* learner varieties
Aussi with scope to the left is used to add a nominal or pronominal item to a list as in (14).

---

13. In Zahra's recordings, on a total of 116 tokens of *aussi* in the data produced over a three-year period, the scope of *aussi* bears on a noun or a pronoun in 111 cases.

(14) Zahra (1.4a)
    I. par exemple? tu peux m'expliquer comment ('c'est')?[14]
        ('for example? Can you explain to me how it is?')
    Z. (oui oui)
        ('yes, yes')
    I. hein ça (en montrant une carte postale) par exemple
        ('this (holding a postcard) for example')
    Z. *les femmes euh pour djellaba* (Focus)
        ('the women for djellaba')
    I. oui et puis
        ('yes and then')
    Z. (rire) *moi aussi comme ça*[15]
        ('[laughs] me too like this').

In (14), *aussi* bearing scope to the left adds *moi comme ça* (me like this) — "AUSSI [moi comme ça]" — following Nølke's notation (Nølke 1993), as a contrastive focus, anaphorically related to *les femmes*. It specifies that *moi* wears djellaba as the set of women on the post card.[16]

B. In *basic* and *post-basic* varieties

In more advanced varieties, the scope of *aussi* on NP is also oriented to the left as in (15), where "AUSSI [moi]" is a contrastive topic.

---

14. The following conventions are used in the transcript: \ indicates interruption by the other speaker; / means self interruption; + (silence); sequences marked () in the transcript overlap; / / stands for phonemic transcription. A broad English translation in parentheses is provided after each line of transcript.

15. One reviewer suggested that the missing predicate could be related to the presence of a scope particle, as observed in the acquisition of Germanic languages. However, this does not apply because utterances like *moi comme ça*, without any scope particle, are also observed in Zahra's learner variety at this stage.

16. One reviewer argues that since *moi* refers to an entity, it should be by definition topical. I disagree with this view on the following grounds: i) Z. is asked to comment a postcard showing Moroccan women wearing djellaba : the whole clause *les femmes euh pour djellaba* is in focus, the question being "what do you see on the postcard"; ii) the new information Z wants to convey is that although she is dressed in a 'European' fashion during the interview session, she also wears djellaba. The same reviewer also notes that this case of contrastive focus does not abide by the definition given above that a contrastive focus answers a disjunctive question. In this example, the implicit disjunctive question introduced by Z, is "these women wear djellaba, what about you?": her answer is "I do too".

(15) Abdessamad (3.3a)
   H. je /uvr/ les yeux je /rogard/ mon père et ma mère et tous les deux + /ife/ la fête de mouton
   ('I open the [my] eyes I look at my father and my mother and both + they make [preparations] for the sheep celebration')
   /ife/ la fête de carême +ah *moi aussi*
   ('they prepare for the celebration of the fast + me too').

7.2.2 *Aussi + jāna X*

A. In *pre-basic* learner varieties

In the thetic construction in (16), the scope of *aussi* extends to the right and the adjacent NP is within the DA of *aussi*.

(16) Zahra (3.5a)
   Z. /jāna/ aussi un / + un monsieur.
   ('there is also a man').

7.2.3 *Aussi + Clause (VP)*

A. In *pre-basic* and *basic* varieties

(17) Zahra (1.7a)
   I. les deux
      ('Both [talking about the legs of Z.]')
   Z. oui ++ quand euh /marʃe/ /li/ /ma/ quand *toujours* euh /dor/ comme ça + /se/ bien le matin
      ('yes ++ when walking it / when always sleep like this + it is fine in the morning')
      /se/ bien et après-midi *encore* quand euh le vent /fi/ chaud + *aussi* + /li/ malade
      ('it is fine and afternoon still when the wind is warm+ also + it aches').

In (17), Zahra uses temporal adverb *toujours* ('always') to mark a causal iterative relation between her state of health and such a factor as a good night's sleep. Additive scalar particle *encore* in the following clause implies that the situation obtains also for the afternoon: "when the temperature warms up, Zahra's legs start aching". *Aussi* with scope to the right adds the state of health depicted by /li/ *malade* to the previous state of affairs. The initial position of *aussi*, ungrammatical in French, in *aussi* + /li/ *malade* favours an interpretation of this particle as a connector (see footnote 1). This position for *aussi* has a low frequency in the data analyzed (see Table 4).

B. In *post-basic* varieties

(18) Zahra (3.1a)
(about the kids of Zahra and Arabic)
I. dehors ils parlent / ils parlent le français et ici ils parlent marocain
('outside they speak/ they speak French and here they speak Moroccan')
Z. oui oui et *aussi le maroc /i parl/ pas français /parle/ l'arabe + marocain.*
('yes and also in Morocco, they don't speak French speak Moroccan Arabic').

In (18), *aussi* is in initial position (see footnote 3 and *supra*). The following clause to the right is in its DA. However, it may be argued that in this position, *aussi* acts as a connector which links what is predicated about /i/ to the previous utterance. The presence of connector *et* ('and') immediately preceding *aussi* is an element in favour of this analysis of *et aussi* as a linking word. Sanell (2007: 124–25) provides similar examples in her analysis of data.

7.3 Summary

Aussi is used by all the informants at various stages of the course of development of their learner varieties. This particle is used both with contrastive focus and contrastive topics. The particle exerts both narrow and wide scope although adjacency to the element within its DA is its most frequent position. It is not the case in MA FSL that *aussi* is used first at the periphery of the clause before working its way to sentence internal position (as opposed to the findings of Benazzo 2005). The scope of *aussi* is oriented mainly to the left.

8. *Même* in MA learner varieties

The number of tokens of *même* collected in the sample of data analyzed is smaller than that of *aussi* (see Table 2).

8.1 Position and DA of *même* (even)

The most frequent position for *même* in the data is utterance initial, with in its DA either NP1 or the whole utterance.

Table 5. Position of *même* in data from Zahra, Abdelmalek and Abdessamad

Informants	Position A Utterance Initial	Position B Adjacent to item in its DA	Position C Internal Preverbal (in utterance with verb)	Position D Internal Postverbal (in utterance with verb)	Position E Utterance Final
Zahra	5	0	0	0	0
Abdelmalek	91	1	4	1	3
Abdessamad	89	0	1	4	0

Même is overwhelmingly present in initial utterance position with narrow and wide scope.

Table 6. Items within the DA of *même* in data from Zahra, Abdelmalek and Abdessamad

	Zahra	Abdelmalek	Abdessamad
NP	5	37	40
Utterance	0	60	52
Other	0	2	2

8.2 Context analysis of *même*

8.2.1 *Même* + NP

In (19), *même* encompasses the contrastive topic, *les jambes* within its scope.

(19) Zahra (2.8a)
 I. Ton mari m'a dit que c'est rien [ça va]
 ('your husband has told me it's nothing you are OK')
 Z. [oui] /se/ rien / et la visite euh pour le coeur pour la tête tout tout bien + *même les*
 ('yes/ it's nothing/ and the visit for the heart for the head everything is OK + even the')
 jambes /se/ bien
 ('legs it's OK').

8.2.2 *Même* + *jāna* X

Example (20) from Abdelmalek provides a good example of the use of additive particles in a MA FSL *basic variety*. *Aussi* has " la police" which is in focus position, within its DA "AUSSI [la police]". *Jāna* + X in focus position is under the scope of *même*.

(20) Abdelmalek (2.7l)
    I. est-ce que tu penses que il était un peu raciste avec toi
        ('do you believe he was a little racist with you')
    A. cent pour cent la police *aussi* /e/ raciste
        ('hundred per cent (sure) the police also is racist')
    I. hm
    A. avant /ja pan/ droit + *même* par exemple comme les Giscard
        ('before there is no right + even for example during Giscard's time')
        …
    I. on peut manifester
        ('one may demonstrate')
    A. oui / po/ / manifeste/ + *même* maintenant / jãn/ pas la police
        ('yes can demonstrate + even now there's no police')
        /ikõntrole/ *pour la carte d'idöntité*
        ('it checks for your ID')
        …
    I. alors y a moins de racistes alors?
        ('then there are less racists')
    A. *même* /jãna/ *beaucoup de racistes euh pour le raciste*/ pour
        ('even there are many racist for')
        le travail pour le logement
        ('the work for the lodging').

In this extract, *même*, in sentence-initial position, has both an additive and a scalar value. Thus, in (20), *même*, as *aussi* above, includes thetic constructions in its DA.

8.2.3 *Même + clause*
In (21) the scope of *même* extends to the right on the following clause. However, /se/ *pas* ('don't know'), which is a meta-comment, is not in the DA of *même*.

(21) Zahra (2.3a)
    I. et au maroc il avait pas de travail
        ('and in Morocco he did not work')
    Z. et /i travaj/ aussi
        ('and he works also')
    I. oui
        ('yes')
    Z. *Même*/ euh /se/ pas co/ euh / *i gan*/ *beaucoup les sous*
        ('even euh I don't know he earned a lot of money').

8.3 Summary

Même seems to be acquired later than *aussi*. The number of tokens of this particle varies from one informant to the other. This could point to a difference in style among the learners although this point is difficult to prove. *Même* is found with NPs, presentationals and clauses containing full finite verbs. The use of *même*, with narrow or wide scope, does not seem to be determined by the presence of inflection on the verb.

9. *Encore* in MA learner varieties

Encore is acquired late and used less extensively than *aussi*, or even *même*.

9.1 Position and DA of *encore*

It is mainly used in utterance initial or final positions, except for Zahra.

Table 7. Position of *encore* in data from Zahra, Abdelmalek and Abdessamad

Informants	Position A Utterance Initial	Position B Adjacent to item in its DA	Position C Internal Preverbal (in utterance with verb)	Position D Internal Postverbal (in utterance with verb)	Position E Utterance Final
Zahra	3	0	8	4	5
Abdelmalek	0	0	0	0	2
Abdessamad	3	0	0	3	8

The DA of *encore* is usually the whole utterance.

Table 8. Items within the DA of *encore* in data from Zahra, Abdelmalek and Abdessamad

	Zahra	Abdelmalek	Abdessamad
NP	4	0	1
Utterance	16	2	13
Other	0	0	0

The late acquisition of *encore* is particularly striking given the translational equivalence that exists between MA *bāqi* and *mā-zāl* and *encore*, which is more straightforward than the relation between MA *həttā* and *même* and *aussi*.

9.2 Context analysis of *encore*

9.2.1 *Encore +NP*

A. In *pre-basic* and *basic* varieties

Example (22) illustrates the use of scalar additive particle *encore* at the BV stage. The scope of *encore* extends to the right over NP *quinze jours* to mark addition, namely "fifteen days more".

(22) Zahra (2.7a)
    I. parce que tu es rentrée à l'hôpital tu as pas travaillé ?
       ('because you came back from hospital you did not work?')
    Z. non euh /dor/ à l'hôpital euh huit jours
       ('no sleep at hospital eight days')
      ...
    Z. après /sort/ à la maison + euh /dorme/ un petit peu +
       ('then come back to the house + sleep a little')
      ...
      + *encore quinze jours* + après /le parti/ maroc
      ('fifteen days still (to go) + then go Morocco').

9.2.2 *Encore + jana X*

In (23), *encore* has within its scope, *jana tu /komãs/ le travail* "ENCORE [/jana/ tu /komãs/ le travail]. It conveys the iterative nature of the process "starting work and going to the end of the month".

(23) Abderrahim (3.1a)
    B. hm /ilerest/ cent francs + /jana/ *encore* tu / komãs / le travail *jusqu*'à la fin du mois + tu /fym/ un paquet de cigarettes.
       ('hm/ there is left hundred francs + there's always you begin the work until the end of the month + you smoke a cigarette package').

9.2.3 *Encore + clause (VP)*

In (24), *encore* is used both in sentence-initial and sentence final positions. In /*itravaj*/ *à six heures encore*, the scope particle conveys a temporal scalar meaning which may be interpreted as "until six o'clock". When *encore* is in sentence initial position, it conveys an iterative value. The difference in temporal reference according to the position of *encore* in the utterance is also signalled by Starren (2001).

(24) Zahra (3.9a)
    I. mais toi comment tu t'organises pendant le ramadan ?
       ('but you how do you get organised during Ramadan?')

Z. /itravaj/ à six heures encore / encore /ātre/ à la
('[I] work [up too, still] at six o'clock / again to the')
maison encore /itravaj/ la cuisine + jusqu à neuf heures quart
('house again I work the kitchen + until nine fifteen')
...

Z. après à trois heures *encore /nu mã3e/*
('after at three we eat again').

9.3 Summary

Encore may be used with NPs, presentationals and clauses containing full finite verbs. It conveys additive meaning (more) and it marks also iteration and continuity. As observed by one reviewer, the tokens of *encore* are often difficult to interpret in early learner varieties. Some of its uses may be due to the transfer of meaning of its Arabic translational equivalent *bāqi* (see example 10 above) as in */itravaj/ à six heures encore*. In more advanced varieties, the interpretation of *encore* with standard temporal values is easier.

10. Discussion

If the positions occupied by scope particles in MA FSL are compared to positions that are acceptable in French (see Table 1), it is possible to assess the point of development reached by the informants.

Table 9. The placement of *aussi, même* and *encore* in MA FSL

	Position A Sentence-initial	Position B Preverbal (adjacent to subject)	Position C Embedded (between Aux and V)	Position D Postverbal	Position E Sentence-final
aussi	+	+	−	+	+
même	+	−	+	+	+
encore	+	−	+	+	+

Non-target-like utterance-initial position is developed with *aussi* and *encore* and internal position of scope particles are less frequent *vis-à-vis* utterance-initial and utterance-final positions. *Aussi* favours adjacency with NP in its DA whereas *même* favours utterance-initial position and *encore* favours utterance final position.

Aussi is the first particle to be acquired by all the informants. In MA FSL learner varieties, it is used in external position (utterance final — 30 tokens out of 128, see Table 3, and ungrammatical utterance initial position — 8 tokens out of 128, and overwhelmingly in adjacent position to an NP (88 tokens out of 128, see Table 3) at practically the same time. Thus, in the MA FSL data, the type of sequence described by Benazzo and Giuliano (1998) for the Spanish learners of French may not be observed. The scope of *aussi* extends more frequently to the left than to the right. Different types of constituents (NPs as well as clauses with presentationals and full verbs) may be found within the DA of *aussi*.

Table 10. Distribution of tokens of *aussi* in 3 different positions in the contexts of presentational and categorical verb clauses

	(aussi) + *jāna* / *se* + X			(aussi) + *Clause* (VP)			
Position	A	B	E	A	B	E	Total
Zahra	0	0	0	3	6	3	12
Abdelmalek	0	4	6	1	15	5	31
Abdessamad*	1	2	6	1	19	6	35
Sub-Total	1	6	12	5	40	14	
Total	19			59			78

* Two tokens of *aussi* in position D have been left out.

As Table 10 shows, 78 tokens of *aussi* occur in the context of presentationals and categorical clauses out of 128 tokens. While in Zahra's data, *aussi* occurs more often in the context of elliptical utterances — 25 tokens — than in the context of a clause (12 out of 37 tokens of *aussi*), in Abdelmalek's — 31 tokens of *aussi* in the contexts of presentationals and categorical clauses out of a total of 38 (see Tables 3 and 4) — and Abdessamad's data — 35 tokens out of a total of 53 —, the reverse situation prevails. Thus, if in Zahra's learner variety, it may be argued that adjacency with NP in the particle's DA is due to elliptical utterances, this does not apply to the data produced by Abdelmalek and Abdessamad. At least in the latter's case, adjacency to NP is not due to the paucity of presentational and categorical clauses.

Aussi is used more extensively by all MA informants than *même* and *encore*. This has also been observed by Benazzo and Giuliano (1998) and by Sanell (2007) in their own data. There is some inter-individual differences in the use of scope particles, compare Abderrahim's and Malika's use of *même* and *encore*.

As in the case of the data analyzed by Andorno (2005) and Sanell (2007), despite a slow development of morphological finiteness on the VP, the integration of scope particles to the core of the utterance is rather slow.

On the basis of a contrastive analysis, the paper posited there would be no direct transfer from L1 in the course of the acquisition of *aussi*, *même* and *encore*. This claim is vindicated both by the quantitative and qualitative analyses developed. It could be argued that:

- the presence of all the scope particles in initial utterance position,
- and, the presence of NP in the DA of all particles,

are due to an indirect influence of L1 (see Sections 3.2 and 3.3 above).

Following Benazzo (2005) and Andorno (2005), TL properties seem to explain the path of development that has been uncovered in this analysis. If scalar particle *encore*, often used to mark temporal and aspectual reference, develops late, this may be due to the semantic and cognitive complexity of this marker. Starren (2001) notes that the presence of *encore* in a position other than utterance initial is a late development.

Although the placement of scope particles is sensitive to the development of finiteness on the verb, finiteness on VP does not play the same role in MA FSL as in the Spanish data studied by Benazzo (2005: 87–88). Scope particles are found both in the thetic and categorical constructions of the learner varieties studied. They occur with contrastive topics and contrastive focus. Thus, it might be argued that the development of scope particles is determined neither by the information structure of the constructions where they occur nor by the development of finiteness on the VP *per se*. The sequence of development observed should rather be explained by cognitive saliency and semantic complexity (Benazzo 2005: 84–89).

Acknowledgement

I would like to thank the anonymous reviewers for their time and insightful comments. Mistakes and shortcomings are mine.

References

Adila, A. (1996). La négation en arabe marocain (le parler de Casablanca). In S. Chaker & D. Caubet (Eds.), *La négation en berbère et en Arabe Maghrébin*, 99–116. Paris: L'Harmattan.

Andorno, C. (2005). Additive and restrictive particles in Italian as a second language. Embedding in the verbal utterance structure. In H. Hendriks (Ed.), *The structure of learner varieties*, 405–444. Berlin: Mouton de Gruyter.

Anscombre, J.-Cl. (1973). Même le roi de France est sage. Un essai de description sémantique. *Communications* 20, 40–82.

Bartning, I. (2009). The advanced learner: ten years later. In E. Labeau & F. Myles (Eds.), *The advanced learner variety: the case of French*, 11–40. Oxford, Berlin, New-York: Peter Lang.

Benazzo, S. (2003). The interaction between the development of verb morphology and the acquisition of temporal adverbs of contrast. A longitudinal study in French, English and German L2. In C. Dimroth & M. Starren (Eds.), *Information structure and the dynamics of language acquisition*, 187–210. Amsterdam: John Benjamins.

Benazzo, S. (2005). Le développement des lectes d'apprenants et l'acquisition de la portée à distance en L2. *Acquisition et Interaction en Langue Etrangère* 23, 65–93.

Benazzo, S. & Giuliano, P. (1998). Marqueurs de negation et particules de portée en français L2: où les placer? *Acquisition et Interaction en Langue Etrangère* 11, 35–61.

Caubet, D. (1993). *L'arabe marocain. Tome II Syntaxe et catégories grammaticales, textes*. Paris-Louvain: Éditions Peeters.

Comrie, B., Haspelmath, M. & Bickel, B. (2008). *Leipzig glossing rules*. Max Planck Institute for Evolutionary Anthropology.

Dimroth, C. & Klein, W. (1996). Fokuspartikeln in Lernervarietäten. Ein Analyserahmen und einige Beispiele. *Zeitschrift für Literaturwissenschaft und Linguistik* 104, 73–113.

Dimroth, C. & Starren, M. (2003). *Information structure and the dynamics of language acquisition*. Amsterdam: John Benjamins.

Dimroth, C. & Watorek, M. (2000). The scope of additive particles in basic learner languages. *Studies in Second Language Acquisition* 22, 307–336.

Dimroth, C., Gretsch, P., Jordens, P., Perdue, C. & Starren, M. (2003). Finiteness in Germanic languages: a stage-model for first and second language development. In C. Dimroth & M. Starren (Eds.), *Information structure and the dynamics of language acquisition*, 65–93. Amsterdam: John Benjamins.

Erteschik-Shir, N. (2007). *Information structure. The syntax-discourse interface*. Oxford University Press: Oxford.

Fuchs, C. (1993). Position, portée et interpretation des circonstants. Encore et les circonstants de localisation temporelle. In C. Guimier (Ed.), *1001 circonstants*, 253–283. Caen: Presses Universitaires de Caen.

Gayraud, F. (2004). Émergence et développement du placement des particules de portée. *Acquisition et Interaction en Langue Etrangère* 20, 172–196.

Giacomi, A., Meyfren, N., Stoffel, H., Tissot, H. & Véronique, D. (2000). Grammaire et discours en L2: l'appropriation des phénomènes de portée en français par des arabophones. In A. Giacomi, H. Stoffel & D. Véronique (Eds.), *Appropriation du français par des Marocains arabophones à Marseille*, 245–271. Aix-en-Provence: Publications de l'Université de Provence.

Harrell, R.S. (1962). *A short reference grammar of Moroccan Arabic*. Washington D.C.: Georgetown University Press.

Harrell, R.S. & Sobelman H. (Eds.) (2004). *A dictionary of Moroccan Arabic*. Harrell, R.S. (Ed), *Moroccan-English*. Sobelman, H. & Harrell, R.S. (Eds), *English-Moroccan*. Washington D.C.: Georgetown University Press.

Hendriks, H. (Ed.) (2005). *The structure of learner varieties*. Berlin: Mouton de Gruyter.

Klein, W. (2008). The topic situation. In B. Ahrenholz, U. Bredel, W. Klein, M. Rost-Roth, & R. Skiba (Eds.), *Empirische Forschung und Theoriebildung: Beiträge aus Soziolinguistik, Gesprochene-Sprache- und Zweitspracherwerbsforschung: Festschrift für Norbert Dittmar*, 287–305, Frankfurt am Main: Peter Lang.

Klein, W. & Perdue, C. (1997). The Basic Variety (or Couldn't natural languages be much simpler?). *Second Language Research* 13, 301–347.

König, E. (1991). *The meaning of focus particles*. London: Routledge.

Lambrecht, K. (1994). *Information structure and sentence form*. Cambridge University Press: Cambridge.

Lee, C. (2003). Contrastive Topic and/ or Contrastive Focus. In B. McClure (Ed.). *Japanese/Korean Linguistics* 12. CSLI: Stanford.

Lyons, J. (1977). *Semantics*. Cambridge: Cambridge University Press.

McCawley, J.D. (1981). *Everything that linguists have always wanted to know about logic**but were ashamed to ask*. Oxford: Basil Blackwell.

Nølke, H. (1980). Le Champ comme notion linguistique et son utilisation illustrée par un examen de ne...que. *Revue Romane* 14, 14–36.

Nølke, H. (1993). *Le regard du locuteur. Pour une linguistique des traces énonciatives*. Paris: Editions Kimé.

Perdue, C. (1984). *Second language acquisition by adult immigrants: a field manual*. Rowley, MA: Newbury House.

Perdue, C. (1996). Pre-basic varieties: the first stages of second language acquisition. *Toegepaste Taalwetenschap in Artikelen* 55, 135–150.

Perrin-Naffakh, A.-M. (1996). *Aussi* adjonctif: de la syntaxe à la sémantique. *Le français Moderne* 64, 136–154.

Quine, W.O. (1960/1977). *Word and object*. Cambridge (Mass.): MIT Press. Traduction française, *Le mot et la chose*. Paris: Flammarion.

Sanell, A. (2007). *Parcours acquisitionnel de la negation et de quelques particules de portée en français L2*, Doctoral Thesis, Stockholm University.

Sasse, H.-J. (1987). The thetic/categorical distinction revised. *Linguistics* 25, 511–580.

Starren, M. (2001). *The second time. The acquisition of temporality in dutch and french as a second language*. Utrecht: LOT.

Stutterheim von, C. & Klein, W. (1989). Text structure and referential movement. In R. Dietrich & C.F. Graumann (Eds.), *Language Processing in Social Context*, 39–67. Amsterdam: North-Holland.

Watorek, M. & Dimroth, C. (2004). Additive scope particles in advanced learner and native speaker discourse. In H. Hendriks (Ed.), *The structure of learner varieties*, 445–488. Berlin, New-York: Mouton De Gruyter.

Watorek, M. & Perdue, C. (1999). Additive particles and focus: observations from learner and native speaker production. *Linguistics* 37, 297–323.

Wehr, H. (1979). *A Dictionary of modern written Arabic*. Edited by J. Milton Cowan. Wiesbaden: Harrasowitz Verlag.

Résumé

Ce chapitre analyse l'acquisition des particules additives *aussi*, *même* et *encore* par cinq locuteurs d'arabe marocain, apprenant le français par immersion sociale et participant au programme de recherche dit ESF. A la suite d'une comparaison entre les particules de portée françaises et leurs équivalents marocains, on formule l'hypothèse que le transfert de L1 ne joue qu'un rôle indirect dans l'acquisition des particules de portée en français L2 à cause des différences sémantiques et syntaxiques entre les unités des deux langues. Le chapitre rend compte de l'émergence et de l'emploi des particules additives dans un échantillon de textes recueillis sur une période d'environ trois ans. Il établit qu'*aussi* est acquis tôt par tous les apprenants. L'appropriation de *même* est différenciée selon les apprenants; *encore* est tardivement acquise. Les résultats de cette étude sont comparés avec ceux obtenus dans des études antérieures.

Development of object clitics in child L2 French

A comparison of developmental sequences in different modes of acquisition

Jonas Granfeldt
Lund University

It has been argued that the study of child L2 development can inform different maturational accounts of language acquisition. One such specific proposal was put forward by Meisel (2008), arguing for a cut-off point for monolingual or bilingual first language acquisition — (2)L1 — type of development at 3–4 years. The paper analyses the longitudinal development of object clitics in child L2 French (L1 Swedish) and compares the developmental sequence in child L2 learners (n = 7) with different Ages of onset of Acquisition (AoA) (from 3;0 to 6;5) to the adult L2 sequence that was found in previous studies (Granfeldt & Schlyter 2004). The study also includes age-matched simultaneous bilingual children (n = 3) and monolingual controls (n = 5). The results show that some of the child L2 learners with an AoA over 4 years display structures that are typical of adult L2 acquisition, whereas these structures were not found in the simultaneous bilingual children or in the child second language acquisition (cL2) children with an AoA under 4 years. It is suggested that differences in developmental sequences are due to a combination of AoA and the level of L1 linguistic development at the onset of L2 acquisition.

1. Introduction

The growing body of research on child L2 (cL2) development (e.g. Schwartz 2004a, 2004b; Unsworth 2005; Haznedar & Gavruseva 2008; Meisel 2008) allows for a renewed discussion of maturational accounts of language acquisition. There are both theoretical and empirical justifications for including the study of cL2 development in this context. Theoretically, cL2 acquisition is highly relevant since, as Schwarz (2004b: 63) puts it, "the L2 child might just be the perfect natural experience". The

L2 child is, at the Age of onset of Acquisition (AoA), more cognitively mature than the L1 child but less mature than the adult L2 learner. With respect to L1 influence, there is by definition an existing L1 present in both adult L2 and child L2 acquisition, but depending on the exact AoA of the L2 child the L1 system will be developed to different degrees. These characteristics, Schwartz (2004b) argues, make cL2 acquisition an ideal test case to tease apart conflicting theories of acquisition. From an empirical point of view, the current situation for researching cL2 development is also promising. There is by now a considerable body of comparative research on monolingual, bilingual L1 (2L1) and adult L2 (aL2) grammatical development in many language combinations.[1] From this research we have substantial knowledge about the properties of grammars at the early or even the initial stage(s), and we know something about the route and rate of grammatical development, i.e. about the developmental sequences of specific grammatical features. If we now analyse new sets of L2 data where the learners were first exposed to the L2 at, for example, age 4 and if we were to find the adult L2 rather than the child L1 developmental sequence for a particular feature, then we have a possible argument in favour of maturational constraints on language acquisition where the effects are seen in early childhood.

Applying this research design, Meisel (2008) studied child L2 learners of French (L1 German) and analysed a set of grammatical features for which the main L1 and L2 developmental properties are thought to be known from previous research. In particular, Meisel analysed the co-occurrence of subject pronouns and seemingly non-finite verb forms in declarative phrases, as in e.g. *il cassE* ('he break/s'), which is a relatively frequent construction in early adult L2 acquisition (Thomas 2009) but virtually lacking at any stage of L1 mono- or bilingual acquisition of French (Meisel 1994; Schlyter 2003). Meisel also looked at subject clitic doubling (structures like *le chat$_i$ il$_i$ grimpe* 'the cat$_i$ he$_i$ climbs') which has also been shown to be a distinctive feature in the comparison between L1 and L2 acquisition of French (Granfeldt & Schlyter 2004). Meisel found that in the cL2 children he studied both these features initially seemed to display properties comparable to adult L2 acquisition of French. On the basis of this and other data, Meisel (2008) suggested the following tentative age ranges for different modes of acquisition:

Table 1 says that, if exposed to a new language at or below the age of 3 years, the child will develop this language as a 2L1, a case of multiple L1 acquisition. If the AoA is between 4 years and 8 years, it will be an instance of cL2 development.

---

1. The seminal work of Inge Bartning on the acquisition of French by adult Swedish learners has been crucial in this respect. Bartning and the *InterFra* group have often focused on the advanced learners whereas we will continue the tradition of the Lund research group and focus on the early and intermediate stages of development in the acquisition of French.

Table 1. Tentative age ranges (adapted from Meisel 2008: 59)

Mode of acquisition	Age of Onset of Acquisition
2L1	≤ 3 years
child L2	≥ 4 years
adult L2	≥ 8 years

From 8 years onwards we can expect adult L2 acquisition. Note that in this model it is no longer a simple question of two modes of acquisition — L1 or L2 — but a tripartite distinction where child L2 development represents a mode on its own, with some aspects being more closely related to L1 acquisition and others closer to adult L2 acquisition. A similar idea has been put forward by Schwartz (2004a), who suggests that cL2 learners resemble L1 children in the domain of bound morphology but not in the domain of syntax (cf. the Domain-by-age model). Meisel argues that it is precisely the other way around: in the domain of syntax the cL2 children resemble L1 children, whereas (bound) morphology develops as in adult L2.

Complement pronouns or object clitics in French, and more generally the grammatical process of cliticisation, is another domain where previous research has shown that there are empirical differences between the acquisition of (2)L1 and adult L2 (Granfeldt & Schlyter 2004; Herschensohn 2004; Hamann & Belletti 2008). Object clitics are interesting because they rely on the one hand on the argument structure of verbs, which is normally an early feature, but on the other hand clitics appear in French in non-canonical positions for arguments, to the left of the main verb. At the level of syntax, cliticisation can be described as the process by which the internal argument of verb moves from its base position to the right of the verb to some position higher up in the structure (see Figure 1 in the next section).

In previous work by Granfeldt and Schlyter (2004) it was found that 2L1 children, aged 2 to 3 years, applied cliticisation in French from early on, whereas it took adults (with L1 Swedish) more than three years of exposure in an immersion setting to develop cliticisation in French. Consider the following example from one of our adult L2 learners:

(1) on prend **le** gaz et refroidir **le** / on refroidir **le** dedans.
one takes the gas and cool.INF it / one cool.INF it in.there
('one takes the gas and cools it off / one cools it off in there')
Karl 2, aL2[2]

---

[2]. Orthographic transcription is used throughout. The sign / indicates a break. Elements of specific interest are in boldface. Learner names are pseudonyms and numbers indicate recording (e.g. Karl 2).

We argued that in (1) cliticisation fails to apply because Karl, who is at the initial stages of development, misanalyses clitic forms and assigns them the same properties as lexical NPs (or DPs in our terminology), like *le gaz* ('the gas') in the above example. In Granfeldt and Schlyter (2004) it was claimed that Karl's lack of cliticisation at this stage was due to an age-related preference for treating all arguments syntactically as lexical expressions. We followed Rizzi (1998) in accounting for this initial preference:

(2) Categorial Uniformity: Assume a unique canonical structural realization for a given semantic type. (Rizzi 1998: 33)

If Karl is assuming Categorial Uniformity, a principle of Universal Grammar, he will assign a uniform analysis to all objects, i.e. to the DP *le gaz* and to the object clitic pronoun *le* rather than assigning them two separate representations. We based our conclusion that (2) is a "maturational preference" on the finding that Swedish-French 2L1 children did not pass through a stage of development where cliticisation is lacking. At no point of development did the bilingual children produce structures comparable to (1), even though Swedish was present as "the other language" in these children and Swedish does not have obligatory cliticisation of the French type (see details below). However, at the time of publication no child L2 data with the same language combination were available, so the account could not be properly evaluated. In this paper some of the analyses in Granfeldt and Schlyter (2004) will be replicated on longitudinal data from cL2 learners with different AoAs. We ask the question whether child L2 learners go through a stage where (1) is possible. In order to control for possible L1 influence and to isolate AoA as the independent variable, cL2 development will be compared with age-matched 2L1 learners from the same setting and with the same language combination (Swedish-French).

The paper is organised as follows. In the next section we present a framework for the description and analysis of pronouns. Section 3 reports on relevant findings in the acquisition of object clitics in French. Section 4 presents the rationale and research questions and is followed by a methodological section where data, procedures and analysis are introduced. Section 6 presents the majority of the results, which are summarised and discussed at the end.

2. A framework for the study of pronouns

2.1 Pronouns in French

Cardinaletti and Starke (1999) argued that pronouns generally come in three different classes: strong, weak and clitic. In French two of the three classes are clearly represented, the strong (or tonic, or disjoint) and clitic pronouns.[3] Strong and clitic forms are with two exceptions (*nous/vous*) morphologically distinct. Accusative and dative clitics generally overlap, with the exception of 3rd person where distinctive dative forms exist (*lui/leur*). French 3rd person accusative object clitics are homophonous with definite articles (*le/la/les*).

In Cardinaletti and Starke's typology the three classes of pronouns display asymmetries in their use at different linguistic levels. With respect to syntax only strong pronouns can be co-ordinated (3a), can occur in isolation (3b) or in peripheral position and can be modified by adverbs (3c).

(3) a. *Il / Lui et son frère sont arrivés hier.
he.WEAK/CLITIC / he.STRONG and his brother are arrived yesterday
('He and his brother arrived yesterday'.)

b. A: Qui l'a fait?
who it.CLITIC-has done
('Who did it?'.)

B: Moi / *Je
me.STRONG / I.WEAK/CLITIC
('I did'.)

c. C'est *il / lui seul qui sait le faire.
it-is he.WEAK/CL(ITIC) / he.STRONG only who can it.CL do
('He is the only one who can do it'.)

The above examples also demonstrate that at the syntactic level strong pronouns such as *moi* and *lui* behave like full nominal expressions, DPs, whereas weak and clitic pronouns do not. Clitics need to be closely related to their verbal 'hosts'.

Cardinaletti and Starke (1999) argue that these and other asymmetries in the distribution and interpretation of the three different classes of pronouns are due to the amount of internal structure that they project. Specifically, clitic and weak pronouns are 'structurally deficient' in the sense that they project less internal structure than strong pronouns.

---

3. Subject pronouns are considered to be clitics in informal registers of French, but it can be argued that French also has weak subject pronouns in formal, especially written, French (see Granfeldt & Schlyter 2004: 386 for discussion).

(4) Clitic < Weak < Strong
    X⁰   XP   XP

It is central to Cardinaletti and Starke, and to the discussion developed here, to regard the weak and clitic pronouns as structurally reduced variants of strong pronouns. Strong pronouns are assumed to have the same internal structure as referential expressions (proper nouns and lexical DPs) and they are predicted to share the syntactic, semantic and prosodic properties of lexical DPs (like e.g. *la femme, les enfants,* etc.). Strong and weak pronouns are phrasal elements in syntax, XPs, whereas clitics are heads, X⁰. This is because clitics lack some of the inherent properties of strong and weak pronouns and therefore clitics need to move and attach to a 'host' in order to 'make up' for these properties.

A movement analysis of object clitics (Kayne 1975) is adopted and it will be assumed together with Cardinaletti and Starke that the movement takes place in two steps. The first movement is an instance of A-movement of an XP to the specifier of an intermediate functional category, SpecAgrOP as suggested by Hamann *et al.* (1996). The second movement is an instance of head movement where the object clitic ends up as a head cliticised onto I⁰.

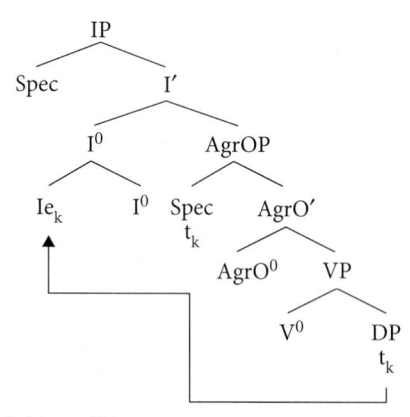

Figure 1. Movement of object clitics

2.2 Pronouns in Swedish

Swedish object pronouns (*mig, dig, honom/henne/den/det, oss, er, dem*) always appear postverbally and are normally considered to be strong pronouns (Hellan & Platzack 1999). Unlike in German and Dutch, they cannot occur in front of the non-finite verb, as in (5a) (*cf.* 5b).

(5) a. *Jag har den sett.
        I   have it seen

b. Jag har sett den
('I have seen it.')

Swedish object pronouns can scramble and they are then analysed as weak in the position between the finite verb and the negation (Hellan & Platzack 1999: 127). In some dialects and informal registers complement pronouns may be cliticised onto the verb. In these cases the pronoun is enclitic to the verb and is produced with strong phonetic reduction:

(6) Jag såg'na   igår   (non-clitic: jag såg henne)
     I   saw-her.CL yesterday
     ('I saw her yesterday.')

According to Cardinaletti and Starke (1999: 65), pronouns like the one in (6) should be analysed as syntactic clitics, which would then imply that clitic complement pronouns are not excluded in Swedish. However, fundamental differences between Swedish and French exist. In French complement pronouns cliticise obligatorlily while this is optional in Swedish and, when they do cliticise, they become enclitic to the verb.

3. Previous research on the acquisition of object clitics

Previous research on the acquisition of object clitics in French has identified three, possibly related, areas where (2)L1 children and/or aL2 learners differ from adult native speaker use: the delay effect of object clitics as compared to subject clitics in (2)L1 acquisition (Jackubowicz *et al.* 1998 among others), early omissions of object clitics (e.g. Herschensohn 2004; Grüter 2006; Pérez-Leroux *et al.* 2009 among others), and placement errors of object clitics (e.g. Towell & Hawkins 1994; White 1996; Hulk 2000; Granfeldt & Schlyter 2004; Belletti & Hamann 2004). For reasons of space, the focus here is on the last property, placement errors of object clitics.

3.1 Placement errors of object clitics in acquisition data

Only placement of object clitics in declaratives is included in this section. The focus is mainly on target deviant structures that are found in data from children in different modes of acquisition, although such occurrences are not very frequent. There are five positions that will be discussed below. Three are target positions and two are non-target positions.

(7) a. *Je vois le   I see it/him   Post-verbal, *V(ERB) CL(ITIC)
     b. Je le vois   I it see   Pre-lexical finite verb CL V

    c. Je veux le voir   I want it see   Intermediate position, Mod(al)Aux CL V
    d. *J'ai le vu   I have it seen   Intermediate position *Temp(oral)Aux CL V
    e. Je l'ai vu   I it have seen   Pre-temporal auxiliary position, CL TempAux V

Note that both (7c) and (7d) are labelled intermediate positions but that only (7c) is target-like. Note also that with respect to clitic status it is clear that the post-verbal position (7a) is indicative of a position where the 'clitic' cannot be analysed as a true clitic because it has not moved out of the VP.

3.1.1 *L1 acquisition*

Non-target placements of object clitics have never been documented in monolingual L1 acquisition (see the overview in Belletti & Hamann 2008). Not a single placement error was found in the large Geneva corpus of three L1 children studied longitudinally (Rasetti 2003). The same finding has been reported for other monolingual children (Hamann et al. 1996; Jakubowicz et al. 1996). According to Jakubowicz et al. (1996), L1 children use all three target positions in declarative clauses correctly (*cf.* 7b, 7c and 7e above) from the time they start producing object clitics, around 2;6 to 3;0.

3.1.2 *2L1 acquisition*

Non-target placements of object clitics have occasionally been found in 2L1 acquisition of French. The post-verbal position (*cf.* 7a) was never found in the Swedish-French (2)L1 children studied by Granfeldt and Schlyter (2004). To our knowledge, the only 2L1 child who has been reported producing clitics in this position is Anouk (Dutch-French) from Hulk (2000):

   (8) Je prends **la**   Anouk 3;03,23; Hulk (2000)
       ('I take it/her')

The intermediate incorrect position (*cf.* 7d above), on the other hand, is well-attested in corpora from (2)L1 children with different linguistic backgrounds:

   (9) a. T'as **le** mis trop chaud   Anouk 3;06,25; Hulk (2000), L1=Dutch
          ('you have it put too hot')
      b. Après il a se réveillé   Ivar 3;02,14; Crysmann and Müller (2000),
          ('then he has himself woken up')   L1=German

In Granfeldt and Schlyter (2004) the intermediate correct position (7c) and the pre-lexical finite verb position (7b) appeared somewhat before the pretemporal auxiliary position (7e), which might then constitute a delay compared to L1 monolinguals where such a sequence has not been reported (Jakubowicz et al. 1996).

3.1.3 cL2 acquisition

While a number of studies on cL2 acquisition have focused on object (clitic) omissions (e.g. Grüter 2006; Prévost 2006), relatively few studies have dealt with the development of object clitic placement in cL2 learners. In her study of the cL2 learners Greg and Kenny (L1=English), White (1996: 356) says that "[a] rare number of such errors is found in the data from Greg in later interviews". Kenny never produced object clitic forms in postverbal position.

(12) Moi, j'ai trouvé **le**   Greg month 14 ; White (1996)
      ('me, I have found it')

Belletti and Hamann (2004) also report occurrences of this position in the spontaneous production of Elisa, a German-French cL2 child. They accounted for this position by assuming transfer from German:

(13) non, on laisse **le**   Elisa 4 ;2 ; Belletti and Hamann (2004)
      ('no one leaves him')

It is interesting to note that, in the case of Elisa, the AoA for French was as low as 2;8. This comes close to one of the cL2 children analysed in the present paper.

3.1.4 Adult L2 acquisition

Although placement errors of object clitics are relatively rare in terms of raw occurrences, placement errors can be used to distinguish adult L2 acquisition of French from other modes of acquisition (Towell & Hawkins 1994; Granfeldt & Schlyter 2004; Herschensohn 2004). Granfeldt and Schlyter (2004) found that the post-verbal position appeared early:

(14) Petra 1, aL2
      elle demande **la**. / elle croit **la**.
      ('she asks her / she believes her')

In Granfeldt and Schlyter (2004) it was suggested that the intermediate positions (*cf.* 7c and 7d above) represented a later step in the developmental sequence of aL2 learners, after the post-verbal:

(15) Karl 2, aL2
      a. je peux **le** faire ...
          ('I can it do')
      b. *j'ai # j'ai **le** vu
          ('I.have I.have it seen')

At least some adult L2 learners acquire all positions of object clitics, including the position before the temporal auxiliary (*cf.* 7e). This structure represents the last step in the developmental sequence, which was attained by naturalistic learners after some 3 years of exposure (Towell & Hawkins 1994; Granfeldt & Schlyter 2004).

3.1.5 *Developmental sequences for object clitics*

Table 2 summarises the developmental sequences known from the literature with respect to the placement of object clitics (note that omission stages are not taken into consideration here).

Table 2. Developmental sequences for object clitics in different modes of acquisition

Stage	L1 sequence	2L1 sequence	Adult L2 sequence
1	All target positions	Pre-verbal and intermediate positions (*je le vois* / **j'ai le vu* / *je veux le voir*)	Post-verbal position **je vois le*
2		Pre-temporal auxiliary position (*je l'ai vu*)	Pre-verbal and intermediate positions (*je le vois* / **j'ai le vu* / *je veux le voir*)
3			Pre-temporal auxiliary position (*je l'ai vu*)

As can be seen from Table 2, the post-verbal position is potentially unique to L2 acquisition of French.

4. Rationale and research question

Object clitics in French have previously been studied in a (2)L1 child — adult L2 comparative perspective and differences in developmental sequences have been found. Much less research has targeted child L2 development. The present study addresses the general question of AoA effects on linguistic development, and in particular the ages ranges proposed by Meisel (2008). The study addresses the following two research questions:

RQ1. Do child L2 learners of French (L1 Swedish) follow the adult L2 developmental sequence over time with respect to object clitic placement?

RQ2. Do child L2 learners of French (L1 Swedish) with AoA under *vs* over 4 years (*cf.* Meisel 2008) follow different developmental sequences over time with respect to object clitic placement?

5. Method and data

5.1 Data and linguistic situation of the children studied

The data were collected within a project focusing on the role of AoA for linguistic development in French (*Startålder och språklig utveckling i franska*) carried out at the University of Lund, Sweden.

The children studied all come from one and the same (pre-)school of the Lycée Français Saint Louis (LFSL) of Stockholm. The LFSL is a French school, accepting children with a somewhat varying background:

a. French-speaking children staying for a short time in Stockholm (L1 group)
b. Bilingual children with one French-speaking parent (2L1 group)
c. A few Swedish-speaking children with two Swedish-speaking parents (cL2 group)

The cL2 children have in principle no French at home and they enter the school either in pre-school, which results in an AoA of around 3–4 years, or in primary school, which leads to an AoA of around 6 years. These cL2 children spend the entire day at school and are almost exclusively exposed to French by the teachers and by their French-speaking peers.

5.2 Data collection procedures

Recordings were made in Swedish and in French four times per school year at regular intervals over a three-year period. Data collection for some of the cL2 children with AoA around 3–4 years is not completed. Tables 3, 4 and 5 present relevant information (mode of acquisition, age range, time of exposure range and range of MLU in words) about the children studied.

As can be seen from Table 5, two of the children, Rachel and Fia, had an AoA in French under 4 years, two children, Patrick and Tony had an AoA of 4 years and some month and three children, Viola, Hannes and Valentine, had an AoA of 6 years and some months.

Time of exposure for the cL2 children was computed on the basis of the school year, excluding two months of summer vacation. Note that the child Tony left the school soon after the recordings began, which explains why there is only one recording with this child.

Recordings were made at the school, in a separate room, with a native French speaker and a native Swedish speaker as principal interviewer in the respective settings. The language situations of French and Swedish were clearly separated.

Each recording session included two different types of procedures:

Table 3. The L1 children

Child / rec	AoA	Age	MLUw
Lorette	Birth	5;1	4.1
Paul	Birth	5;2	3.9
Noa	Birth	5;5	4.9
Lucie	Birth	5;5	4.2
André	Birth	6;5	4.0
Antoine	Birth	6;5	8.6

Table 4. The 2L1 children

Child / recs	AoA	Age range	MLUw range
Lars 1–4	Birth	5;9–7;9	2.6–3.9
Linnea 1–4	Birth	5;9–7;5	4.3–8.2
Louise 1–5	Birth	5;9–7;9	3.4–9.4

Table 5. The cL2 children

Child / rec(s)	AoA	Age range	Exposure range	MLUw range
Rachel 1–5	3;5	3;7–5;0	4–18 months	1.2–5.6
Fia 1–4	3;0	3;3–3;10	3–13 months	0–3.4
Tony 1	4;5	5;0	7 months	3.5
Patrick 1–4	4;8	6;3–7;6	17–30 months	2.6–3.5
Viola 1–7	6;5	6;11–9;4	7–30 months	2.3–4.8
Hannes 1–7	6;6	7;1–9;0	7–27 months	4.7–9.6
Valent. 1–7	6;7	7;2–9;1	7–28 months	5.4–7.7

- Free conversations about the past and the future (in order to elicit tense markings).
- Different elicitation tasks in order to elicit specific grammatical constructions or form (object clitics, hypothetical conditionals, passives, tense, narratives).

The object clitic elicitation procedure consisted of 12 pictures describing a boy or a girl, an event and an object. The procedure created a natural context for anaphoric use of an object clitic in the child's response. Consider example (16).

(16) *INV: on a Félix encore mais qu'est-ce-qu'il a dans la main Félix ?
('we have Félix again but what does he have in his hand Felix')
*CHI: un [Sic !] balle.
('a ball')

*INV: une balle et qu+est+ce+qu'il va faire avec la balle ?
('a ball and what is he going to do with the ball')
*CHI: il va **la** jeter.
('he will it(cl) throw')
*INV: très bien.
('very good')

Among the 12 items there were three different target structures in order to create contexts for different positions of the object clitic:

4 pictures targeted CL V (*cf.* 9b)
4 pictures targeted Mod CL V$_{[inf]}$ (*cf.* 9c)
4 pictures targeted CL TempAux V$_{[ptc]}$ (*cf.* 9e)

For the purpose of this study all occurrences in the transcriptions were pooled.

The data were transcribed by students or members of the research team. For this purpose the CLAN editor was used, and the transcriptions follow the mid-CHAT transcription conventions (MacWhinney 2000) with some project-specific additions. All transcriptions were checked by a second member of the research team. Divergences were discussed between the transcribers where necessary.

6. Results

6.1 Object clitic placement in the L1 children

Jakubowicz *et al.* (1996) had found that L1 monolingual children use all positions available with object pronouns from the time they start producing object pronouns. Not a single occurrence of a misplaced object pronoun has occurred in

Table 6. Distribution of object clitics (ocl) in L1 children (all data)

	Age	Distribution of object pronouns				
Structure		*V CL	*TempAux CL V	ModV CL V$_{[inf]}$	CL V$_{[fin]}$	CL TempAux V$_{[ptc]}$
Example		*je vois le	*j'ai le vu	je veux le voir	je le vois	je l'ai vu
Child						
Lorette	5;1	–	–	3/3	5/5	4/4
Paul	5;2	–	–	4/4	8/8	7/7
Noa	5;5	–	–	7/7	8/8	5/5
Lucie	5;5	–	–	5/5	8/8	2/2
Total		–	–	18/18	29/29	18/18

any corpora of L1 children (Rasetti 2003; Hamann & Belletti 2008). The results in Table 6 confirm this picture. In total 65 occurrences of pronominal objects were found in the four L1 children. Not a single occurrence of a misplaced pronoun was found. Furthermore, all three target positions in declarative sentences were used, including the position before the temporal auxiliary (e.g. *je l'ai vu*). This is the last position to emerge in adult L2 acquisition.

6.2 Object clitic placement in the 2L1 children

The results in Table 7 show that in two of the 2L1 children, Lars and Linnea, there are in total six non-target occurrences. These occurrences appear in the so-called intermediate position, between the temporal auxiliary and the past participle (e.g. *j'ai le vu*). These occurrences confirm findings in the literature suggesting that 2L1 children may occasionally use this position (Belletti & Hamann 2004; Hamann & Belletti 2008). All of these occurrences, with one single exception, appear in the very first recording of each of the two children (Lars 1 and Linnea 1). On a more careful analysis, we see that in these very recordings there is in fact a complete *complementary distribution* between object clitics in the intermediate position and the CL TempAux V[$_{ptc}$] position (e.g. *je l'ai vu*), indicative of stage 3 in the developmental sequence of adult L2 learners. To illustrate this point, we can look at Lars' production in his first recording.

Lars produces two contexts for this pre-temporal auxiliary position, but on both occasions he places the object incorrectly between the temporal auxiliary and the verb:

(17) Lars 1, Age 5;9
    *INV: elle lui met un pansement ?
          ('she him puts on a band-aid')
    *CHI: oui.
    *INV: pourquoi ?
    *CHI: qu'il a **se** fait mal.
          ('"cause he has himself hurt')
    *ASS: avec quoi ?
          ('with what')
    *CHI: un pansement.
          ('a sticking plaster')
    *ASS: et où est+ce+qu'il a trouvé le pansement ?
          ('and where has he found the sticking plaster')
    *CHI: le oiseau [= zoiseau] il a **t**'aidé
          ('the bird he has you(him) helped')

Table 7. Distribution of ocl in 2L1 children (all data)

Structure		*V CL	*TempAux CL V	ModAux CL V$_{[inf]}$	CL V$_{[fin]}$	CL TempAux V$_{[ptc]}$
Example		*je vois le	*j'ai le vu	je veux le voir	je le vois	je l'ai vu
Child (rec)	Age					
Lars 1	5;9	–	2	1/1	2/2	0/2
Lars 2–3	6;2–7;6	–	1	4/4	10/10	2/3
Lars 4	7;9	–	–	–	7/7	4/4
Linnea 1	5;9	–	3	3/3	9/9	0/3
Linnea 2	6;9	–	–	6/6	10/10	5/5
Louise 1	5;9	–	–	4/4	2/2	–
Louise 2–4	6;9–7;6	–	–	17/17	12/12	5/5
TOT		–	6	35/35	45/45	16/22

The data suggest that the CL TempAux V[$_{ptc}$] structures (e.g. *je l'ai vu*) emerge, and are possibly acquired, in the second or third recording of the 2L1 children, and thus we find signs of a development with respect to placement of the object clitics still at age 5 to 6 years. This confirms a similar observation made in Granfeldt and Schlyter (2004) for other 2L1 children, suggesting a delayed development as compared to L1 monolingual children (*cf.* also Pérez-Leroux et al. 2009 for results on delay in English-French bilinguals with respect to object clitic omissions). The new data analysed here, however, indicate a considerably longer delay than previously thought.

Nevertheless, despite not mastering placement of object clitics, the 2L1 children do not produce occurrences of clitics in the post-verbal position. The same result was found in our previous study with younger 2L1 children between 2 and 3 years (Granfeldt & Schlyter 2004). Crucially for the purposes of the present paper, it can be concluded that the post-verbal position is not part of the developmental sequence in the acquisition of 2L1 French where the other language is Swedish.

6.3 Object clitic placement in the cL2 children with AoA over 4 years

Turning now to the distribution of complement pronouns in the cL2 children, we first look at the five children with an AoA of above four years. In three out of the five children studied here, we find evidence of structures at the Stage 1 of development, the post-verbal position (**je vois le* type). As in previous research (Towell & Hawkins 1994; Granfeldt & Schlyter 2004; Hamann & Belletti 2008), raw numbers are small, in this case six occurrences. Examples are presented below:

(18) a. Tony 1 (AoA 4;5) Age 5;0, Exposure 7 months
 *CHI: il va casser **le**
        ('he will break it')
 b. Viola 1 (AoA 6;4) Age 6;11, Exposure 7 months
 *INV: et qu+est+ce+qu'il fait ?
        ('and what does he do')
 *CHI: mange **le**
        ('eat it.')
 c. Valentine 2–3 (AoA 6;6) Age 7;11–8;2, Exposure 12–15 months
 *CHI: et après il y avait deux garçons qui étaient amoureux de **les**
        ('and then there were two boys who were in love with them')

Two factors make these rare occurrences important with respect to the overall research questions. First, we can confirm again that only L2 learners produce occurrences of post-verbal clitic placement, (2)L1 children do not. Post-verbal placement of complement pronouns could thus be a specific and discriminative feature of L2 acquisition of French (where the L1 is Swedish or possibly another Germanic language). Second, the post-verbal occurrences systematically appear in the very first recording(s), i.e. in the early stages of acquisition. The post-verbal placement of complement pronouns is thus confirmed to be a Stage 1 structure. In the same recordings there are no or very rare evidence for Stage 3 structures. In fact only one child, Valentine, shows an overlap between the stages in her first three recordings.

With the exception of Valentine, occurrences of the ungrammatical intermediate position (*TempAux CL V) are in complementary distribution with occurrences of the post-verbal position (*V CL). In other words, we do not tend to find an overlap of post-verbal object pronouns and ungrammatical intermediate object pronouns. Even though it is not completely systematic in the data it, would seem as if the ungrammatical *TempAux CL V position emerges after the post-verbal position (*cf.* Patrick 3–4 and Viola 6). This can be interpreted as additional evidence of the cL2 children following the adult L2 developmental sequence.

Finally and most importantly, the cL2 children with AoA above 4 years reach the third stage of development and produce CL TempAux V$_{[ptc]}$ structures (e.g. *je l'ai vu*) in the last recordings analysed here. This happens after approximately two years of exposure.

Overall, these findings point to a relatively systematic emergence and development of object clitics in the child L2 learners with AoA above 4 years. The development sequence thus resembles the one in adult L2 development.

Table 8. Distribution of ocl in cL2 children (all data)

Structure		*V CL	*TempAux CL V	ModAux CL V$_{[inf]}$	CL V$_{[fin]}$	CL TempAux V$_{[ptc]}$
Example		*je vois le	*j'ai le vu	je veux le voir	je le vois	Je l'ai vu
Child (rec)	AoA					
Rachel 1–2	3;5	–	–	–	–	–
Rachel 3		–	–	1/1	–	–
Rachel 4–6		–	–	1/1	4/4	6/6
Fia 1–2	3;0	–	–	–	–	–
Fia 3		–	–	2/2	–	–
Fia 4		–	2	3/3	1/1	0/2
Tony	4;5	2	–	0/1	1/1	–
Patrick 1–2	4;8	–	–	3/3	–	–
Patrick 3–4		–	3	5/5	2/2	0/3
Viola 1	6;5	1	–	–	0/1	–
Viola 2–5		–	–	–	6/6	–
Viola 6		–	1	1/1	2/2	0/1
Viola 7		–	1	5/5	7/7	4/5
Hannes 1–2	6;6	–	2	3/3	1/1	0/2
Hannes 4–5		–	3	–	7/7	3/6
Hannes 6–7		–	–	9/9	3/3	10/10
Valent. 1–3	6;7	3	3	6/6	8/8	3/6
Valent. 4–6		–	4	5/5	3/4	3/6
Valent. 7		–	–	4/4	5/5	4/4
Total		6	19			

6.4 Object clitic placement in the cL2 children with AoA under 4 years

Turning to the two younger children with AoA in French under 4 years, Rachel and Fia, we find both differences and similarities compared to the older children. First, Table 8 shows that if object clitic forms appear in the first recordings after some seven months of exposure in the older cL2 learners (with AoA over 4), it takes somewhat longer before they appear in the recordings with Rachel and Fia (ten months). The later appearance in the younger children is most probably an effect of AoA. Second, the same table shows that neither of the two children with AoA under 4 years produces any post-verbal occurrences of object clitics (e.g. *je vois le*). This result would be in line with a cut-off point between 3 and 4 years for L1 type of development, as suggested by Meisel (2008). Since, however, no occurrences of the post-verbal position were found in two of the children with AoA above 4 years either, the issue cannot be settled on the basis of this data (see further discussion below).

Some other properties of object clitics in the younger children, however, point to other qualitative differences with respect to adult L2 learners. In the recordings Rachel 4 and 5 object clitics appear more regularly and quite soon they also appear in the pre-temporal auxiliary position (e.g. *je l'ai vu*).

(19) Rachel 5 (AoA 3;4) Age: 4;8, Exposure: 14 months
 *CHI: il a donné Lille Skutt et Bamse, mais pas Skalman.
  ('he has given (to) Lille Skutt and Bamse but not (to) Skalman')
 *CHI: mais moi je l'a vu, Skalman.
  ('but me I him have seen, Skalman')

The right-dislocated proper noun in (19) is interesting. Right-dislocation is a frequent construction in French L1 child data but more or less lacking in adult L2 French, at least at low and intermediate stages of development. In fact, structures similar to (19) are also found in Fia 3, even though the interpretation is less clear than in the previous example:

(20) Fia 3 (AoA 3;0) Age 3;10, Exposure 10 months
 *INV: alors regarde qu+est+ce+qu'il fait là ?
  ('so look what does he do there')
 *CHI: veut **le** manger le petite chat
  ('wants it eat the small cat')

Further research is needed to determine the exact significance of (right-)dislocated structures in child L2 French with different AoAs. In the data analysed so far right-dislocation seems to appear in the children with AoA under 4 years but not in the children with AoA over 4 years.

7. Summary and discussion

The objective of this study was to analyse the longitudinal development of object clitics in child L2 learners of French with different AoAs. The development of object clitics has previously been studied in a (2)L1-adult L2 comparative perspective and differences have been found (Granfeldt & Schlyter 2004). A specific adult L2 developmental sequence of object clitics has previously been argued for. Therefore, the following research questions were developed:

RQ1. Do child L2 learners of French (L1 Swedish) follow the adult L2 developmental sequence over time with respect to object clitic placement?
RQ2. Do child L2 learners of French (L1 Swedish) with AoA under *vs* over 4 years (*cf.* Meisel 2008) follow different developmental sequences over time with respect to object clitic placement?

With respect to RQ1 it was found that three out of the seven cL2 children produced structures compatible with the first stage of development in adult L2 (e.g. **je vois le*). In all seven cL2 children there was evidence of a developmental sequence such that the pre-finite lexical verb (*cf.* 9b) and/or the intermediate position (correct or incorrect, *cf.* 9c and 9d) emerged before the pre-temporal auxiliary structure (*cf.* 9e). As in previous research reported in the literature, the post-verbal position of object clitics turned out to be a discriminative feature of L2 acquisition. An analysis of three age-matched 2L1 children from the same school showed that these children did not produce occurrences of the post-verbal position even though they were still in a phase where they did not yet completely master all target positions. With respect to RQ2 it was found that the younger children with AoA below 4 years did not produce structures of the post-verbal type, the only position which is truly incompatible with a clitic status. The three children who did produce this structure all had an AoA above 4 years.

The empirical conclusion so far has to be that the crucial post-verbal position of object clitics is a possible, but not obligatory, first stage of development in child L2 French, at least when the AoA is over 4 years.[4] How can this individual variation be explained? Besides a trivial but obvious explanation of a sampling effect, the data also allow for a more principled discussion, and the paper will end with a sketch of a possible account that integrates the age ranges proposed by Meisel (2008) but offers a somewhat different explanation for them.

What the findings suggest is that at least some of the children with an AoA above 4 years initially treat French object pronouns as weak or possibly even strong pronouns. Arguably, these children initially assign a uniform XP-representation to all objects which results in both lexical DPs (*la maison*, 'the house', etc.) and object 'clitics' (*le, la, les,* etc.) in post-verbal position. In other words they do not apply cliticisation systematically and the pronoun stays, at least occasionally, in its base position (*cf.* Figure 1). Granfeldt and Schlyter (2004) argued for precisely this interpretation of the adult L2 learners and accounted for the findings by assuming

---

4. In fact, omission of the clitic is the first stage of both (2)L1 and cL2 acquisition but we do not deal with omissions here. A thorough study of object clitic omissions would, in our view, have to deal with object omissions in the childrens' language more generally and this is beyond the scope of the present article.

that Categorial Uniformity was guiding initial stages of adult L2 acquisition (see example (2) above).

The data in this study suggested that at least some children with an AoA of above 4 years start out with the same initial representations of object "clitics". What we argue here is that the development of the other language, the L1, is important for a principle like CU in initial stages of L2 development, and that this can account for the differences between the 2L1 children and the cL2 learners on the one hand and for the possible difference between the cL2 learners with different AoAs on the other. Moreover, this interpretation is in fact in line with the cut-off point around 3–4 years as suggested by Meisel (2008). But rather than a general cognitive maturational approach, we want to argue for a specific linguistic developmental approach where the degree of (structural) development of the L1 plays a central role and, in turn, leads to a transfer of representation.

We follow Rizzi (1998, 2005) in thinking that CU does not come into play at the initial stages of L1 grammatical acquisition.

> As for development, we can think that the issue of categorial uniformity does not arise in the initial period, when the child's system only deals with root declaratives. […] The issue of uniformity only arises <u>when the child has mastered embedded declaratives</u> […]. (Rizzi 1998: 34, emphasis added)

Rizzi suggests that CU is dependent on linguistic development to become active. It is only when the child starts producing subordinate clauses that the issue of a uniform structure of all declarative clauses becomes important. Put simply, it is only when children acquire subordination, realisations of the C-system, that they realise that root declaratives also should be analysed as CP-clauses. The uniformity principle might first become an issue in the acquisition of phrase structure in the L1, but then it can be assumed to be at play independently of linguistic structure and independently of type of acquisition (L2, L3 etc.). If we believe that CU is important for the initial stage of L2 acquisition and we want to know when such a principle might start to become active for the child, we could look at the age when subordination emerges in the first language. By what age do children acquire subordination in Swedish?

Håkansson and Hansson (2007: 157) say in their overview of stages of grammatical development in Swedish that different types of subordinate clauses are acquired between 3 and 4 years. This coincides exactly with the time-span that Meisel (2008) suggests to be end-point of (2)L1-type of acquisition. If this account is on the right track it has the potential of being precise. The point in time when uniformity becomes a factor will vary somewhat in different languages and in different learners, depending on a range of external and internal factors such as language-specific properties, frequency of use, saliency of the involved elements, language aptitude etc. (see Ågren *et al.* submitted, for discussion of the effects of external factors on the rate of development in these children). Håkansson and Hansson (2007) note, for example, that Swedish children develop subordination at an earlier age than English monolinguals.

The prediction for future research, which needs to include L1 data, is that if the age of onset of an L2 occurs when the children have developed their L1 phrase structure up to the C-level, evidenced for example by a productive use of a varied set of subordination, the principle of uniformity will have a bearing on the initial stages of development of this L2. In the case of object clitics in French L2 where the L1 is Swedish, this will lead to an initial transfer of representation where objects are assigned a uniform XP-representation as evidenced by the post-verbal placement of clitics (see Granfeldt *et al.* 2007 for additional discussion). Support for this hypothesis, which admittedly is presented briefly here due to space limitations, comes from the fact that none of the 2L1 children studied here or previously (Granfeldt & Schlyter 2004), produced any post-verbal 'clitics' (e.g. *je vois le*) which would be inconsistent with a clitic status. In the 2L1 children the presence of the same other language does not at any stage of development seem to lead to a uniform analysis of objects in French.

Acknowledgements

A previous version of this paper was presented at the Conference Workshop on Critical Period(S) and Successive Acquisition in Childhood, Hamburg, 4–5 June 2009. The audience present is thanked for valuable comments. I wish to thank three anonymous reviewers for constructive criticism. All remaining errors are mine. This research was supported by a grant from the Swedish Research Council (Vetenskapsrådet) to the project *Startålder och språklig utveckling i franska*.

References

Ågren, M., Granfeldt, J. & Thomas, A. (submitted). The impact of external factors in French cL2 and 2L1: quantity and quality of the input. Ms University of Lund.
Ågren, M., Granfeldt, J. & Thomas, A. (in press). Combined effects of age of onset and input on the development of different grammatical structures: A study of simultaneous and successive bilingual acquisition of French. *Linguistic Approaches to Bilingualism* 2014, Issue 4, Volume 4.
Belletti, A. & Hamann, C. (2004). On the L2/bilingual acquisition of French by two young children with different source languages. In P. Prévost & J. Paradis (Eds.), *The acquisition of French in different contexts*, 147–174. Amsterdam: John Benjamins.
Cardinaletti, A. & Starke, M. (1999). The typology of structural deficiency: a case study of the three classes of pronouns. In H. van Riemsdijk (Ed.), *Clitics in the languages of Europe*, 145–233. Berlin: Mouton de Gruyter.

Crysmann, B. & Müller, N. (2000). On the non-parallelism in the acquisition of reflexive and non-reflexive object clitics. In C. Hamann & S. Powers (Eds.), *The acquisition of clause-internal rules: scrambling and cliticization*, 207–236. Dordrecht: Kluwer.
Granfeldt, J. & Schlyter, S. (2004). Cliticisation in the acquisition of French as L1 and L2. In J. Paradis & P. Prévost (Eds.), *The acquisition of French in different contexts: focus on functional categories*, 333–370. Amsterdam/Philadelphia: John Benjamins.
Granfeldt, J., Schlyter, S. & Kihlstedt, M. (2007). French as cL2, 2L1 and L2 in pre-school children. In J. Granfeldt (Ed.), *Studies in Romance bilingual acquisition — age of onset and development of French and Spanish*, 6–41. PERLES 24. Centre for Languages and Literature, University of Lund.
Grüter, T. (2006). Object (Clitic) Omission in L2 French: mis-setting or Missing Surface Inflection? In M.G. O'Brien, C. Shea, & J. Archibald (Eds.), *Proceedings of the 8th Generative Approaches to Second Language Acquisition Conference* (GASLA 2006), 63–71. Somerville, MA: Cascadilla Proceedings Project.
Håkansson, G. & Hansson, K. (2007). Grammatisk utveckling. In U. Nettelbladt & E.-K. Salameh (Eds.), *Språkutveckling och språkstörning hos barn*, 171–198. Lund: Studentlitteratur.
Hamann, C., Rizzi, L. & Frauenfelder, U. (1996). On the acquisition of subject and object clitics of French. In H. Clahsen (Ed.), *Generative perspectives on language acquisition*, 309–334. Amsterdam/Philadelphia: John Benjamins.
Hamann, C. & Belletti, A. (2008). Developmental patterns in the acquisition of complement clitic pronouns: comparing different acquisition modes with an emphasis on French. *Rivista di Grammatica Generativa* 31, 39–78.
Haznedar, B. & Gavruseva, E. (Eds.) (2008). *Current trends in child second language acquisition: a generative perspective*. Amsterdam/Philadelphia: John Benjamins.
Hellan, L. & Platzack, C. (1999). Pronouns in Scandinavian languages: an overview. In H. van Riemsdijk (Ed.), *Clitics in the languages of Europe*, 123–144. Berlin: Mouton de Gruyter.
Herschensohn, J. (2004). Functional categories and the acquisition of object clitics in L2 French. In P. Prévost & J. Paradis (Eds.), *The acquisition of French in different contexts: focus on functional categories*, 207–242. Amsterdam/Philadelphia: John Benjamins.
Hulk, A. (2000). L'acquisition des pronoms clitiques français par un enfant bilingue français-néerlandais. *The Canadian Journal of Linguistics* 45, 97–118.
Jakubowicz, C., Müller, N., Kang, O., Riemer, B. & Rigaut, C. (1996). On the acquisition of the pronominal system in French and German. In A. Stringfellow, D. Cahana-Amitay, E. Hughes & A. Zukowski (Eds.), *Proceedings of the 20th Annual Boston University Conference on Language Development*, Vol. 1, 374–385. Sommerville, Mass.: Cascadilla Press.
Kayne, R.S. (1975). *French syntax*. Cambridge, Mass.: MIT Press.
MacWhinney, B. (2000). *The CHILDES project: tools for analyzing talk*. 3rd edition. Mahwah, NJ: Lawrence Erlbaum Associates.
Meisel, J.M. (1994). Getting FAT: finiteness, agreement and tense in early grammars. In J.M. Meisel (Ed.), *Bilingual first language acquisition*, 89–130. Amsterdam/Philadelphia: Benjamins.
Meisel, J.M. (2008). Child second language acquisition or successive first language acquisition? In B. Haznedar & E. Gavruseva (Eds.), *Current trends in child second language acquisition: a generative perspective*, 55–82. Amsterdam/Philadelphia: John Benjamins.
Pérez-Leroux, A.T., Pirvulescu, M. & Roberge, Y. (2009). Bilingualism as a window into the language faculty: the acquisition of objects in French-speaking children in bilingual and monolingual contexts. *Bilingualism: Language and Cognition* 12, 97–112.

Prévost, P. (2006). The phenomenon of object omission in child L2 French. *Bilingualism: Language and Cognition* 9, 263–280.

Rasetti, L. (2003). *Optional categories in early French syntax: a developmental study of root infinitives and null arguments.* PhD thesis. Université de Genève.

Rizzi, L. (1998). Remarks on early null subjects. In A. Greenhill, M. Hughes, H. Littlefield & H. Walsh (Eds.), *Proceedings of the 22nd Annual Boston University Conference on Language Development*, 14–39. Sommerville, Mass: Cascadilla.

Rizzi, L. (2005). On the grammatical basis of language development: a case study. In G. Cinque, R. Kayne (Eds.), *Handbook of comparative syntax*, New York/Oxford: Oxford University Press.

Schlyter, S. (2003). Development of verb morphology and finiteness in children and adults acquiring French. In C. Dimroth & M. Starren (Eds.), *Information structure, linguistic structure, and the dynamics of learner language*, 15–44. Amsterdam/Philadelphia: John Benjamins.

Schwartz, B.D. (2004a). On child L2 development of syntax and morphology. *Lingue e Linguaggio* 3, 97–132.

Schwartz, B.D. (2004b). Why child L2 acquisition? In J. van Kampen & S. Baauw (Eds.), *Proceedings of GALA 2003*, Vol. 1, 47–66. Utrecht: Netherlands Graduate School of Linguistics (LOT).

Thomas, A. (2009). *Les débutants parlent-ils à l'infinitif ? Influence de l'input sur la production des verbes par des apprenants adultes du français.* PhD thesis. Lund: Etudes romanes de Lund 87.

Towell, R. & Hawkins, R. (1994). *Approaches to second language acquisition.* Clevedon: Multilingual Matters.

Unsworth, S. (2005). *Child L2, adult L2, child L1: differences and similarities: a study on the acquisition of direct object scrambling in dutch.* Utrecht: LOT.

White, L. (1996). Clitics in L2 French. In H. Clahsen (Ed.), *Generative perspectives on language acquisition*, 335–368. Amsterdam/Philadelphia: John Benjamins.

Résumé

Selon certains auteurs, l'étude du développement précoce des enfants L2 peut permettre une nouvelle discussion de différentes théories de l'acquisition selon lesquelles il existerait des contraintes de maturation sur l'acquisition du langage. Une telle proposition fut avancée par Meisel (2008). Meisel propose un âge de début d'acquisition critique pour l'acquisition du type (2)L1 entre 3 et 4 ans. Dans notre étude, nous analysons le développement longitudinal des objets clitiques en français chez des enfants L2 précoce (n = 7) dont la L1 est le suédois. L'âge de début d'acquisition des enfants varie (de 3;0 à 6;5) et nous comparons leur développement à celui des apprenants adultes que nous avons étudiés préalablement (Granfeldt & Schlyter, 2004). L'étude inclut aussi des enfants bilingues simultanés du même âge (n = 3) et des enfants monolingues (n = 5) comme groupe contrôle. Les résultats montrent que les enfants dont l'âge de début d'acquisition est supérieur à 4 ans produisent des structures typiques pour l'acquisition L2 adulte alors que de telles structures ne sont attestées ni chez les enfants bilingues simultanés, ni chez les enfants dont l'âge de début d'acquisition était inférieur à 4 ans.

Subject index

A
additive 35, 36, 40, 117, 119, 120, 120n1, 121, 122, 124, 125, 131, 133, 134, 136, 137, 139–141
adjacency 124, 125, 132, 137, 138
advanced stages 25, 76, 82, 86, 88, 93, 95, 99, 103, 108, 112, 113
adverb 30, 35, 47, 107, 131
Age of Onset 145
allemand 17, 49
anglais 14, 17, 34, 49, 56, 56n5, 57
argument structure 145
argumentative 29–31, 33, 34, 39, 41, 45–48
aspectual 33, 139
auxiliary 104, 150, 152, 156, 160, 161

B
bilingual acquisition 144, 163, 164
bilingue 23, 164

C
CAF 22
categorical 117, 118, 121n3, 126, 138, 139, 141
CEFR 14, 25, 78, 93
child L2 143–146, 152, 158, 160, 161, 165
chinois 54
chunks 36, 77, 95, 99–102, 114
clitic 100–103, 112, 120, 143–152, 154–161, 161n4, 162–165
comment 40, 118, 134
concessive 35–38, 40, 46

connecteur 12, 13, 15, 26
connective 36, 37, 39
connector 120n1, 131, 132
continuity 37, 125, 137
contrastive 47, 48, 50, 57, 65, 118, 119, 124, 130, 130n16, 132, 133, 138–140
CP 162
CU 162

D
declarative 27, 47, 96–99, 102, 108, 111–113, 144, 150, 156, 162
development 24, 25, 27–31, 33, 41, 42, 48, 73, 75–79, 81, 86–88, 91–94, 99–102, 104, 110, 111, 113, 114, 124, 132, 137–140, 143, 144, 144n1, 145, 146, 151–153, 157, 158, 160–165
discourse 24, 26, 30, 31, 34, 38, 39, 41, 48–50, 72, 77, 99, 118, 124, 140, 141
DP 25, 146
Dutch 80, 124, 148, 150

E
émergence 13, 16, 17, 140, 141
enclitic 149
English 31, 50, 77, 80–82, 86n4, 92–94, 102, 104, 109, 110, 114, 139, 140, 151, 157, 163
ESF 9, 54, 55, 117, 124, 127, 141

F
finiteness 27, 103, 124, 138–140, 164, 165

fluency 22, 26, 27, 77, 94, 95, 104, 108, 109, 114
focus 119, 121n3, 124, 130, 130n16, 132, 133, 139–141
formulaic 24, 25, 75–79, 81–85, 85n2, 87, 88, 90–95, 97, 99, 101, 114
français 7–9, 12, 14–20, 22–27, 49, 50, 53–55, 56n5, 58–61, 66, 68–72, 92–94, 140, 141, 164, 165
French 24–32, 43, 47–50, 71–73, 75–83, 83n1, 84, 85, 85n2, 86n4, 90–95, 99, 100, 102, 104, 106–110, 113, 114, 117, 120, 120n1, 122, 122n4, 123–126, 131, 137–139, 143, 144, 144n1, 145–147, 147n3, 149–153, 157–161, 163–165
frequency 42, 48, 75, 76, 78–80, 82–85, 85n2, 85n3, 86, 86n4, 86n5, 87–91, 94, 104–107, 112, 126, 127, 129, 131, 162
full noun phrase 100

G
genre 12–14, 16, 17, 19, 20, 27, 56
grammaticalisation 12, 25, 50

I
idiomaticity 75, 77, 85, 94
individual variation 41, 42, 49, 108, 112, 161
inferential 38, 39, 41, 46–48
initial stage 95, 99, 100, 102, 113, 144, 146, 162, 163
interactive 33–35, 38, 41, 47, 55

InterFra 7–10, 14–16, 18, 19, 28, 29, 32, 33, 55, 58, 62n10, 76, 82, 144n1
interrogative 34, 35, 100, 102, 114
IPU 41–43, 47
iterative 124, 131, 136
itinéraire 12, 14–16

L

L1 14, 15, 17, 24–26, 29, 31, 45, 49, 50, 72, 77, 85, 92, 93, 95–97, 102, 103, 108, 110–113, 117, 124–127, 138, 139, 141, 143–146, 149–158, 160, 161, 161n4, 162–165
L1 acquisition 102, 144, 145, 149, 150
L1 influence 144, 146
LoR 82, 83, 89

M

marker 29–33, 38–49, 59, 77, 119, 127, 139
maturational 26, 114, 143, 144, 146, 162
MLR 109–111, 113
Moroccan Arabic 117, 120, 122, 132, 140
morphological 99, 102, 112, 138
movement 114, 118, 141, 148

N

nativelike 76–78, 81, 84, 86, 88, 90–92
near-native 25–29, 81
negation 105, 106, 119, 124, 140, 141, 149
NP 101, 102, 122, 126, 126n9, 129–133, 135–139, 146

O

object clitics 143, 145–152, 154–161, 163, 164
oral 12, 14–16, 19, 25–27, 31, 53, 73, 75, 76, 80, 85, 87, 90, 92–94

P

particle 49, 50, 117, 119, 120, 121–128, 130n15, 131–133, 135–141

particules 6, 16, 27, 49, 50, 140, 141
polarity 122, 124, 125
post-basic variety 117, 127
post-verbal 126, 149–152, 157–161, 163
postverbal 120, 121, 129, 133, 135, 137, 151
pragmaticalization 29–31, 39, 43, 48, 49
pre-basic variety 117
presentational 118, 126, 129, 135, 137, 138
procedural 27, 96–99, 101, 108, 112, 113
proceduralisation 111, 112
proceduralise 95
processing 24, 26, 27, 73, 95, 99, 101, 108, 109, 113, 141

Q

quaestio 118
quantifier 107
quasi-natif 7, 16, 14, 18, 22, 23

R

référent 54, 56, 57, 61, 63–66, 69, 70
reorienting 38, 39, 46, 48
right-dislocation 160

S

scalar 33–38, 41, 119–122, 126, 131, 134, 136, 139
scope 31, 37, 117–126, 126n9, 127, 129, 129n13, 130, 130n15, 131–141, 161n4
semantics 50, 78, 119, 122, 125, 140
speaking rate 109, 110, 112
spoken 25, 26, 29, 30, 43, 49, 50, 73, 75, 77, 82, 85, 86n4, 92, 93, 114
stade 7–9, 12–14, 16, 17, 19, 23–25, 49, 55, 58, 59, 61–71, 92, 124
stage 9, 10, 12, 25, 27, 28, 30, 32, 36, 37, 39, 41, 42, 47, 48, 72, 76, 80, 82, 83, 86–91, 93, 95, 99–103, 108–110, 112, 113, 117, 118, 124, 130n15, 132, 136, 140, 141, 144, 146, 152, 156–158, 160–163
strong pronouns 147, 148, 161
subject pronouns 103, 144, 147n3
suédois 15, 25, 53, 58, 63, 69, 71, 165
surface 37, 95, 97, 98, 108, 112, 113, 164
Swedish 32, 47, 73, 75, 76, 80–82, 93, 124, 143, 144n1, 145, 146, 148–150, 152, 153, 157, 158, 161–163
syntax 96, 97, 99, 100, 103, 104, 113, 114, 119, 122, 125, 140, 145, 147, 148, 164, 165

T

temporal 25, 26, 29–31, 33, 35, 40, 41, 43, 44, 47, 48, 121, 122, 125, 131, 136, 137, 139, 150, 152, 156, 160, 161
textual 26, 29–31, 33, 35, 36, 38–45, 47, 48, 77, 109
the TH model 95, 101, 103, 108, 111–113
thematic 36–38
thetic 117, 118, 121n3, 126, 131, 134, 139, 141
topic 30, 38, 39, 41, 46–48, 72, 73, 77, 84, 118, 119, 124, 130, 132, 133, 139, 140
topique 54, 56, 57, 63–66, 69, 70, 72
transfer 96, 97, 99, 117, 125, 137, 138, 151, 162, 163

U

Universal Grammar 95, 98, 114, 146
utterance position 125, 133, 139

V

verb phrase 100, 102–104, 112
verb raising 96, 104, 107, 108

W

weak pronouns 147, 148
working memory 96, 98, 108